MAKING THE INVISIBLE VISIBLE

REVIEWS
for
Making the Invisible Visible

'Managing knowledge in a company begins with using information effectively. This book helps senior managers to measure and manage their information, people and IT capabilities to create business value with information for innovation, growth and customer focus. A must read!'
Dipak Rastogi, Executive Vice President, Emerging Markets, Citibank N.A., London, UK

'Finally, a practical approach to the use of IT to manage information that takes into account all the non-IT parts, the parts that really determine success or failure.'
Steen Riisgaard, Corporate Executive Vice President, Novozymes, Copenhagen, Denmark

'The Information Orientation of companies could be the key to unlocking the true potential of Information Technology which has eluded us for decades.'
Jim Barrington, Senior Vice President and CIO, ABB Group, Zurich, Switzerland

'*Making the Invisible Visible* is the first complete and practical reference helping Senior Managers to optimize Information, People and Technology resources to compete and win in the new digital era.'
Frederick Wohlwend, Vice President, IS/IT, Ares Serono International, Geneva, Switzerland

'This book provides a roadmap to how high performing companies really extract the business value of IT in today's knowledge and information intensive economy.'
Sukanto Tanoto, Chairman, RGM International, Singapore

'We at Nestlé have often said that "people and products are more important than systems" to achieve winning business performance. Don Marchand's excellent book provides a systematic framework to understand clearly the powerful potential of using information systems intelligently. This refreshing piece of work will help managers at all levels to make better use of their growing investment in information systems and technology.'
Mario A. Corti, Executive Vice President and CFO, Nestlé S.A., Vevey, Switzerland

'The philosophy and process of Information Orientation integrates all "hard" and "soft" factors of corporate behaviours with information management and IT practices. Information Orientation provides companies in the Financial Services industry with a great opportunity to transform their information delivery and use, from art form to a strong institutional discipline, leading to improved business performance and competitive advantage for those companies that manage their information capabilities extremely well.'
Yury Zaytsev, Group Information Officer, Swiss Re, Zurich, Switzerland

MAKING THE INVISIBLE VISIBLE

How companies win with the right
information, people and IT

Donald A. Marchand
William J. Kettinger
John D. Rollins

JOHN WILEY & SONS, LTD

Chichester · New York · Weinheim · Brisbane · Singapore · Toronto

Other Wiley Editorial Offices

John Wiley & Sons, Inc., 605 Third Avenue,
New York, NY 10158-0012, USA

WILEY-VCH GmbH, Pappelallee 3,
D-69469 Weinheim, Germany

John Wiley & Sons Australia, Ltd, 33 Park Road, Milton,
Queensland 4064, Australia

John Wiley & Sons (Asia) Pte Ltd, 2 Clementi Loop #02-01,
Jin Xing Distripark, Singapore 129809

John Wiley & Sons (Canada) Ltd, 22 Worcester Road,
Rexdale, Ontario M9W 1L1, Canada

British Library Cataloguing in Publication Data

A catalogue record for this book is available from the British Library

ISBN 0-471-49609-X

Typeset by Dorwyn Ltd, Rowlands Castle, Hampshire.
Printed and bound in Great Britain by Biddles Ltd, Guildford and King's Lynn.
This book is printed on acid-free paper responsibly manufactured from sustainable
forestry, in which at least two trees are planted for each one used for paper production.

To the daughters in our lives who constantly strive to be different from their dads, but who never cease to delight them with their accomplishments, enthusiasm and love.

Lauren Marchand, Lindsey Kettinger, Anne and Margaret Rollins

CONTENTS

Part III   Managing Information Capabilities

AUTHOR BIOGRAPHIES

Donald A. Marchand is Professor of Information Management and Strategy at the International Institute of Management Development in Lausanne, Switzerland. He specializes in information and knowledge management as business capabilities, e-business, demand/supply chain management and the strategic roles of information and technology in global companies. He has directed several major research projects and has authored eight successful books and over 150 articles and cases in his specialist fields. Professor Marchand earned a PhD and MA at UCLA and a BA at the University of California, Berkeley (Phi Beta Kappa), after which he held academic posts at the Syracuse University and the University of South Carolina, USA.

Professor William J. Kettinger is Director of the Center of Information Management and Technology Research at the Darla Moore School of Business, University of South Carolina. He teaches management information systems in the Masters of International Business Studies program and is a visiting faculty at IMD. He has 25 years of consulting experience and has over 100 publications including four books and articles in journals such as *MIS Quarterly* and *Sloan Management Review*. In 1995 he received the Society of Information Management's Best Paper Award, honouring outstanding work in the field of information systems. He earned a PhD and MS from the University of South Carolina and an MPA from the University of Massachusetts, USA.

John D. Rollins is the managing partner of Strategic Information Technology Effectiveness for Accenture (formerly known as Andersen Consulting), a leading global management and technology consultancy. He works with client companies in setting direction for the appropriate use of information and technology in support of business and competitive strategies. He also consults with organizations that are undertaking substantial change, or transformation initiatives where information and technology will play critical driving or enabling roles. He received an MBA in Corporate Finance & Investment Management from the University of Pennsylvania Wharton School and has a BS in Chemistry from the Carnegie Mellon University, USA.

FOREWORD

Managers and people in companies act on what they know, even if what they know is not nearly enough! Companies like my own, with a lot of smart people, have little choice but to excel in sharing and using information about customers, products, markets and operations, if we wish to continue to achieve superior business results.

Whether you are in an e-smart established company or a new e-venture, you must do two things very well to succeed in today's fast-paced business climate. First, you must invent creative strategies to grow your business and you must implement the right business capabilities, including information capabilities, to sustain your growth. Second, you must be passionate about creating a culture of proactive information use and sharing through every level of your company, including with your customers, partners and even markets.

This book is not about a new management fad or passing fashion. It elevates the singular importance of effectively managing information, people and information technology (IT) to achieve superior business performance to its rightful place in the 21st century. This book tracks winning companies in diverse industries globally pursuing a passion – yes, that's the right word – for managing how information and IT are effectively used by their people each day to create outstanding business value.

What do winning companies know about building excellent information capabilities for growth that competitors do not know or cannot act upon? After e-business and e-commerce have become parts of the general business vocabulary, the mastery of growth through excellence in information capabilities will remain a cornerstone of business success. Read this book and discover what you suspected was right to do all along, but may not have gotten around to implementing fully within your company.

Learning to see, measure and manage the way your company uses and manages information, people and IT to grow and prosper is what *Making the Invisible Visible* is all about.

Matti Alahuhta
President, NOKIA Mobile Phones

PREFACE

This book is about management mindsets – how managers see, measure and manage information and knowledge to achieve superior business performance. It moves beyond the popular, but oversimplified, view that IT leads to competitive advantage by focusing on how people use information and IT to impact business performance. Moreover, this book suggests that creative business strategies, even e-business strategies, are not sufficient to win in today's global markets unless managers can develop the right information capabilities to leverage their staff, processes, structures and external relationships with business partners and suppliers. The winning companies in this book know which business capabilities lead to superior growth and performance. They are moving beyond the 'e' in business to leverage how information, people and IT can be effectively used to differentiate their companies in markets increasingly converging on priced-based competition.

This book is different from most business books that create interesting stories and prescriptions around a few well-known companies. Rather, this work is the product of rigorous, international and scientifically validated, empirical research about how senior managers deploy information, people and IT to impact business performance, and their expectations about future industry leadership in competing with information. The cases and prescriptions highlighted in the book were selected from a global sample of hundreds of managers in companies across diverse industries and countries, to offer a representative view of business today. From the empirical results of our international sample, we identified companies whose 'real world journeys' would best help us learn about how companies win and lose based on the way they configure and use their information, staff and IT. This book combines business relevance with scientifically validated and tested frameworks. It pinpoints business strategies and practices that impact business performance positively, and those that do not.

Most importantly, this book is about a passion. A passion to proactively use information about customers, products, services, operations, finances and markets to achieve great things. This passion drives managers to a deeper understanding of how to use the power of information and people to lead their companies to exceptional operational excellence, customer delight and exciting new business opportunities. This passion is what guided us to discover a new way for managers to recognize, measure and build the information capabilities to relentlessly compete in the global economy.

Finally, this book is about new beginnings in the lives of the authors. For Don and Bill, this book culminates over 25 years of joint research and practice in information management and technology in business on both sides of the Atlantic. It also represents the start of a promising new company, enterpriseIQ, and the journey of bringing scientifically validated business measures and metrics of information and knowledge-use to companies over the Internet, to improve their information capabilities and performance with employees, customers, and partners.

For John, this book encapsulates nearly 25 years of assisting clients to manage information and IT to improve the performance of their businesses. It also represents the development of new management insights that directly support John's ongoing efforts to change the way clients of Accenture (as of 1 January 2001, Accenture became the new name of Andersen Consulting) think and work.

We hopethat you enjoy reading the results of our international journey of management research and that you join us in our new ventures to improve the information capabilities of your company.

D.A.M.
W.J.K.
J.D.R.

ACKNOWLEDGEMENTS

This book is one of several major publications reporting the managerial results of a 28-month research project entitled 'Navigating Business Success'. The project was conducted at IMD with the participation and support of Accenture (at the time known as Andersen Consulting) from September 1997 to December 1999. The Project involved over 1200 senior managers in 103 companies in 26 industries and 37 countries, including over 330 managers from the Global Financial Services company included for the first time in this book. Our first 'thank you' goes to the senior managers who participated in this international research project from all over the world.

In addition, we conducted interviews with and worked alongside senior managers in 24 companies, including the companies highlighted in this book, to understand the managerial implications and lessons learned from our empirical research. In particular, we owe special thanks to the managers who gave their professional time to provide us with insights into how their companies manage information, people and IT to impact performance. Most importantly, we wish to offer our specific gratitude to the senior managers of Hilti Corporation, Banco Bilbao Vizcaya Argentaria, Skandiabanken, as well as The Bank, who graciously provided us with detailed profiles of their companies.

We also wish to thank the hundreds of managers involved in IMD Executive Programmes and Discovery Events for their significant 'real world' insights and responses to our research and case studies. These sessions gave new meaning to our motto: 'Real World, Real Learning'.

To distill and develop our learning into this book, we benefited greatly from a disciplined and productive research and writing team. In particular, the dedicated analytical and writing support provided by Katarina Paddack was outstanding throughout the production of the book. In addition, Joyce P. Marchand, the manager of the research project, and Dr Andreas Wildberger provided both coordination and direct contributions to the development of the manuscript. Dr Choong C. Lee of Yonsei University, Korea, provided valuable statistical consultation. Finally, our IMD editor, Lindsey McTeague contributed greatly to turning our early drafts into polished and readable prose after giving us an abundance of author queries.

At John Wiley and Sons, Claire Plimmer, Publishing Editor for Business and Management, was committed to this book from the proposal onwards and led a dedicated team of Wiley staff to move the book from manuscript to global release in a few short months.

At IMD, the research project and the book were actively encouraged by Dr Peter Lorange, the President, with his positive spirit and support of research that makes a difference to managers. At Accenture, Vernon Ellis, the International Chairman, was instrumental in sponsoring the Partnership Project at IMD and taking a personal interest in its development and success.

The book writing process involved a personal journey with the full participation of our families. To Joyce, Lynda and Theresa and all our children, who support our intellectual passions and professional pursuits wherever they take us, a very big thank you for your love and understanding.

INTRODUCTION

There is a well-known saying in management that 'You can't manage what you can't measure.' However, there is an even more basic reality underlying this adage which is 'You can't measure what you can't see.' This book is about seeing information in a new way so you can both measure its use and manage it to improve business performance.

It is with information that people in business express and convey their knowledge about markets, competitors, customers, products, services and operations. If knowledge—consisting of experience, skills, expertise, judgement, and emotions—primarily resides with people, in order to share knowledge and increase business performance, managers and employees need to use information. Information, or more precisely data, is around us like the air we breathe, yet few companies and managers perceive its importance to business success. Managers complain about either information overload—as they are barraged by e-mails, voice mails, cell phone calls, and reports—or information scarcity—when they prepare to make decisions about key strategies or customers, but have little or no meaningful information available to them.

You may be asking yourself: 'Well, if information is so important to the ways companies perform today, why haven't managers already learned to manage information better?'

The answer is that some companies have indeed learned to use information effectively to achieve superior performance. These managers understand how to leverage information, people and information technology (IT) to systematically improve business performance. We call these three capabilities 'information capabilities'. They are not only essential for executing business strategies today with speed, agility and responsiveness, but they can also be employed to enhance, substitute or reduce the use of people, organizational structures or business processes. Companies that develop superior levels of information capabilities in the ways they integrate their people, information practices and IT can be more profitable and innovative than their competitors.

You may also be thinking: 'Isn't effective information use what information technology and e-business are all about?'

The answer to this question is yes and no. During the last half of the twentieth century and into the twenty-first, managers have been trying primarily to use information technology, rather than to manage information—all too often with mixed success. They have been preoccupied with the 'T' in IT, to the detriment of the 'I', which seemed to fade away as business managers learned to use IT to transact orders, issue payments, plan manufacturing and service customers. Just learning about each new wave of IT, and buying and deploying the latest hardware and software, has filled the scarce time available to managers. And senior managers seemed to take it for granted that the 'I' was part of running a business; they rarely worried about it. They seemed to believe that, if necessary, they could rely on IT and information specialists for advice.

This focus on technology has also de-emphasized one critical component of information use—people. While managers have worked on learning how to manage technology and information, they have not yet developed a full understanding of how people's behaviours affect information use within their companies. After more than 40 years of IT in business, and with the rapid evolution of the Internet and e-business, one conclusion is certain: the Internet and IT have become competitive necessities in industry worldwide. So today, to differentiate themselves from their competitors, managers must focus on the ways people use information. Our research showed us this: senior managers believe that the competitive advantage goes to companies that create superior business results by synchronizing the management of their people with information and IT.

STORIES OF TWO COMPANIES

Let's take a look at two companies in very different industries and see how they manage people, information and IT to achieve superior business performance. Although these two companies use different business models, they exhibit similar characteristics of effective information use.

Hilti Corporation

Founded in 1941 in the principality of Liechtenstein, Hilti is one of the world's leading companies specializing in drills, fasteners and demolition systems for the construction industry.

Founder Martin Hilti's belief 'that market share is more important than factories' has led, over the years, to an obsession with understanding and responding to customers. From its beginnings, Hilti employed a direct sales force, rather than using distributors or dealers as most of its competitors did. This internal group sells the company's products and provides knowledgeable advice on the best use of Hilti products on construction sites. Today, Hilti's management recognizes the value of the over 70,000 contacts per day its 7,000 sales representatives have with customers. They provide hands-on advice and training in the use of Hilti's products, which usually sell for significantly higher prices than its competitors' products.

From the beginning, Martin Hilti considered a corporate culture of high employee involvement and communications to be 'very special'. The primary values of the culture were—and continue to be—openness, integrity, tolerance, responsibility and teamwork. These values are central to both individual and organizational behaviour at Hilti today.

In the 1990s, Hilti experienced several key changes in strategy (from a geographic to a market segment-based approach) and organizational structure (from a very decentralized country-based operation to a more global approach with local adaptations). The company needed to respond better to construction industry shifts as well as to more intense competition in its key markets.

Through these changes, senior managers recognized the crucial role that each employee plays in adapting to constantly changing business conditions and in contributing to the company's success. Senior managers worked aggressively to develop new ideas and business concepts with high employee involvement. Managers were convinced that employees who clearly understand and are informed about the business, as it changes, are more motivated to achieve shared performance goals.

For example, Hilti's managers have, in recent years, refined the process of educating Hilti's 12,000 employees about the business and its performance through the use of 'cockpit charts' in every work area. The charts identify key performance information to the shop-floor workers and sales representatives. To do this, Hilti developed a common language and understanding of performance criteria and measures at every level. Their e-mail network and intranet is used to share this information across the company.

In addition, senior managers and employees constantly seek direct contact with their customers—from both inside and outside the company. These exchanges with customers are critical for the information and ideas that they provide. Customers use Hilti tools on a daily basis. Their insights and reactions to these products promote further improvements and new product development at Hilti. Each senior manager spends at least two days each month speaking with customers. In addition, the company regularly surveys its key accounts and collects information from call centre interactions with customers in after-sales service.

To deepen their knowledge of customers and their understanding of employees, senior managers are in constant contact with employees through their open communications network. Monthly breakfast meetings are held for groups of employees with executive board members. This transparency in employee communications, supplemented by regular surveys of employee attitudes, allows employees to voice their work-related concerns with managers and to enhance individual, team and company performance.

The daily outputs of this highly transparent, open and proactive information culture contribute to Hilti's continued growth and profitability. In addition, Hilti's senior managers continually question existing performance and business realities. 'We can do better' is an often-heard phrase at Hilti. In fact, this constant questioning of current work practices and the search for new information has changed the information practices of Hilti staff at every level. Employees in geographically dispersed locations regularly exchange information about customers and products. Operational and product development units also share customer and product intelligence to improve products. Repositories of product information and customer knowledge are available company-wide through the company's global IT network.

To enable all these information management changes, the company's IT department is headed by a chief information officer (CIO) with a strong business and IT background. All business applications and IT investments at Hilti require strong business and senior management support and understanding. Hilti has focused its IT practices on improving business processes first; for example, supply chain management, determining the right time to market new product offerings, and innovation in both product development and management decision-making, especially with performance-based information. For Hilti managers, IT is a key tool for managing their business and, like all the company's tools, must deliver business value.

Banco Bilbao Vizcaya (BBV)[1]

Banco Bilbao Vizcaya was created in 1988, the product of a merger between two large Spanish banks, Banco de Bilbao, founded in 1856, and Banco de Vizcaya, founded in 1878. This merger followed Spain's entrance into the European Union (EU) in 1986 and placed the new bank in a leading position in the Spanish retail banking market. Since 1997, BBV has outperformed its largest rival, Banco Santander, and is recognized as one of Europe's most successful banks.

BBV's managers have always placed great emphasis on the correlation between customer and business value. Like most retail banks in the 1980s, BBV organized its banking around branches as the centre of the bank's value-creation activities. But, instead of focusing on pushing banking products and completing transactions like most traditional banks, all BBV branches were responsible for developing and enhancing the bank's information about customers. BBV began to build a customer sales support system that would enable branch employees to collect individual customer profiles, offer a personalized service and cross-sell banking, insurance and financial products to customers. Also, BBV's managers viewed the bank's headquarters as supporting, not directing, the branches—a view not widely held in the retail banking industry at that time.

After a series of management crises in the 1980s and early 1990s, including the unexpected death of its CEO, BBV's new leadership decided, in 1994, to start a three-year growth initiative called the 1,000-day Programme. The main focus of the programme was to 'unleash BBV's hidden value'. At the start, the CEO nominated six executive champions to lead the programme. The whole of the bank's management met off-site to outline the main purpose and guidelines of the 1,000-day Programme. 'The CEO even placed a bet and put his position at stake,' commented one of the programme's executive champions. 'In fact, he would have quit had the programme not been successful.'

The 1,000-day Programme set ambitious growth and profitability goals. As one of BBV's executive champions noted:

> We planned yearly business volume growth of 10 per cent, which was higher than that of our competitors. Our employees became very motivated and set out to use all the tools available to achieve these ambitious goals. They used, for instance, customer and segment information and IT applications to cross-sell products to existing customers. The bank exceeded growth plans and scored yearly growth rates of 25 per cent.

At the end of the first 1,000-day Programme, BBV experienced substantial growth in market capitalization—from $5 billion in 1994 to $22 billion in 1997. Based on the success of the first programme, the bank's senior managers initiated a second 1,000-day Programme, Programme Dosmil—a word game in Spanish that means both 'second 1,000-day programme' and 'programme 2000.' The second 1,000-day Programme has set equally ambitious growth, capitalization and profitability goals.

In pursuit of value creation in a very mature retail banking market, BBV places strong emphasis on implementing clear business processes that integrate the ways in which people use customer and product information to deliver services and cross-sell to new and existing customers. Unlike other retail banks, BBV uses its IT infrastructure to unify in one customer record every single contact that the customer has with the bank, whether through the branch or through direct channels. This means that while developing automated teller machines (ATM), call centre, and Internet banking channels, BBV has consolidated all its customer transaction records in one file to make sure its employees can see all the information held on each customer at once. Branch employees are assigned specific customers to contact regularly, regardless of the mix of channels that these customers employ. The bank encourages its employees to personalize the bank's relations with customers, especially those who use only direct channels.

At BBV, teamwork and a transparent business culture are the key principles according to which the branches operate. Every branch employee is evaluated on the branch's overall success, rather than on his/her personal achievement alone. All performance-based information is shared within and between branches to encourage performance improvements overall and to practice sharing.

Teamwork is also the cornerstone of the IT department's interactions with business functions. As the IT director notes: 'Our department always works with the business functions when a new IT application needs to be developed. Our bank does not invest in IT unless the business value of the application is explicit.' The business and customer focus of the bank is reflected in the way it categorizes its IT applications:

- Business intelligence systems
- Management information systems
- Customer knowledge systems
- Business development systems.

Although the bank operates IT systems for operational support, the business and IT management perspective is to make every BBV IT application contribute to the bank's growth and customer focus.

MANAGEMENT LESSONS FROM THESE STORIES

Both Hilti and BBV are high-performing companies in two very different industries—construction and retail banking. Yet, after examining the recent five to ten year histories of the companies and speaking to their managers and employees at different levels, we believe that their management styles have a lot in common.

The senior managers and employees of both companies are energized by ambitious business growth and customer focus. Their strategic focus concentrates on an externally driven view of the business and on explicit performance criteria and measures, which all managers and employees understand appropriately at their levels. These companies value the proactive seeking of information about markets, customers and competitors and the sharing of this information at all levels. The value of information to managers and employees is not an abstract or vague concept, but a day-to-day operating reality. Managers and employees in both companies know which customer, product and operational information creates business value in their company. They use and improve this information daily.

The senior managers in both companies also believe that the development and effective management of the three information capabilities leads to superior business performance. By personal example, they foster people behaviours that promote information sharing, transparency and integrity. Mistakes and failures in these companies are not penalized, but treated as opportunities to learn.

Information about team and business performance is understood and shared among all operational levels in these companies. People are actively encouraged to test the validity of their knowledge of customers, competitors and markets against the daily conduct of their jobs and business functions. In these companies, new business intelligence is actively sought, even if it runs against the mind-sets supporting current practices.

Managers introduce process changes in both these companies to simplify and eliminate unnecessary complexity and data and to introduce IT systems that focus on helping people better use targeted information. Business changes in information uses and IT systems and to support people's behaviours are introduced concurrently rather than sequentially. These are not companies where IT is introduced for every information problem. IT is not perceived as a 'quick fix' but as a key enabling tool. Senior managers in both companies are deeply involved in IT and information decisions that impact on the business. They manage people, information and IT holistically, rather than discretely as separate functions.

Functional and business unit managers in these companies seek to optimize information for the business rather than for their function or business area. Managers do not invest in IT unless the new systems support well-defined information uses and processes across the company.

Finally, in each company, senior managers seek to build information capabilities that can leverage their staff, customers and partners as a substitute for unnecessary processes, organizational structures and business complexity. In both Hilti and BBV, senior managers studiously avoid confusing people with the latest management innovations and buzzwords. While they welcome change and respond rapidly to it, they concentrate on translating new business ideas and concepts into terms that other managers and people can comprehend. In both these companies, the emphasis is on having people understand the business, on linking people's performance to the company's performance, and on using information and IT clearly and consistently to run the business.

In this book we have chosen to illustrate our ideas through the use of three main case studies, supported by a number of smaller examples. All cases are drawn from our experience with companies who have successfully built information capabilities—Banco Bilbao Vizcaya, Hilti Corporation and SkandiaBanken—or who are struggling to build them over the next few years. We chose to highlight these companies based on their success at attaining excellent information capabilities and performance leadership in their industries, not on their mass market appeal. They were also chosen to represent different business models—including newer e-business as well as more traditional business models—to illustrate that building information capabilities is not just an issue for new economy companies focusing on e-business, but for all companies seeking to create competitive advantage.

WHO SHOULD READ THIS BOOK

This book was written for managers. The ideas presented in this book are the result of empirical research conducted with over a thousand senior managers internationally. We attempted to simplify and populate these ideas with real case studies to give managers a practical guide for effectively managing information to improve their company's business performance. Readers looking for detailed methodology and explanations of our study and statistical analysis should refer to *Information Orientation: The Link to Business Performance*, by Donald A. Marchand, William J. Kettinger and John D. Rollins, Oxford University Press, UK (2001).

HOW TO GET THE MOST FROM THIS BOOK

This book is not about a new management fad or IT trend. The focus of our two-year research study is on how senior managers in a global sample of companies perceive people, information and IT as capabilities associated with effective information use to be managed in order to achieve superior business performance. There are companies that have excelled at this in various industries. We have looked at several of these to learn how they do so and how they have figured out the formula for their winning performance.

Now it is time to ask yourself a few pertinent questions:

- Do you know where your company is today in managing people, information and IT effectively—and where you could be?
- Do you know how to measure the effective use of information in your company to improve business performance?
- Do you know if you have a competitor in your industry, or perhaps even outside your industry, that is building these capabilities systematically to beat your company?
- Will your company need to use information, people and IT more effectively in the future to compete in—or even lead—your industry?

These are the managerial questions you should consider while reading this book. The questions may not sound new or radical, but we believe that the answers require a new or different management mind-set. We believe that we have discovered a new way to 'see' the business value of information, people and IT and to measure and manage these capabilities.

The aim of this book is to make visible a previously invisible dimension of business management. This book shows you how information capabilities can improve your business and your performance as a manager. As a manager, after reading this book, you will be able to see, measure and manage the information resources, people and IT in your company to improve business performance. Some managers are already doing this. Others will want to learn.

HOW THE BOOK IS ORGANIZED

The book is divided into five parts, with one or more chapters per part. The parts are as follows: Improving business performance through effective information use; Measuring information capabilities; Managing information capabilities; Strategy and competing with information capabilities; and Putting information capabilities into practice starts with you.

In Chapter 1, we explain ways to discover how people, information and IT interact to affect business performance in your company. We present the information orientation (IO) model, which is the 'lens' that we discovered through our extensive survey research. This initial study involved 1,009 senior managers representing 169 senior management teams in 98 companies in 25 industries and 22 countries. The IO model is composed of three information capabilities which are as follows:

- the information behaviours and values capability (IBV)
- the information management practices capability (IMP)
- the information technology practices capability (ITP).

We explain our basic discovery that improving any single information capability does not lead to better business performance. It is only when managers improve all three information capabilities concurrently that higher levels of business performance are achieved.

In Chapter 2, we discuss three obstacles that have prevented managers from seeing the link between their information capabilities and business performance. We present the 'IO dashboard' as a tool that managers of a company or business unit can use to evaluate its level of information orientation and IO's link to business performance. For the first time, managers have a business metric, which is grounded in proven statistical and psychometric research techniques, to measure the levels of information capabilities in their company. With the IO dashboard, companies can benchmark their information capabilities over time, or compare their information capabilities against other companies based on a global benchmark database. By learning to interpret the IO dashboard, managers can identify deficiencies in information capabilities and target actions to improve them.

Part III focuses on what we learned about managing information capabilities to achieve superior performance. We believe that companies progress down paths that lead them to increase the maturity of their information capabilities. Mature IO companies are good at all three information capabilities and typically have worked at improving them over several years. In Chapter 3, we demonstrate how three companies have achieved IO maturity and how highly mature companies benefit from the cross-capability links between information behaviours and values, information management practices and IT practices. We explain the 'IO interaction effect' that occurs between the three information capabilities and show how a company can begin to identify and improve specific deficiencies in each capability to improve its IO maturity to create higher IO.

The next three chapters in this part concentrate on making specific improvements in each of the three information capabilities.

Chapter 4 focuses on changing people's information behaviours and values. How do managers in a company instil and promote the specific people behaviours and values that lead to proactive information use and IO maturity? We explain how managers can influence six specific behaviours that result in effective information use by themselves and their staff.

Chapter 5 reveals the five key areas of information management practices that lead to the improved processing and use of information in companies and to IO maturity. It describes how managers can set about unleashing the power of better information management in their company.

Chapter 6 focuses on using IT to support business value creation. Which IT practices should business managers implement to achieve IO maturity for higher IO in their business unit or company? This chapter provides managers with specific performance criteria and practices to help them evaluate and transform the way IT is deployed, to enhance the ways people in their company use information to improve performance.

While Part III is about helping to improve the management of information capabilities, Part IV offers ways to compete with information capabilities.

In Chapter 7, we show how information capabilities are linked to a company's strategic priorities and relate to four recognized business capabilities of people, processes, organizational structure and external relationships. Based on our discovery that managers view the way people use information and the way the firm manages its information and IT as a single strategic business capability, we present information capabilities (IC) as a key business capability. We show how companies follow either a proactive or a reactive strategic priority bias, and discuss the specific mix of business strategies and capabilities that lead to improved IO and business performance and those that do not. We also discuss research findings that indicate that there are three distinct strategy groups among our study sample. Lastly, managers are provided with a quick self-assessment method to evaluate their own company's business strategy, as well as the relationship of their information capabilities investment to that strategy.

In Chapter 8, we present another major finding of our survey research. It explores how each of our three strategy groups views the future, with the specific emphasis on the role of information capabilities within this mix. We also introduce the IC maximization effect, which permits high IO companies to deploy IC to save on or enhance people, processes, organizational structures and external relationships. We discuss how companies in our three strategy groups face different challenges in the future to close the gap between past and future levels of information capabilities, and how a well thought-out action plan is essential to achieve IC investment and development. We show how companies have been able to close the gap by developing plans based on becoming future leaders in competing with information in the e-business era. The chapter concludes with some concrete steps that managers can take to begin to formulate an information capabilities strategy for future action.

Chapter 9 looks at improving information capabilities and the IO scores of companies with multiple business units worldwide. What are the issues concerning managing information capabilities and achieving IO maturity in a global, multiple business unit company? This chapter presents the case study of a global financial services company for which we surveyed 48 senior management teams comprising 336 managers in 32 countries. Using the same analysis techniques as our main study sample, we discovered that the IO model was validated in the global company and was linked to business performance and future industry leadership in competing with information. We found that the business units of a global company are not homogeneous in their measurement of IO, business performance or future industry leadership. Thus the corporate managers of the global company must employ a portfolio approach in managing the information capabilities of its business units. The chapter explains how a portfolio approach can be used to create the right mix of business strategies and capabilities to lead to superior business performance in a global company.

Part V focuses on how IO begins with the individual manager—your mind-set, behaviours and practices, which are connected to effective information use. Chapter 10 presents seven key principles that managers should follow to improve information capabilities in their business unit or company through their personal conduct and mind-set. The good news is that managers can have a direct and major impact on the information capabilities and IO maturity of their business unit or company. The bad news, or at least the personal challenge for many managers, is that they may need first to change their personal mind-set and behaviours to do this. You cannot talk about information capabilities if you do not practice them yourself.

HOW TO READ THIS BOOK

We recommend that you read Chapters 1 and 2 to gain a good under-standing of the link between information orientation and business perfor-mance. These chapters provide a clear explanation of the significance of measuring your company's IO and show you how to use the IO dashboard to evaluate the strengths and weaknesses of your company's information behaviours and values, information management practices and IT practices.

If you are a manager who wants to learn immediately about managing and improving your company's information capabilities, then review Part II, Chapters 3 to 6 in detail. These Chapters offer case studies and hands-on management prescriptions for you to implement in your company.

If you are a manager who wants to understand how to compete with information capabilities and to link them with business strategy, or to learn the right mix of business capabilities for your company today and for future industry leadership, then go to Part IV, Chapters 7 and 8. In these chapters, we present the strategic paths that companies can follow to achieve the right mix of strategies and business capabilities to improve business performance and position the company for competing with in-formation in the future.

If you are a manager of a global company overseeing multiple business units, read Chapter 9 to understand how a portfolio approach to improving information capabilities leads to overall superior company performance.

If you want to understand what this book means for your personal leadership role in your company and discover the challenges you face in developing the right mind-set and behaviours associated with effective information use to increase business performance, then Chapter 10 is for you. Think about our seven principles of personal leadership to 'walk the talk'. They will help you gain credibility with your staff and help you to make the changes needed in information values and behaviours, as well as in information and IT practices, which will lead your company to superior business performance and position it for future leadership in competing with information.

NOTE

1. The corporate entity, Banco Bilbao Vizcaya (BBV), no longer exists. In January 2000 BBV merged with Spain's Argentaria to form Banco Bilbao Vizcaya Argentaria (BBVA), one of Spain's two largest banks.

I

IMPROVING BUSINESS PERFORMANCE THROUGH EFFECTIVE INFORMATION USE

INFORMATION CAPABILITIES IMPROVE BUSINESS PERFORMANCE

All managers develop a distinctive mind-set about how they interpret events in their business—about what other people (including customers and employees) do, and how they should think about and influence events, people and their business to achieve the desired results. Much of what managers 'manage' each day is the mind-sets of their staff and their own mind-sets to achieve a mutual understanding and agreement about the meaning of perceptions, events and actions that influence change in a company. A fundamental assumption underlying this book is that the mind-sets and perceptions of managers count. How a manager sees events, behaviours and actions in the world will directly influence first, his or her diagnosis of what is good or bad about a situation, and second, which course of action to pursue to improve the situation.

This chapter is about your mind-set as a manager and how you see the relationships between people, information, IT and business performance in your company. We will start by setting a scene and asking you to interpret what you see as the key elements influencing the customer interaction with the company. Then we will present a new 'lens' or way of seeing the interactions between people, information and IT and the way they relate to business performance, based on our research. In this way, you can appropriately interpret and intervene in business situations in your own company. Finally, we provide an example of how to see business events differently using the new lens or mind-set.

INTERPRETING A BUSINESS SITUATION

European Regional Bank

A long-time customer walks into the regional branch of her bank in a city she is in on business. She is not familiar with this branch. She gives her account number to the branch representative, who enters the code into the bank's customer support system and addresses her by name. 'Good afternoon, Ms Alvarez. I see that you are visiting our branch for the first time. How can I help you?'

Ms Alvarez explains that she needs to transfer funds from her main account into her stock fund account for a new investment. The branch representative checks the computer screen and says:

> I see that you are currently investing only in individual stocks. I don't know if you are already aware of this, but you can take advantage of new retirement legislation that allows you to invest up to 20 per cent of your yearly salary in a tax-free investment fund. Our bank offers several different funds that you can choose from if you are interested.

Ms Alvarez indicates that she would be interested in getting information about the funds, but is concerned that she might not be able to invest since she works for a company based in another country. The branch representative says that he will try to find out for her, picks up the phone, and calls the bank group responsible for these funds. Within three minutes, the question is answered for the customer, and she leaves the branch thinking that these fund investments might be a good idea.

The next day, the customer accesses her main account through the Internet and opens the investment fund account that she feels is most attractive to her. The bank, in turn, captures the new fund subscription by Ms Alvarez in her main account record and customer profile. It identifies future investment fund information to offer her the next time she accesses her account through the Internet or walks into a branch of the bank.

What exactly does this business interaction illustrate? Some managers might comment that it is a good example of responsive and informed customer service. Others might perceive a well thought-out product cross-selling strategy designed to offer a specific customer the right product information at the appropriate time. Still others might conclude that the whole customer interaction was enabled by an IT system providing very thorough customer information wherever the customer chooses to do business with the bank.

In fact, this customer has just experienced the customer service and cross-selling practices of Banco Bilbao Vizcaya (BBV). The customer profile of Ms Alvarez accessed by the branch representative was not simply her transaction record, as other retail banks might have available. In BBV, branch representatives access the customer support system, which identifies the customer's segment type from a choice of eight options. Also listed is the product portfolio for each segment and the customer profile and transaction history, including all contacts with the bank through ATMs, the Internet and branches visited. By comparing the financial products/services the customer already has to the products/services held by members in the same customer segment, the customer support system identifies cross-selling opportunities on-line for the branch representative during interactions with the customer.

During each customer interaction, every representative is responsible for cross-selling at least one product and updating the customer profile with the outcome of the offer. At BBV, product cross-selling is carefully planned at branch and head office levels. Each branch conducts daily, weekly and monthly reviews of cross-selling opportunities using reports supplied by the customer support system. Having identified the product profiles of the branch customer segments and compared them with the actual products that each customer uses, branch managers—with head office support—define the cross-selling opportunities for the next day, week and month. Every branch and its employees are scored in a rating system that compares performance across all branches in every customer segment across all products.

Both customer and product information used by branch representatives and managers in BBV are maintained by the customer support system, which seamlessly combines on-line customer profiles with product offers by customer segment. As a result, BBV has been able to implement an extremely successful product cross-selling strategy, retain high levels of customer loyalty and achieve high business growth.

BBV's story shows a company whose staff are able to use customer and product information, enabled by a well developed IT system, to effectively serve customers and sell products at the same time—and on every occasion of customer contact. From the customer's perspective, Ms Alvarez's interaction with the bank contributes to her willingness to do more business with the bank. BBV facilitates contact with customers, no matter where the customers are located or which contact channel they use. Branch representatives are encouraged and trained to be proactive in questioning customers about current and future needs and can provide accurate and specific product information and advice in a timely manner. They can also provide customer feedback to aid in new product development. Moreover, they are rewarded for going out of their way to respond to customer questions with information from their colleagues or head office.

To sum up, this is a story about a company's abilities to do three things that are critical to its superior performance:

1. The company has the ability to instil in its employees and managers the right information behaviours and values, which affect how information is used for customer interactions and internal management.
2. The company is able to manage information across all branches in a consistent and timely way while ensuring that the information is accurate and of high quality.
3. The company can deploy IT systems to support operational and management levels of decision-making as well as to innovate with new products.

In the next section, we will see that BBV's managers are not alone in thinking that focused and proactive management of people, information and IT capabilities leads to improved business performance.

THE NEW LENS: LINKING INFORMATION CAPABILITIES TO BUSINESS PERFORMANCE

If companies and industries are becoming increasingly information intensive and information-based, how do senior managers know whether their company is using information effectively to achieve better business performance? The practical answer is, they don't—or at least they didn't, until now. Over the last two and a half years, we have conducted a major, international research study called Navigating Business Success, which has provided us with a clear answer to this question.[1]

From the beginning, our study sought to establish the link between three key capabilities that influence information use in companies— people's behaviours and values, information management practices and information technology practices. In addition, the study aimed to discover how these information capabilities are linked to business performance. If our study could confirm a predictive link between the way senior executives manage people, information and IT and the way in which they achieve superior business performance, then the study could make a major contribution to management practice in two key ways: by providing a new business metric to measure effective information use, and by delivering a new framework or lens to enable executives to manage these capabilities to improve business results.

The Information Orientation (IO) Model

Through our study, we know that senior managers recognize that moving a company to effective information use requires the active management of three unique information capabilities:

- *Information behaviours and values (IBV)* is the capability of a company to instil and promote behaviours and values in its staff for the effective use of information and IT.
- *Information management practices (IMP)* is the capability of a company to manage information effectively over its life cycle, which includes sensing, collecting, organizing, processing and maintaining information.
- *Information technology practices (ITP)* is the capability of a company to effectively manage appropriate IT applications and infrastructure to support operational, decision-making and communication processes.

Senior managers view the interaction of these three unique information capabilities as one fundamental idea or measure, which we call information orientation, or IO.

Moreover, our study went a step further and tested the link between each of the information capabilities of a company and business performance. Did senior managers believe that any one capability was linked to business performance or did they perceive another relationship?

Our study showed that there is no causal link between any one of the information capabilities and business performance. Being good at one of the information capabilities does not lead to improved business performance. Focusing on people behaviours and values at the expense of information management practices, or focusing on IT practices at the expense of information behaviours and values, will not lead to improved business results. This is a sobering finding given the time, effort and expense some companies spend in optimizing one capability over another.

However, our study did find that a company must be good at managing all three information capabilities in order to achieve superior business performance. As the senior managers participating in our research confirm, the three information capabilities work together to produce a set of interactions between them that predicts business performance.

Our core finding is that the interaction of the three information capabilities, which is the information orientation of a company, constitutes the key link to business performance (see Figure 1.1). Companies with high IO (those that are good at implementing their information capabilities) will be high on business performance. Companies with low IO will, in turn, be low on business performance.

Our basic conclusion is that higher IO predicts higher business performance and thus can act as the measure of effective information use in companies. To achieve superior business performance, companies must be good at managing all three information capabilities. Each of the information capabilities alone is necessary, but not enough, to improve business performance.

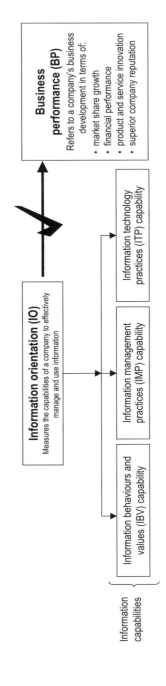

Figure 1.1:   Higher information orientation (IO) predicts higher business performance

Applying the IO Model

From a practical perspective, there are three managerial implications of our findings:

1. Our research confirms that each of the three information capabilities is a distinct and valid concept in the minds of senior managers. Companies that are good at managing information behaviours and values, information management practices and IT practices achieve superior interactive effects. By managing all three information capabilities concurrently, companies achieve higher IO and, thus, better business performance.

2. Our study establishes for the first time that there is a definitive measure of effective information use—IO. High IO predicts superior business performance. Managers can now use information orientation to analyse and benchmark the degree to which their company possesses high or low levels of effective information use. They can therefore find out if they are successful in deploying their information capabilities effectively enough to improve business performance.

3. Our study concludes that if a company invests too little in any of the three information capabilities, business performance will suffer. Companies that want to improve their business performance need to manage all three information capabilities well. Focusing on just one information capability, at the expense of the others, will not significantly improve business performance.

The IO model, presented in Figure 1.2, provides managers with a powerful new lens through which to manage and improve their company's performance.[2] This new lens permits managers to measure how proficient their company is at using information effectively and to understand what actions need to be taken to improve the three information capabilities.

Let's take a look at each of the information capabilities incorporated in the IO model.

Influencing Information Behaviours and Values

Every company tries to promote a set of behaviours and values (that is, create a culture) that managers believe will improve business performance. However, not every company understands which specific behaviours and values will best promote effective information use. During our study, we identified six dimensions of information behaviours and values that directly contribute to effective information use in companies.

Information orientation (IO)
Measures the capabilities of a company to effectively manage and use information

Information technology practices (ITP) capability
The capability of a company to effectively manage appropriate IT applications and infrastructure in support of operational, decision-making and communication processes

Information management practices (IMP) capability
The capability of a company to manage information effectively over its life cycle

Information behaviours and values (IBV) capability
The capability of a company to instil and promote behaviours and values in its staff for effective use of information

IT for operational support
includes the software, hardware, telecommunication networks and technical expertise to ensure that lower-skilled workers perform their responsibilities consistently and with high quality and to improve the efficiency of operations

Sensing
involves how information is detected and identified concerning: economic, social and political changes; competitors' innovations that might impact the business; market shifts and customer demands for new products; and anticipated problems with suppliers and partners

Integrity
is an organizational value manifested through individual behaviour that is characterized by the absence of manipulating information for personal gains such as knowingly passing on inaccurate information, distributing information to justify decisions after the fact or keeping information to oneself. Good information integrity results in effective sharing of sensitive information

IT for business process support
focuses on the deployment of software, hardware, networks and technical expertise to facilitate the management of business processes and people across functions within the company and externally with suppliers and customers

Collecting
consists of the systematic process of gathering relevant information by profiling information needs of employees; developing filter mechanisms (computerized and non-computerized) to prevent information overload; providing access to existing collective knowledge; and training and rewarding employees for accurately and completely collecting information for which they are responsible

Formality
refers to the degree to which members of an organization use and trust formal sources of information. Depending on the size, virtualness, and geographic dispersion of an organization, this balance shifts towards more formal or informal information behaviour

IT for innovation support
includes the software, hardware, telecommunication networks and capabilities that facilitate people's creativity and that enable the exploration, development and sharing of new ideas. It also includes the hardware and software support to develop and introduce new products and services

Organizing
includes indexing, classifying and linking information and databases together to provide access within and across business units and functions; training and rewarding employees for accurately and completely organizing information for which they are responsible

Control
is the disclosure of information about business performance to all employees to influence and direct individual and, subsequently, company performance

Sharing
is the free exchange of non-sensitive and sensitive information. Sharing occurs between individuals in teams, across functional boundaries and across organizational boundaries (i.e., with customers, suppliers and partners)

IT for management support
includes the software, hardware, telecommunication networks and capabilities that facilitate executive decision-making. It facilitates monitoring and analysis of internal and external business issues concerning knowledge sharing, market developments, general business situations, market positioning, future market direction and business risk

Processing
into useful knowledge consists of accessing and analysing appropriate information sources and databases before business decisions are made. Hiring, training, evaluating and rewarding people with analytical skills is essential for processing information into useful knowledge

Information transparency
occurs when an organization's employees trust each other enough to talk about failures, errors and mistakes in an open and constructive manner and without fear of unfair repercussions

Maintaining
involves reusing existing information to avoid collecting the same information again, updating information databases so that they remain current and refreshing data to ensure that people are using the best information available

Information proactiveness
occurs when an organization's staff actively seek out and respond to changes in their competitive environment and think about how to use this information to enhance existing and create new products and services

Figure 1.2:   The IO model

These dimensions are integrity, formality, control, sharing, transparency and proactiveness. These are defined in Figure 1.2.

We know that companies with high IO understand how to instil these behaviours and values in their staff. Senior managers continually and explicitly promote these values by personal example and, at every opportunity, recognize good behaviour and discourage bad. They also know how to derive the most value from the way these behaviours work together to make a company proactive in innovation and using information to respond to business changes.

As an example, companies with high IO understand how information integrity facilitates the formal use of information. Since people share values—honesty, candour, and openness—they trust their formal information sources inside the company. Trusting formal information is also necessary for information control. The willingness of people to trust the performance-based information they get from their senior managers relates directly to the amount of trust they have in the integrity of the managers and the quality of the shared performance information.

In addition, integrity and a positive view of sharing performance-based information create a climate of transparency, in which people are willing to expose failures, mistakes and errors for remedy. A company that treats mistakes and failures as opportunities to learn creates an atmosphere of trust and openness necessary for employees to share all information willingly.

Only when employees understand their impact on company performance and willingly share sensitive information whenever needed will conditions be right for them to seek information proactively inside and outside the company.

Companies with high IO not only understand the interactions among these information behaviours and values, but also know how to improve them over time and instil in their staff a consistent view of how to use information effectively in their company and externally.

Leveraging Information Management Practices

For many years, companies have recognized that effectively managing each phase of the information life cycle—sensing, collecting, organizing, processing and maintaining information, as defined in Figure 1.2—improves how they use information. Nevertheless, recognizing the need to manage information does not necessarily mean that they will do it well.

Ironically, the focus of many executives—either on managing people or on coping with IT challenges—has obscured the practices in their company that have a direct impact on the content and quality of the information used by people internally and externally. What types of information should the company sense and collect? How good is the information the company organizes and processes for decision-making? How well does the company reuse, update or renew the information sources that are most critical to responding to customers, providing product information and running the company?

Companies high in IO address each phase of the information life cycle to improve information use. They also understand how each of the information management phases sharpens the company's skills in learning what information and which information practices create the most business value.

For example, sensing information from outside the company on market shifts, customer needs and new technology changes influences how information is collected. By sensing, a company's staff continually test their perceptions and views against new information about changing business conditions. Collecting relevant, focused information not only prevents information overload, but also directly determines how a company organizes information (that is, how well a company indexes and classifies information and links databases together to promote access and use by its employees).

Organizing information properly, in turn, enables managers and their employees to process it so that they can operate effectively and change the business. Companies that know what information to process and how to maintain it avoid retaining irrelevant information or failing to reuse or update information, thus saving other employees from having to re-collect and organize it in order to make decisions.

Getting the IT Pay-off

For many managers and companies, the link between IT investments and practices and improving business performance remains elusive. Companies spend more and more on IT, but many gain little advantage from their IT practices. Instead, companies use IT to lower costs and improve productivity. Their competitors, however, quickly follow suit, passing the same benefits on to customers in the form of more and cheaper products and services. As the spiral of IT-enabled competition intensifies in every industry, companies seem locked into IT spending more out of competitive necessity than for competitive advantage.

Companies with high IO effectively manage four dimensions of IT practices—IT for operational support, IT for business process support, IT for innovation support and IT for management support—as shown in Figure 1.2. High IO companies know how to break out of the cycle of spending more on IT and getting less pay-off on their bottom line. The break-out strategy depends on knowing how to use IT practices across a range of applications and infrastructure that a company can only develop and implement over time.

For example, IT for operational support focuses primarily on controlling business operations, processing transactions and making sure less skilled employees carry out their work consistently. However, using IT well for operational support provides the infrastructure—and technical knowledge—from which to develop IT for business process support, networking employees, improving business processes and bringing suppliers and customers together. A company that excels at using IT for operational support has an easier time using IT for innovation support. Why? Because using IT for operational support facilitates the sharing and use of information company-wide and thus improves product development and creativity.

Further, companies that use IT well for business process support can more effectively develop their IT practices for management support. They leverage information across their business processes and with customers and suppliers to gain better knowledge for developing new products, spotting emergent customer needs, forming strategy and analysing risk.

Companies with high IO understand that to retain their position among industry leaders, they must use IT effectively to run today's operations and business processes. In the pursuit of competitive necessity, these companies get the most from their IT investments and practices. But they also build for the future. They leverage their IT practices in support of operations and business processes to build a platform for IT to support innovation and create value. In contrast to companies with low IO, high IO companies have developed their IT capabilities to improve their processing and use of information. They have also taught their employees to use information and IT proactively and continuously to improve business performance.

SEEING INFORMATION ORIENTATION (IO) CLEARLY: A PRELUDE TO MANAGING

The first step to being able to manage information capabilities to improve a company's IO level is to be able to see and recognize how a company improves these capabilities over time. High IO does not 'just happen' in companies. It is the outcome of how real managers think about managing people, information and IT to improve performance and how they aid in implementing change in their company.

Let's take a look at another case study that was first presented in the Introduction, but this time through the new lens of the IO model.

Hilti Corporation: Improving the Information Capabilities of the Direct Sales Force

During the early 1990s, Hilti's senior managers found that sales increases were not accompanied by equivalent increases in profits. This finding required senior managers to reassess their company's strategy and identify areas where the capabilities of the company needed improvement. This strategic reassessment led senior managers to reaffirm their strong focus on the customer, along with more attention to excellence in marketing and product innovation. In addition, senior managers decided to substantially improve the information capabilities and business performance of the direct sales force.

Hilti's first attempt to improve the direct selling of its 7,000-person sales force worldwide had focused on an IT-led initiative to equip Hilti's sales force in the United States, Belgium, and Germany with linked laptop computers. This attempt to automate the sales force did not lead to any increase in sales or profitability in these countries. Hilti senior managers wanted to know why.

They discovered that sales people were reluctant to collect information from their sales calls and enter the information into their laptops to forward to the Hilti sales force automation (HSFA) database because they did not see how these new daily tasks improved the way they carried out their job. After some months of frustration and concern, senior managers intervened and gave the chief information officer (CIO), the leader of the initiative, a deadline of nine months either to achieve measurable business results (that is, sales increases) through the IT initiative or terminate the project. The CIO together with local line management proceeded to redefine the initiative and focus on an approach to the project more in line with the company's culture and attitudes toward using information.

Hilti's culture had developed with a strong disposition to behaviours and values that reflected high levels of information integrity, transparency, control and sharing, as noted in Figure 1.2. Martin Hilti's management philosophy emphasized proactive information use by employees through candid and open communications between employees and managers, high levels of information sharing and clearly targeted and understandable performance criteria and indicators.

As senior managers examined the causes of the failure in automating the sales force, they also re-examined how they could further improve the information behaviours and values of their employees.

First, to increase communications and greater information sharing at every level, senior managers surveyed all employees to get honest feedback, to improve working conditions and to stress the need for candour and integrity in the company. This effort began to address the underlying reasons why the first sales force automation project had not been well accepted by the sales force.

Second, to improve control through better communication of business performance information, the company refined its performance 'cockpit charts' to make them more understandable and reflective of employee inputs. The company also improved training at every level. This effort reinforced the notion that sales people needed to understand how information responsibilities at Hilti would be evaluated and directly contribute to business performance.

During the same period, while information behaviours and values were being strengthened in Hilti, the CIO and his team set out to enable the sales force to increase sales through improved information management and IT practices.

The new project team started by profiling the information needs of individual sales people in Hilti to determine the specific types of information to collect and organize. At the same time, they began to map the behaviours and practices that constituted a successful sales person and to discover how these behaviours and practices could be supported with better information and IT. For example, they asked questions like: 'How often does a sales person call on his or her customers?' 'What ancillary products or product information could a sales person offer to existing customers?'

During this process, the project team also identified relevant information needs of the marketing and customer service departments, such as capturing suggestions from customers about service and product improvements as well as new product ideas. This information, which could be directly collected by the sales person on the construction site in conversations with customers, could also improve the information sensing and processing abilities of these departments and the decision-making about future product and customer service strategies and practices.

By defining the information needs underlying the sales process— highlighting the connection between collecting information at the sales person's level and the use of that information by marketing, customer service and product development groups within Hilti—the project team designed an information system, rather than an IT solution. The new HSFA system would improve sales, service and new product development, as well as respond to customer complaints. In addition, to enhance the way this information would be maintained, all unnecessary or redundant data were filtered out of the new system. Sales people would now collect only the information that was useful to them or to their colleagues. This contributed to their success in satisfying Hilti customers. Moreover, the project team made sure that each sales person was fully trained in using the new system and IT, and that the reward system for sales people reflected the new emphasis on information management practices. As a result, Hilti sales people became better at sensing information from customers and forwarding that information to the appropriate people or departments in the company.

Finally, the project team defined a new IT approach that would put in place well-defined information management practices to support the sales force. The new systems would provide operational support to facilitate order fulfilment and deliveries, as well as business process support, by linking the international sales force to the home office and support units in marketing, services and new product development.

Over time, the new system provided sophisticated management support tools to assist the sales efforts, such as prompts that would alert the sales person to call on a key customer after a certain amount of time had elapsed since the previous call. The new system also prompted sales people to promote and cross-sell other related products or product applications to customers, based on the customer's history and profile.

Overall, the new HSFA system focused sales people on the information required to do their job better and make more money themselves as well as serve the interests of the company in sharing customer information and ideas among other departments company-wide. As the CIO noted: 'The new system leaves the sales people no choice but to share the required information, as the other functions depend on it.'

The Hilti HSFA project shows that when information capabilities are managed and changed holistically and concurrently, rather than one set of capabilities being optimized at the expense of others, then the information orientation of the company will improve and so will its business performance.

CONCLUSION

In this chapter we have shown you how to see your business reality through the new lens of our information orientation model and the three information capabilities associated with the model. We also applied our lens to Hilti to assist you in understanding how a company combines or weaves together these information capabilities in order to improve business performance.

However, being able to see a business situation in a new light, or reading a case study from another company, does not ensure that you, as an executive, will be able to manage your situation any differently. For you to close the loop between new management theory and practice, you must have a way of diagnosing and measuring your own information capabilities and how they contribute to better business results.

In the next chapter we will show you how to measure IO in your own company and how to benchmark your information capabilities and business performance against a core sample of companies and senior management teams. We will introduce you to the information orientation dashboard and show you how to use this tool to diagnose the strengths and weaknesses in your company's information capabilities.

NOTES

1. A team of 10 researchers and staff from the International Institute for Management Development (IMD) in Lausanne, Switzerland, sponsored by Accenture, conducted a two and a half year international research effort called Navigating Business Success to understand how senior managers perceive the relationship between three information capabilities—IT, information management and people's behaviours and values pertaining to the use of information—and business performance. Detailed statistical results of the study and full research methodology can be found in Marchand, D.A., Kettinger, W.J. and Rollins, J.D. (2001) *Information Orientation: The Link to Business Performance*, UK: Oxford University Press.
2. The IO model is an empirically-validated model representing the ways in which senior managers view effective information use.

II

MEASURING INFORMATION CAPABILITIES

2

HOW TO MEASURE INFORMATION CAPABILITIES

Measurement counts. What a company measures and the way it measures influence both the mind-sets of managers and the way people behave. The best measures are tied to business performance and are linked to the strategies and business capabilities of the company.

Many managers espouse interesting management concepts and ideas such as knowledge management or learning organization, but fail to measure the relationship between the company's actions and the outcomes to be achieved, especially increases in business performance. Without clear definitions and measures, managers take various leaps of faith hoping that if they follow a certain course, such as investing in knowledge repositories, these investments will lead to improved performance. Managers are left with no way to assess their progress or the return from investing in one set of actions versus another.

When we began our research study, we were convinced that advancing new management prescriptions in line with our information orientation (IO) model would be interesting, but not compelling, to senior managers, unless we could develop a business metric directly tied to business performance that would assist managers in measuring their information capabilities. As the first business metric of its kind, information orientation measures the extent to which senior managers perceive that their organization possesses the practices and behaviours associated with effective information use to improve business performance. Using the IO metric,[1] we can show managers the strengths and weaknesses of their company's information capabilities, and help them to identify key areas for focused, strategic change.

In this chapter we explain why efforts in the past to link people's behaviours and values, information management practices or IT practices to business performance have been unsatisfactory. We then introduce our new measurement tool, called the information orientation dashboard, and explain how we developed and tested it. We explain how managers can use the IO dashboard inside and outside their company as a benchmark, how to interpret the IO dashboard and how managers can benefit from its use in their company.

WHY HAVE INFORMATION CAPABILITIES NOT PREVIOUSLY BEEN LINKED TO PERFORMANCE?

Perhaps the main reason why information capabilities have not been satisfactorily tied to business performance is because, in the past, companies have not explicitly managed their people behaviours and values, information management practices and IT practices in a holistic way.

Instead, each of these capabilities, when it was managed explicitly at all, was perceived as separate from the others. Information systems and IT departments were charged with the management of IT; libraries and records departments with the management of information; and human resources departments (HR) with the management of people. In the cases of the IT and HR departments, the separation was functional—one focused on technology management, while the other focused on people management, including appropriate rewards and controls. In the case of information practices, the focus was either on the activities of information specialists in corporate libraries, information centres and market research units or was perceived as embedded in the business activities and processes of the company. If information was everywhere in business life like the air we breathe, then measuring its value did not seem to be necessary.

Missing from all three functional views was the responsibility to actively improve the ways in which people use information and the behaviours and values associated with effective information use. While companies pumped millions of pounds into IT investment (without seeing comparable increases in performance), they failed to invest in more formal ways of understanding and improving people's information behaviours. As a result, this area has remained a relatively informal management activity, and for the most part been left out of the measurement management equation (see Figure 2.1).

In the absence of a comprehensive measure of information effectiveness such as IO and a proven predictive link between this new measure and business performance, approaches to the measurement of a

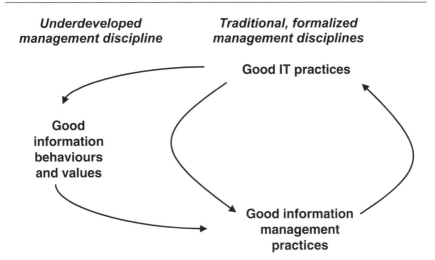

Figure 2.1: A key gap in formalizing management activities

company's information capabilities in the past were either rather narrowly focused, not articulated explicitly or not linked to performance.

Let's take a closer look at why this fragmentation occurred in business measurements of information capabilities.

People Count in Business, But So Does Control

Today, in a global economy in which knowledge and its application are critical to competitive survival and advantage, most companies subscribe to the view that 'people are our most important asset'. Moreover, many managers accept the view that a company's culture (that is, its values and behaviours) counts.

However, while managers and HR professionals recognize that the behaviours and values that a company instils in its people are important to performance generally, companies have not directly addressed the relationship between the management of people and the ways that people use information to achieve business results. What specific behaviours and values lead some companies toward effective information use, and how can these be instilled in people over time to improve, rather than degrade, performance?

In recent years, managers in the finance and accounting professions, in particular, have placed a lot of emphasis on improving global measures of business performance. These focus on implementing management control systems such as value-based management or the balanced scorecard. They are also concerned with developing appropriate performance criteria and measures such as economic value added or activity based costing and applying this information at various levels to influence working behaviour consistent with improving the company's performance.

While the advocates of better management controls and performance measures recognize the role of control-oriented information in managing people and linking their performance to business performance, they do not identify other behavioural issues that are linked to business performance and are essential for the effective use of information.

Measuring Information's Business Value: Grasping the Intangible

If it has been difficult in the past for managers to identify the behaviours and values linked to business results, the search for a way to understand and measure good information practices and their link to performance has been no less frustrating.

One reason is that managers and IT people see information everywhere in the business and have difficulty in assessing how much is too much or how much is enough. Information takes on meaning, and therefore value, for managers and employees only when the context of its use is clear. However, the same information may be used by people in many different contexts or decision-making processes in which the information employed may also be poorly understood or structured.

These difficulties in valuing information have led to two views of how companies should measure and manage information:

View A: The Process View of Information

In the process view, information use goes through a life cycle, from sensing and collecting, through organizing and processing, to maintaining information. Each step in this life cycle can add or subtract value from the use of the information in a company. Managing information means making information relevant for decision-making, therefore the value of information is closely linked to the context for decision-making in a company.

Managing information as a process also means understanding the role of information in business processes. Improving business processes depends on the quality of the information that is used in the process as well as on how it can be changed and improved. Little progress has been made, however, in linking information used for business processes or decision-making to overall business performance.

View B: The Resource View of Information

In this view, information is perceived as an organizational 'resource' like people, capital or technology. As in the process view, information is seen as inherently contextual, that is, its value can vary according to the context in which it is used, the people involved in its use and the criteria applied to its use. Since, according to this view, the value of information is a function of an individual's viewpoint, managers play an important role in shaping the business contexts in which information is used and the criteria for the ways in which information management practices enhance or dilute decision-making by people in the company.

Both views—of information as a process and as a resource—have suggested important criteria through which its value in a company can be evaluated. However, until now, neither business practitioners nor academics have developed measures that could be used to link information management to business performance. Where there have been serious attempts to measure information value, the focus has been on measuring the usefulness of corporate libraries and information centres from an individual user's perspective, rather than from the perspective of company performance.

Measuring IT Practices: Focusing on the Means, not the End

Many companies attempt to assess the value of IT through metrics not linked to business performance. The IT field has a rich tradition of building IT metrics. Unfortunately, for the most part, these metrics are biased towards the IT function, based on user satisfaction with the computer systems, on levels of IT acceptance, or on the service quality and responsiveness of the IT department. While it is useful for managers to have this sort of knowledge, most of these metrics have not been linked to the broader criteria of business performance such as profitability or growth in market share.

In addition, IT metrics have generally focused on information use in relation to information systems developed or purchased within the domain of the IT function. As a consequence, these measures are not only biased toward the IT function, but are also employed primarily by IT managers in the company, rather than by business managers. Thus IT metrics have for the most part not been developed from the perspective of senior managers. They have emphasized the perceptions of users of computer systems or the IT function, rather than clear business performance criteria.

Efforts to measure the link between IT investment and business performance from an economics perspective have also failed to establish a
consistent causal linkage with sustained business profitability. Despite
considerable effort, no practical model has been developed to measure
whether a company's IT investments will definitely contribute to sustainable competitive advantage.

Lastly, IT metrics have captured little of the behavioural capability of
information use. Understanding how human behaviours and values influence information use has remained an ancillary area of research and
management concern.

To sum up, we can conclude that managers and functional professionals representing the three information capabilities have in the past
treated them quite separately from each other in terms of measuring
information behaviours and values, information management practices
and IT practices and their contributions to business performance. A visible void in measurements concerning people's information behaviours
and values marks all three areas. Information orientation represents the
first comprehensive measure of the relationship of information capabilities to improved business performance.

MEASURING INFORMATION CAPABILITIES

Knowing what you have to measure is not good enough. A manager must
have a way of visualizing the information orientation of the company that
shows how good it is at each of the information capabilities, how it scores
on IO and how all this is related to business performance. We have
developed a diagnostic tool, known as the information orientation
dashboard. Figure 2.2 shows the IO dashboard for Hilti—a company that
we have seen is high on IO and high on business performance.

The IO dashboard can be used by managers to evaluate each of the
three information capabilities in their company. The dashboard gives
percentage rankings of each capability—and its dimensions—relative
to our overall research study benchmark sample. In a simple, clear
picture it shows companies which dimensions they need to improve in
their information capabilities to achieve higher IO. With a quick glance
at the dashboard, managers can identify areas of strength, as well as
areas in need of improvement in their company. The IO dashboard is
also a powerful management tool for internal or external benchmarking. Since, as we noted in Chapter 1, higher IO results in higher
business performance, improvements in the three information capabilities and their dimensions should lead to gains in business
performance.

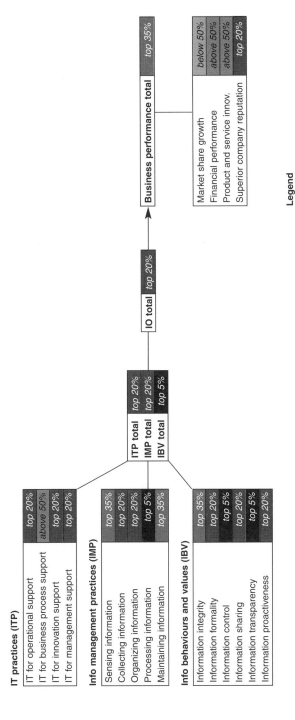

IT practices (ITP)

IT for operational support	top 20%
IT for business process support	above 50%
IT for innovation support	top 20%
IT for management support	top 20%

Info management practices (IMP)

Sensing information	top 35%
Collecting information	top 20%
Organizing information	top 20%
Processing information	top 5%
Maintaining information	top 35%

Info behaviours and values (IBV)

Information integrity	top 35%
Information formality	top 20%
Information control	top 5%
Information sharing	top 20%
Information transparency	top 5%
Information proactiveness	top 20%

ITP total	top 20%
IMP total	top 20%
IBV total	top 5%

| IO total | top 20% |

Business performance total | top 35%

Market share growth	below 50%
Financial performance	above 50%
Product and service innov.	above 50%
Superior company reputation	top 20%

Legend

Top 5% (top 8 SMTs)	top 5%
Top 20% (top 34 SMTs)	top 20%
Top 35% (top 60 SMTs)	top 35%
Above 50% (upper 84 SMTs)	above 50%
Below 50% (lower 85 SMTs)	below 50%
Bottom 35% (lower 60 SMTs)	bottom 35%
Bottom 20% (lower 34 SMTs)	bottom 20%
Bottom 5% (lowest 8 SMTs)	bottom 5%

Explanations

The information orientation dashboard depicts the ranking of a senior management team (SMT) within the benchmark sample of the IMD/AC Partnership Project Navigating Business Success.

By using the legend to the right you can identify the relative position of the displayed SMT within the benchmark sample.

Figure 2.2:   The Hilti Corporation information orientation dashboard

Developing the IO Dashboard

Our research study utilized a representative, international benchmark of 169 senior management teams (SMTs) from 98 companies; 1,009 individual senior managers responded to the survey. Chief executive officers (CEOs) represented the highest concentration of responses within an individual management-position category. The majority of survey responses (58 per cent) came from CEOs, executive and senior vice presidents, and general managers/directors. See Figure 2.3 for a full breakdown of the study sample and benchmark.

- 1,009 Senior Managers from 169 senior management teams
- 58% CEOs, executive and senior vice presidents and general managers/directors
- 22 countries represented
- 25 industries (IT industry excluded)
- Companies ranged from very small to global enterprises
- 94% male and 6% female respondents
- 62% of respondents between 41 and 55 years old
- 58% have been in their positions between 1 and 5 years
- 51% have been associated with their company for over 11 years

---

Figure 2.3:   The study and benchmark sample

Why Focus on Senior Managers and Senior Management Teams?

Throughout our research study and in this book, our basic point of reference is the perceptions and perspectives of senior managers in a broad sample of manufacturing and service-oriented companies—ranging in size from small, family-owned businesses to large, global enterprises—across 25 industries in 22 countries. Why are the perceptions of senior managers so important?

First, the perceptions of senior managers drive strategic decisions and actions in companies. Closely examining these perceptions leads to better understanding of how senior managers view the deployment of people, information and IT to achieve their business objectives or intended strategies. Also, it is senior managers who must strike the balance between pursuing an intended strategy, articulated and implemented by a senior management team, and an emergent strategy that typically arises at various levels of the organization as people search for opportunities and solve new or unexpected problems. Even though, as Henry Mintzberg has observed,[2] intended and emergent strategies coexist in most companies, it is the senior managers who somehow have to find a way to deliberately pursue intended strategy while also creating the conditions for emergent strategies to evolve. How rigidly they expect to implement their intended strategy and how willing they are to recognize emergent strategies in their company—to respond and change course—will condition the ways they motivate their people to use information effectively.

Second, for senior managers, achieving business results for their company and business unit is a never-ending challenge. And previous management researchers have shown that senior managers' choices do influence the performance of their company and business unit.

Third, senior managers do not work alone. They are members of senior management teams or groups. (We define a senior management team as 'a relatively small senior leadership group of the most influential corporate, division and/or business unit executives'.) They represent the key areas of business or functional responsibility in their organization. They formulate the basic strategies of the organization, allocate resources and implement strategies to achieve the right business results.

Reading and Using the IO Dashboard

To read the IO dashboard, first look at the legend at the bottom of Figure 2.2 (see p. 41). Note that 169 senior management teams (SMTs) have been categorized in percentiles, based on their scores relative to the average sample scores across all measures of the study. The legend is coded in a graduated scale from dark (very high) to light (very low) relative to the total benchmark.

At the far left of the dashboard are the dimensions within each of the three information capabilities. Each of the dimensions, in this case for the Hilti Corporation, has been ranked according to the legend. To the right is a score for each of the information capabilities, based on the statistical analysis of the dimensions. The total IO score for the company (or a business unit) follows. To the right of the IO total score is the company's (overall) business performance score. At the far right of the dashboard are the items that make up the scores for business performance—market share growth, financial performance, product and service innovation and superior company reputation.

A manager can scan the IO dashboard in order to:

- get a snapshot of where his or her company stands in using information effectively, and
- understand the relationship of the company's information use to overall business performance.

Once a company has identified a problem in an information capability, it can further ask which of its problematic, or weaker, dimensions need to be improved in order to raise its scores. At a glance, managers can identify areas of strengths and areas in need of improvement.

In addition, using the benchmark database, we can visualize the relative position of each individual company or business unit to our benchmark of 169 senior management teams on a plot of the two main study variables—information orientation and business performance.[3] This is a useful benchmarking tool to quickly evaluate an individual company or business unit by comparing its position relative to the position of the senior management teams in our benchmark database. Figure 2.4, for example, shows the position of Hilti's corporate senior management team. Each number on the chart represents one senior management team's perceptions of the information orientation and business performance of their company, division or business unit.

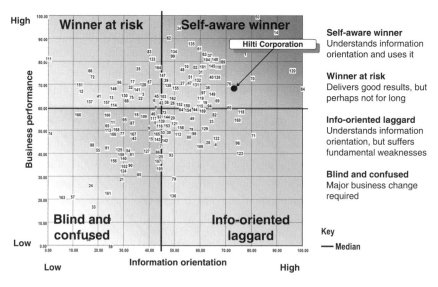

Figure 2.4: To benchmark: compares Hilti's information orientation to business performance

For descriptive purposes, we have grouped the participating SMTs in four quadrants:

1. *Self-aware winner*   Companies, divisions or business units in this quadrant understand how to manage their information capabilities to improve their information orientation and to achieve superior business performance.

2. *Winner at risk*   Companies, divisions or business units in this quadrant deliver good performance results at present, but lack the information capabilities to improve IO in the future. Given their current strong business performance, they may be unaware of the need to improve IO, and thus may be at risk of diluting their future business performance.

3. *Info-oriented laggard*   Companies, divisions or business units in this quadrant understand how to improve their information capabilities to improve IO, but suffer from other fundamental business weaknesses. For example, external environmental changes beyond the company's control, such as sudden national economic crises or fluctuations in currency markets may be constraining performance, despite good information capabilities.

4. *Blind and confused*   Companies, divisions or business units in this quadrant have not improved information capabilities in the past and have suffered poor performance. These companies are in need of a major business change to significantly transform their information capabilities and business performance.

Companies with multiple divisions or business units can create an internal benchmark sample, along the lines of Figure 2.4. This can be used to define a portfolio approach (see Chapter 9) to raising the IO levels across business units and thus strengthen the IO score and business performance of the company or group as a whole.

Periodic Benchmarks

Managers can use the IO measures and benchmarks at various times to assess management decisions and efforts at improving IO and business performance. Figure 2.5 looks at three sample companies.

Company A

This company scores very low on IO at Time 1. Senior managers in this company may take immediate action to address the causes of low IO.

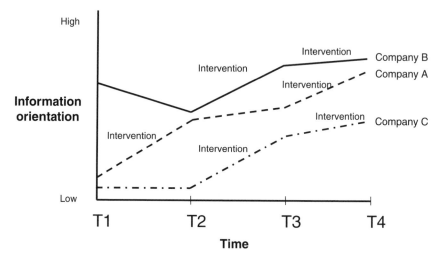

Figure 2.5: Assessing a company's information orientation over time

Such an intervention can directly address a serious deficiency in one or two of the IO dimensions. For example, this company may be low in information behaviours such as transparency and sharing, which makes people very reactive in sensing and collecting information about key customer needs.

A second assessment at Time 2 might indicate some improvement, but not at the level desired. Managers can take further steps to improve key behaviours and values as well as launch a plan for implementing a new IT system to support customer sensing and information collection by sales people. A third assessment at Time 3 may show a slight, but slowing, improvement in IO, suggesting a need for further efforts to improve behaviours and perhaps increase the pace of IT system implementation.

Finally, at Time 4, the marked improvements in IO might indicate that the company is achieving significant benefits from concurrently changing behaviours and values and introducing a new IT system to improve information management practices.

Company B

This company shows an average IO compared with its competitors. If the company's managers are not proactive in sustaining the current level of IO, however, it may decline. For example, if the company engages in an acquisition, the process of integrating the two companies may dilute the information capabilities of the acquiring company as well as the acquired company for a year or more. It is important to recognize that a company's

IO level is never constant or fixed, but changes continually with business conditions. An IO assessment in Time 2 indicates a drop in IO, perhaps following the acquisition, which could worsen unless appropriate actions are taken to reverse the decline in information capabilities.

Company C

Both Time 1 and Time 2 indicate very low IO. Senior managers in this company will need to dramatically transform their information capabilities to improve the company's IO over time.

INTERPRETING AND ACTING ON THE IO DASHBOARD RESULTS

By looking at a company's IO dashboard, you can immediately see whether it is high on IO and/or business performance.

A High IO, High-performing Company: Staying Ahead

If you examine the IO total and the business performance total cells in the middle of Figure 2.6, you can readily see that the company is high on both measures. On IO, the company ranks in the top five per cent of the benchmark companies (dark). On business performance, the company ranks in the top 20 per cent of the benchmark (located in the Self-aware winner quadrant of Figure 2.4).

The challenge for managers in this company is to stay ahead with information capabilities so that they continue to excel in the future. Taking a closer look at the IO dashboard reveals that there is room for improvement, even in this high-performing company. Across several of the IO dimensions, the company does not score dark, such as IT for innovation support in the ITP capability; sensing information in IMP and information integrity and information transparency in IBV.

At this point, we need to ask why these lower scores are present and what actions could be taken to raise these specific areas over time—even though the company overall is high on IO.

Managers could focus on why the company has not fully exploited IT for new product development. As in a lot of companies over the last five years, the focus of improvements has been on using IT for basic operational support and for business process support. Similarly, the company may not have developed its abilities to sense customer needs and use this information in product innovation or customer service. Perhaps managers have not placed enough emphasis on improving the

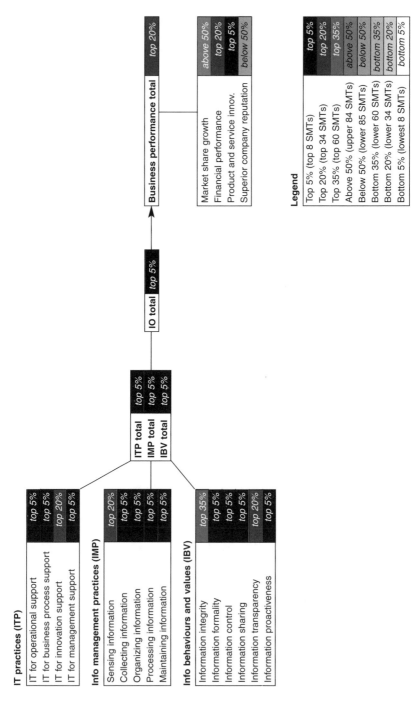

Figure 2.6: The IO dashboard of a high IO, high-performing company

process of sensing information, involving people at all levels in the company.

The deficiencies in transparency and integrity may raise important concerns about how well managers and people in the company respond to errors and mistakes and whether they seek to correct them both internally and for customers. Are people in the company hesitant about sharing information about errors and mistakes as they occur and seeking to resolve them constructively? Have there been incidents when employees reporting errors have been embarrassed or reprimanded unfairly by managers? Are people in the company passing on inaccurate information, or even manipulating information, to cover operational problems or difficulties with customers, because employees feel that certain managers do not want to hear 'bad news'?

These behavioural deficiencies may also be affecting the company's business performance, especially with regard to market share growth (above 50 per cent) and company reputation (below 50 per cent). Is this high-performing company beginning to lose its edge with customers because it is not perceived as innovative or as responsive to customer complaints and problems? Is the IO measurement within the information capability dimensions beginning to register a dilution of information capabilities at precisely a time when the company's IO and business performance scores are high? How should the company's managers interpret these signals and what actions can they take to stay ahead with IO and business performance?

Even when a company is high on IO and business performance, it is unlikely that there are no information capabilities that can be improved to sustain superior IO and business performance.

A Low IO, Low-performing Company: Breaking Out

A company that is low on IO and performance (see Figure 2.7) must move beyond incremental improvements, such as those outlined above, and think about breaking out of its current mind-set to transform its information capabilities. This company falls in the bottom 35 per cent of the benchmark sample on IO and business performance. The managers responsible for this company have led it into a state of being 'blind and confused' (lower left quadrant in Figure 2.4).

The first question is: Does this team of managers have the mind-set and motivation to transform the information capabilities of this company as part of an overall effort to redefine company strategy and business capabilities? The board of directors may have to ask some serious questions about how the company got into this predicament with the current

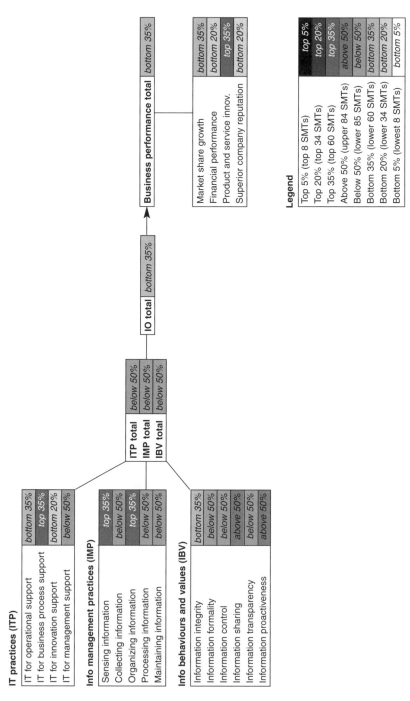

IT practices (ITP)

IT for operational support	bottom 35%
IT for business process support	top 35%
IT for innovation support	bottom 20%
IT for management support	below 50%

Info management practices (IMP)

Sensing information	top 35%
Collecting information	below 50%
Organizing information	top 35%
Processing information	below 50%
Maintaining information	below 50%

Info behaviours and values (IBV)

Information integrity	bottom 35%
Information formality	below 50%
Information control	below 50%
Information sharing	above 50%
Information transparency	below 50%
Information proactiveness	above 50%

ITP total	below 50%
IMP total	below 50%
IBV total	below 50%

IO total	bottom 35%

Business performance total	bottom 35%

Market share growth	bottom 35%
Financial performance	bottom 20%
Product and service innov.	top 35%
Superior company reputation	bottom 20%

Legend

Top 5% (top 8 SMTs)	top 5%
Top 20% (top 34 SMTs)	top 20%
Top 35% (top 60 SMTs)	top 35%
Above 50% (upper 84 SMTs)	above 50%
Below 50% (lower 85 SMTs)	below 50%
Bottom 35% (lower 60 SMTs)	bottom 35%
Bottom 20% (lower 34 SMTs)	bottom 20%
Bottom 5% (lowest 8 SMTs)	bottom 5%

Figure 2.7: The IO dashboard of a low IO company

management team and how willing—or capable—this team is to lead the company out of this situation.

The existing senior management team can use the IO dashboard to develop the best mind-set and set of actions for improving serious deficiencies in information capabilities and business performance over time. The shadings for each dimension of the three information capabilities, and their pattern, raise key questions about how to interpret these measures and what to do to transform them.

For example, how would managers explain the low scores in IT practices? What is the connection between the low score for innovation support and the higher score for process support? Did the company place too much emphasis on IT for process support at the expense of IT for new product development or innovation?

Also, the managers of this company rated the company quite high on the product and service dimension of business performance. Are they focusing too much attention on Sensing information and Proactive information behaviours without giving their people the right IT tools to share information about emerging customer needs and being more innovative in the future?

What constrains this company from collecting information, if both sensing and organizing information seem to work reasonably well compared with the benchmark? Why is the company not better processing the information it organizes before decisions are made or converting the information into useful knowledge?

Why does the company rate itself high on sharing information (above 50 per cent), but very low on information transparency and integrity?

Do people share information that is of low value and withhold information that is sensitive or even negative? Do managers penalize bearers of bad news so that information about errors and mistakes is suppressed by employees?

In terms of business performance, we can examine each dimension of information capabilities and see where specific improvements could lead to changes in business performance. What mix of business strategies and capabilities will lead this company to better financial performance and company reputation when it ranks in the bottom 20 per cent of the benchmark sample?

Without the IO model and the measures of information capabilities, IO and business performance, managers in these two companies would be unable to see where they are deficient and in need of changes. They would not know how their company stands relative to other companies on IO and performance. Nor would they be able to ask the right questions about their situation and improve their information capabilities over time.

HOW MANAGERS CAN BENEFIT FROM THE IO DASHBOARD

The core benefit of the IO dashboard is that it closes the loop in advancing a new management theory about information capabilities, information orientation and business performance and putting it into practice. It actually measures the key variables in the IO model to permit managers to act on what they know. By interpreting the IO dashboard, you as a manager can discover strengths and weaknesses within the information capabilities of your company. You can start asking the right questions and taking steps to improve or sustain your information capabilities.

The IO dashboard also offers managers a 'reality check' over time. Carrying out the IO assessment periodically (for example, annually or bi-annually) permits an evaluation of the journey the company is taking toward higher IO and more effective information use. With these periodic IO measures, you can ask the following questions: Which actions to improve information capabilities have worked? Which ones have not? Which dimensions of information capabilities does the company need to work harder and smarter on? How has the level of IO to business performance improved or declined?

Moreover, if there are multiple business units in the company, corporate managers can assess the IO levels of all of them. Knowing the relative information capabilities of the business units, corporate and business unit managers can develop a portfolio approach (see Chapter 9) to improving information capabilities and IO levels to raise the business performance of the group or company as a whole. Managers can learn about best practices in managing information capabilities from high-performing business units and transfer them to lower performing business units.

However, the IO dashboard is more than a new set of operational measures. Managers can employ the IO dashboard as a strategic management approach to linking long-term improvements in information capabilities to business strategies, as we will explore in Chapters 7 and 8. Companies can employ the IO dashboard to achieve some critical management objectives.

First, the IO dashboard can help to clarify the set of business strategies and capabilities that a company must build over time to succeed. The senior management team must be explicit about IO goals and how to achieve improvements to its information capabilities. In doing so, the senior managers can use the IO model and dashboard to develop a common or shared language for themselves and their staff.

Second, the IO dashboard offers a clear and consistent way to communicate and cascade key messages about improvements in information capabilities throughout a business unit or company. The IO dashboard can signal to employees the objectives to be achieved if a company's business strategies are to succeed. The IO dashboard can act as a 'cockpit chart' to help people communicate about improvements to information capabilities with corporate executives or the company's board of directors and build commitment to a business unit's or company's IO approach.

Third, the IO dashboard can be used to plan and set targets to align information capabilities with business strategies. The targets for the changes to information capabilities are derived from the IO dashboard and aimed at improving business performance. Managers can use the dashboard to build consensus and teamwork around information capability improvement projects.

Fourth, the IO dashboard can enhance strategic feedback and learning over time. It enables managers and employees to monitor and make adjustments in the implementation of initiatives to improve information capabilities. If necessary, fundamental changes to accelerate or redefine initiatives can be made over time in response to rapidly changing business conditions. Managers and employees can discuss not only how past initiatives have improved IO and business performance, but also—more importantly—whether expectations for competing with information in the future in their industry or industries remain on track.

Fifth, the IO dashboard permits the senior management team to hold a mirror in front of itself that reflects its mind-set or views about information capabilities and business performance. We know that the mind-sets of senior managers directly affect the actions they will support and take to improve business performance. Therefore, their mind-sets concerning how they individually and collectively think about information capabilities, especially information behaviours and values, are critical to building credible improvement efforts among employees in their company or business units.

Senior managers and senior management teams must 'walk the talk'. Their personal and team challenge is to practice good information behaviours, good information management practices and good IT practices themselves to demonstrate to other managers and their employees that improving information capabilities is not just for others in the company, but starts at the top.

CONCLUSION

In Chapter 1, we presented the IO model as a new lens for seeing how information capabilities are linked to business performance. In Chapter 2, we presented the IO dashboard as an innovative and powerful diagnostic tool to measure information capabilities, IO and business performance. The IO dashboard not only provides a link between our IO model and management mind-sets, but can also lead managers to actions that, over time, can improve information capabilities and thus business performance.

In Part III, we will focus on what we know about how companies with high IO achieve high performance and which specific management actions lead to improved information behaviours and values, information management practices and IT practices. How do the winners tie the dimensions of the three information capabilities together to achieve superior business performance today and to stay ahead in the future?

NOTES

1. The IO metric is grounded in proven statistical and psychometric research techniques—confirmatory factor analysis (CFA) and structural equation modelling (SEM)—that establish a predictive link between IO and business performance.
2. Mintzberg, H., Ahlstrand, B. and Lampel, J. (1998) *Strategy Safari*, London: Prentice Hall. See pp. 10–11.
3. The IO benchmark is designed as a managerial positioning tool to help senior managers identify where their company is in relation to other multinational companies faced with the challenge of competing in the 'information age'. The IO benchmark uses a scatterplot to visualize the relative position of the 169 SMTs in terms of the two main study variables, information orientation and business performance. In order to derive a 0 to 100 scale, the SMT data was normalized: the lowest value scored on any of these three variables became '0', the highest score became '100'. Subsequently, all SMTs were set in relation to this defined spectrum by simple mathematical transformation. These calculated values were then used as x and y coordinates for the benchmark plot. The medians for each variable were plotted on the chart to gain additional descriptive depth and thus create a high-level categorization of study SMTs. It should be noted that while the IO benchmark is an extremely useful managerial positioning framework for initiating management discussion and forms the basis of further probing of information usage practices within a company, it is not a validated statistical framework and was not the basis for our primary study findings.

III

MANAGING INFORMATION CAPABILITIES

Part III is all about making information orientation (IO) happen by managing information capabilities to achieve superior performance. In Chapter 3, we focus on the journeys that companies take to become excellent at managing all three information capabilities. We present case studies of three companies that have worked—and continue to work—diligently on improving their information capabilities, thus achieving the paybacks from the interaction, or cross-capability, effects of very good information behaviours and values, information management practices and IT practices. We explain the power of these cross-capability linkages in our IO maturity model and outline how companies can get started in attaining higher levels of IO to improve business performance.

In Chapters 4 to 6, we show how to make specific improvements in each of the three information capabilities that lead to IO maturity and higher IO. The four chapters in Part III provide hands-on management prescriptions and case studies to help your company attain IO maturity and improve business performance.

3

ACHIEVING HIGH INFORMATION ORIENTATION (IO): MAKING IT ALL HAPPEN

In Chapter 2, we showed how to measure the strengths and weaknesses of a company's information capabilities. In this chapter, we will begin to explore how managers can prioritize changes to their information capabilities to best attain high IO through what we call the 'IO maturity model'.

Building information capabilities takes time. A company cannot be high-performing unless its managers and staff take the time to develop their company's information capabilities. A basic lesson that we have learned from companies with high IO and business performance is that improving information capabilities involves a considerable journey. This lesson may seem somewhat paradoxical in the age of 'Internet-time' and fast-paced business changes. But we believe that managers of high performing companies understand and work on two levels at once:

- they carefully build information capabilities over years, and
- they make sure their companies exploit these capabilities to compete with information in their industries and markets—smarter, faster and keener.

This dual strategy means that companies are always moving to different levels of IO maturity. The natural differences between companies that are high or low on IO come about in two ways. First, within the three information capabilities, companies work on different practices and behaviours, and second, over time, some companies implement these practices and behaviours more successfully than others do.

Due to these realities, the task of developing information capabilities may seem daunting. Given limited time and resources, how should managers start to improve their company's IO? Do companies with high IO follow similar paths to building their information capabilities that can act as a guide for others?

Let's look now at how companies with high IO make it happen.

WINNERS TIE IT ALL TOGETHER: LEARNING FROM COMPANIES WITH HIGH IO

Companies with high IO are good at managing all three information capabilities and typically have focused on improving them over several years. Regardless of how the company has undertaken the journey, senior managers in companies with high IO know that all three information capabilities must be worked on simultaneously. Unlike companies with low IO, companies with high IO have an understanding of the fundamental relationships between these capabilities and are able to use these relationships to build 'IO maturity'.

Companies with IO maturity know that certain relationships or linkages exist between the key dimensions *within* each of the information capabilities. They also know that, if managed well, these linkages help to generate and accelerate the interaction that we believe exists among the three information capabilities—and therefore, help to increase IO.

What Do Companies with IO Maturity Know?

Companies with IO maturity are good at managing all three information capabilities, and do three things especially well:

- *IT practices*   More mature IO companies not only use IT systems to support operations, business processes, and product innovation, but also enhance *management-level decision-making*.
- *Information management practices*   More mature IO companies manage information in a consistent and timely way while ensuring that information is accurate and of high quality. In addition to collecting, organizing and maintaining information well, more mature organizations continue to enhance the *sensing* and *processing* practices—the most difficult information management dimensions to improve.
- *Information behaviours and values*   More mature IO companies instil in their employees precisely those behaviours and values that affect how the company best uses information for customer, supplier and partner

relationships as well as for internal management control. By instilling this set of good information behaviours and values, employees develop strong *proactive* information behaviours.

More mature IO companies understand that these four key dimensions interact with each other across the three information capabilities to create higher IO. We call this the 'IO interaction effect'. This effect is greatest when a company has established good *proactive* information behaviours; when it is able to *sense* the right information; and when it has solid *processing* and *IT support of management decision-making* (see Figure 3.1).

- Build proactive information use among all people in the company

- Develop information processing practices linked to business strategies and changes in future business conditions

- Improve sensing capabilities of all employees to anticipate the future today

- Invest in IT for management support

Figure 3.1:   Prescriptions from mature IO companies

The IO maturity model in Figure 3.2 shows the results of statistical path analysis.[1] The arrows indicate the dimensions that influence each other (are causally linked), and the direction of the relationship. For example, the arrows in Figure 3.2 indicates that within the IBV capability, proactiveness is influenced directly by sharing and control. The arrows also indicate, however, that proactiveness is influenced by a dimension outside the IBV capability—IT for management support. Proactiveness, in turn, has a direct effect on the information management practice of sensing, which in turn influences IT for management support. Both proactiveness and IT for management support directly influence the processing practice. By following the direction of the arrows, this model identifies the 'paths' that companies should follow to improve their IO maturity.

This model also allows us to define IO maturity in a direct way: companies with less mature IO tend to focus on those dimensions found towards the bottom of the IO maturity model. Those companies desiring more mature IO strive to move up the paths in the model, developing all IO dimensions to eventually capitalize on the IO interaction effect between proactiveness, sensing, IT for management support and processing.

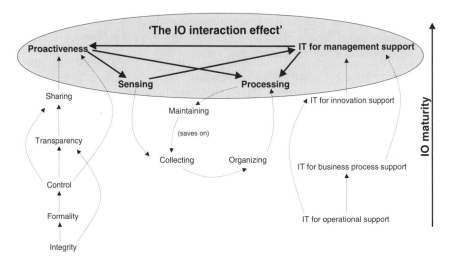

Figure 3.2:   The IO maturity model: cross-capability linkages

As seen in the shaded area of Figure 3.2, more mature IO companies work on these key dimensions simultaneously and create a powerful interaction effect among the three information capabilities that lead to higher IO. A deficiency in any one of these cross-capability dimensions will diminish a company's ability to create effective information use, decreasing its effect on business performance.

Companies with mature IO also know that certain relationships or linkages exist between the dimensions within each information capability. For example, as shown in Figure 3.2, IT for operational support has a direct influence on IT for business process support and IT for innovation support. It also serves as a building block for the entire IT capability, indirectly influencing IT for management support through these linkages. Companies with IO maturity know that, if managed well, these linkages help to generate and accelerate the interaction effects among the dimensions across the three information capabilities. The relationships and linkages within the dimensions of each of the information capabilities will be discussed in detail in Chapters 4—6.

Companies with Low IO: 'Can't Get It Together!'

Companies with low IO may superficially embrace the idea of sharing information in the company, but fail to create the conditions in which sharing of important information actually occurs. A strong culture based on individual achievement and personal competition, hoarding information for personal gain, and punishing people who report errors, mistakes or failures will discourage information sharing.

Although companies with low IO do collect and organize lots of data, they have few or no information sensing abilities to focus on new market and customer trends, or to detect changes in business conditions that make existing business practices less effective. The result is that the data they collect is never tested against outside realities, creating an inward-looking and reactive view of information, which is at odds with current business practices.

There are several reasons that these companies may not focus on information processing to facilitate better decision-making. They either cannot attract people with well-developed analytical skills; or they lack the appropriate training programmes to develop good analytical skills in their workforce; or they do not promote the information behaviours that encourage people to anticipate new information needs or be proactive in using information inside the company. Similarly, these companies usually find it difficult to know what information to maintain over time. They may create vast databases, but fail to exploit them for business value. These companies may either be collecting too much data for unclear purposes or they may not be allocating sufficient resources or attention to updating or reusing the information they have.

One executive suggested that managers in such companies behave a lot like homeowners who buy fresh buckets of paint each time they paint a room in their house and leave the leftover paint in used buckets in the garage for many years. The used paint buckets stack up until the home-owner decides to throw them all out. Many companies collect and maintain data in the same way. Lots of data is stored in computers and servers after it is first used, and people fully intend to access this data again one day. However, at some point people either forget that they have already collected the data or decide to collect fresh data because the old data is inaccessible or out of date.

Although companies with low IO may have highly developed IT for operational support to automate basic transaction processing in their business, they may not be investing in IT to make the company more innovative or for managerial and other forms of decision-making. These companies tend to invest in IT for the necessary or essential aspects of their business today, but neglect IT investments that would give them distinctive abilities to compete with information in the future.

To sum up, companies with low IO display a mix of information practices and behaviours that operate more or less haphazardly in their business. They are unable to link these behaviours and practices together and so can derive little leverage or synergy from the three information capabilities.

Companies with low IO need roadmaps to show how improvements in one dimension can affect improvements in other dimensions. Once these relationships are clear, managers can set priorities and chart the best way to improve their information capabilities and, in doing so, raise their overall IO score.

Let's take a look at three different journeys undertaken by high IO companies to develop their information capabilities and leverage the interaction effects between information proactiveness, sensing and processing, and the use of IT for management support. As we will see in each company journey, senior managers are able not only to build these cross-capability dimensions, but also to understand the importance of continually improving them to avoid complacency, even in a high IO company.

SkandiaBanken—Achieving High IO and Superior Performance in Direct Banking

At SkandiaBanken, managers needed to build information capabilities around a new, direct approach to retail banking. From the beginning, senior managers were aware of the importance of developing information capabilities to attain the IO interaction effect at all levels of the company. Since they realized that the financial services business would experience rapid and disruptive changes in the years ahead, they recognized that their information capabilities had to be effective in responding quickly to market shifts.

The Start-up: Learn from Your Competitors

In October 1994 SkandiaBanken, one of Sweden's first direct banks, opened for business. With only one Stockholm-based branch (required under banking regulations then in effect), this telephone and Internet bank decided to compete head-to-head with the large established banks that dominated the Swedish retail banking market. Created by Skandia, one of Sweden's best known and most respected insurance companies, the direct bank planned to leverage the Skandia brand name and compete by offering account interest rates that were 1–3 percentage points higher than those paid by more established banks in Sweden. Public dissatisfaction with a government bailout of two of Sweden's well-known banks, Nordbanken and Gota Bank, as well as growing market receptivity to direct banking, favoured the start-up of this venture.

In addition, during this period, several established banks attempted to start direct banking services with mixed results or outright failure. These banks attempted to use direct banking as an additional service channel to their predominantly branch-oriented approach. Since managers and employees in branches saw direct banking as a potential threat to their jobs through the gradual loss of good customers to the new channel, the direct banking efforts, grafted as they were on to the more traditional branch banking, were perceived more as a threat than an opportunity for these banks.

Senior managers at SkandiaBanken learned from these experiences and designed a direct banking approach that avoided channel conflicts and promoted a new image for direct banking in Sweden.

A Business Vision with a Bias towards Action

SkandiaBanken's vision was not just to be a deposit bank, but to create a point of customer contact that could offer opportunities to cross-sell many different financial service products. Managers aimed at developing long-term customer relationships and a product portfolio that would be attractive and convenient for customers to access.

To achieve these objectives, senior managers knew that all employees would have to develop a focused and service-oriented approach to customers, since their main contacts with customers would be over the telephone or via the Internet. The managing director commented:

> Motivating our employees is a key factor in managing this type of operation. Our employees *are* the bank. Every time a customer calls, he or she speaks directly to one of our employees. It is imperative that each employee knows how to achieve solutions for the customer.

The chief information officer (CIO) also explained the company approach: 'We are expected to act upon problems, not talk about them, at every level of the company. It is a very action-oriented, problem-solving atmosphere.' The general manager of stock-brokering services added: 'We are expected to take the initiative and to inform ourselves about things that we need to know.'

Leveraging the Right Information Behaviours

Senior managers knew that control, transparency and sharing were critical behaviours to create a work environment that allowed for proactive behaviours to occur. Simple, yet specific, performance criteria and measures were developed and shared with all employees. Transparency of all information, including performance information, was a key goal advocated and practiced by senior managers. 'Everyone knows who is doing what. Everyone knows and is trained to understand his or her targets and calculations for revenues and costs.' To further encourage transparency, there were employee surveys to evaluate managers, and problems were shared among employee and managerial teams. 'We spend a lot of time listening to our employees,' commented one senior manager. 'They are the ones on the front line and their experience is important knowledge.' To promote transparency in their own group, for example, the IT staff adopted a saying: 'Success in software development depends on making a carefully planned series of small mistakes in order to avoid making unplanned large ones.' The IT teams had one person in charge of keeping track of the mistakes that occurred and passing on solutions to the rest of the teams.

Touching the Information Means Touching the Customer

Direct banking also requires carefully developed information management practices. At SkandiaBanken, these were designed around employee routines in interacting with customers and were well defined at each level and within each business area of the company. Managers paid special attention to the information processing and analytical abilities of telephone representatives in each of the four main business units—car financing, home mortgages, banking operations and stock trading. They focused on the information representatives needed to inform customers and help them make good decisions for their investment needs. Information captured by these representatives was recorded daily in databases and reviewed by employees and managers to improve each group's abilities to sense new market and customer needs. Customer representatives were divided into small call groups with team leaders acting as information specialists to identify and share problems and their solutions within and across call groups. The company's bias for proactive behaviours towards finding customer solutions encouraged all employees to actively sense for new customer and market information.

Business-led IT Practices

Senior managers at SkandiaBanken paid close personal attention to the development of IT systems support, since these information systems were the glue holding the direct banking model together. These managers believed that the appropriate IT tools enabled proactive information use and promoted transparency and open access to all information to run the business. They also supported operational and managerial decision-making through on-line access to analytical tools and relevant information. When designing these systems, IT programmers were excluded from the discussion. Instead, the managers went straight to the users—those people whose job it was to sense changes in market environments and customer needs—to design appropriate systems for improved decision-making at both the operational and management levels of the company.

Standardizing operational functions, including bank administration, allowed representatives more time to focus on customer interactions. The company also used IT for business process support to link SkandiaBanken directly to the databases and IT network services of the national bill paying clearing house, employer salary accounts, credit records, car registrations, mortgage approval systems, stock exchanges and international bank transfers. In addition, the bank employed its IT for operational and business process support as a platform for innovative Internet services, which earned SkandiaBanken its rating as the best bank in 1998 and 1999 by one of Sweden's major business magazines, *Privata Affärer*. IT systems also supported management decision-making needs through careful monitoring of employee performance, business performance, and scenario decision tools in areas such as credit risk and preferred payment plans. Finally, senior managers strongly encouraged modularity in IT systems design, since they anticipated a future filled with product and service innovations.

Lessons Learned: Attaining High IO Makes Your Company More Flexible

Senior managers at SkandiaBanken do not view the building of information capabilities as a journey with an end. Gaining the business impacts of high IO requires constant manager and employee attention and evolution. However, senior managers do understand that, once strong information capabilities are in place, the company can sense and respond to business and market shifts more quickly and flexibly and can build new IT support applications to meet these needs.

Proactive Information Use with Customers Sustains Superior Business Performance

As we suggested in Chapter 1, Hilti's managers realized early on that creating a proactive information environment was critical to the company's success. They know that this environment would encourage their employees to actively sense information about changes in the company's external business environment and respond quickly with new or enhanced products or services, as these changes became competitively meaningful. Moreover, information proactiveness depends on good control and sharing—behaviours that together encourage people as individuals to contribute their knowledge willingly to others and to act in the company's interest, not just their own. Hilti's managers know that instilling information proactiveness in their employees is not sufficient unless the right information is sensed, captured and maintained with IT systems that support good operations and managerial decision-making and product or service innovations simultaneously.

Hilti's unique competitive advantage, as we saw in the Introduction and Chapter 1, lies in its obsession with delighting its customers, who are challenged every day on construction sites by new demolition and drilling requirements. The next case study illustrates how they do this.

Hilti Corporation: Delighting Customers with Good Information Creates Profit

Our case study illustrates Hilti's journey in building information capabilities and achieving high IO. Hilti is structured in a two-dimensional matrix with business units and market organizations, each with its own profit and loss (P&L) responsibility. In 1996, Hilti's executive board devised a new strategy called Champion 3-C to further enhance their customer focus at all levels in the company. In a break from their previous strategy, business units and market organizations were responsible for defining their own strategies and adapting the overall company strategy to local conditions and needs. The previous corporate strategy had focused on a single, centrally controlled system, which had increased sales tremendously, but had not improved profitability enough.

The new approach depended on higher levels of customer involvement, local adaptations and more market organization commitment.

The Champion 3-C strategy was clear and compelling. 'Champion' meant being among the top three companies in the world in each business line. '3-C' referred to:

- Customer—absolute customer focus
- Competency—direct selling, effective marketing, total quality, excellence in innovation
- Concentration—focus on products and markets with which and in which leadership positions can be achieved and sustained.

Senior managers understood that deep-rooted elements of the company culture such as integrity, transparency and employee loyalty would promote more proactive behaviours by employees at all levels. However, they also knew that significantly increased information sharing within and between market organizations and business units would be critical to the success of the new strategy.

Instilling the Right Information Behaviours across and down the Company

During the mid-1990s, a worldwide employee survey indicated that employees were concerned about poor communication between senior managers and employees and a lack of information about individual performance criteria and compensation schemes tied to company performance. To address these concerns and really engage employees in the Champion 3-C strategy, senior managers began a project to improve information control by defining and sharing performance criteria and measures across the company.

The company developed 'cockpit charts', with eight or nine key performance measures, in each work unit. Employees at all skill levels were taught how to read and use the charts as well as understand the relationship between their personal performance and that of the team or work unit. Managers were required to review performance objectives with their employees every two months.

To improve information sharing among market organizations, senior managers organized 'experience workshops' for country-based managers to meet each other and exchange information about practices. The company organized similar programmes to improve information exchange between market organizations and business units worldwide.

Proactively Sensing and Processing External Information

In an attempt to better understand the threats and opportunities in Hilti's competitive situation worldwide, senior managers asked their 7,000-person field force to act as radars: What is happening in your specific market? What do the customers really want? How does the competition respond to customer needs?

The international field force answered these and other questions in their local environments. Their answers were collected and organized. Then managers sent these analyses back to the field force asking, 'Is this a good reflection of the world as you see it every day?' They wanted to make sure that no important information had been deleted or changed during the processing and analysing of the data. They knew that the field force staff were the closest to the customers and wanted to avoid losing any valuable information. Based on the sales force responses, adjustments in the analyses were made as required.

The results of this initiative were compelling. Managers now had detailed analyses of their customers and competitors worldwide and could use this information for product and service innovation, strategic planning, and improved operations and business processes. Hilti also now possessed a people-driven information system to facilitate sensing of new information and to maintain and refresh the existing information. To reinforce this competitive radar and to keep information up-to-date, market managers from twenty countries around the world speak every two months through telephone conferences to exchange ideas and find out about market changes. These managers then share information gathered at these meetings with their sales forces, setting goals to respond to new market trends. A consistent set of information management practices was now in place to collect, organize, process and maintain information on customers, competitors and markets worldwide. Through this initiative, the field force and other employees discovered which information it was relevant to collect and share with one another and the importance of continuing to sense new information as well. Most importantly, perhaps, everyone realized how important their information management practices were to the company, which in turn motivated people to sense and collect better information about customers, competitors and markets.

Exploiting IT for Decisions about the Future

In addition to the Hilti sales force automation project (HFSA) described in Chapter 1, the company continued with an aggressive programme to exploit IT for managerial and innovation support. It deployed new market analysis programmes for market organizations; it invested in data analysis tools for 'data mining' of customer and market information; and it employed scenario creation software to test alternative business futures. The company used sophisticated computer-aided design (CAD) and testing software to simulate the applications of its products at the customer construction site.

The attitude of Hilti managers was to apply IT to support product and service innovation and to discover new insights about customers, markets and external business conditions.

Lessons Learned: Attaining High IO Makes Your Company Compete for the Future Today

The road to reaching high IO has not been easy at Hilti. The senior managers of the company have focused for several years on their efforts to improve information capabilities at all levels of the company. It is clear that by persistently working on the dimensions of each information capability, the company has learned to manage well the interactive effects of being high on each information capability. Hilti managers created a proactive sales force over many years of careful attention to behaviours such as integrity, transparency and sharing; within this environment, the sales force was asked to sense and collect information to better determine new market trends. This information was then used to create appropriate IT tools for higher-level decision-making concerning market and customer needs to support better decisions and inspire further proactive behaviours by providing employees with tools that help them to make better decisions.

Moreover, as good as Hilti is in IO, managers feel a sense of urgency to prepare for the future each day. This is a company obsessed with knowing about its customers, markets and competitors better than any other company in its industry. Creating the future at Hilti means proactively managing information about the future today and knowing how to lead the market, not react to the market.

Exploiting High IO Maturity for Sustained Growth

Since 1994, Banco Bilbao Vizcaya (BBV) has been on an extraordinary journey in which the bank has worked on all three information capabilities and built its strategy of growth around being very high on IO. From 1994 to 1997, the bank doubled its business volume in a saturated banking market, increased its earnings per share by 131 per cent and its market capitalization by four times. For customers, BBV wants to be the bank with the highest yields and the best service. For employees, BBV wants to be the best place to work. In pursuing these strategies, the bank has created an environment of proactive information use around its branches, its direct channels—including ATM, telephone and Internet banking—and its home office, which works in support of the branch concept. We have already glimpsed the BBV approach to customers, along with its customer sales support system, in Chapter 1. Now we will take a look behind the scenes to see how BBV leverages its information capabilities.

Banco Bilbao Vizcaya: Transforming the Role of People and Information in the Branch

On the surface, BBV looks like a traditional-style retail bank serving its national market. BBV serves over 6.5 million individual customers and over

500,000 shops and companies in Spain. The bank has over 2,800 branches, employs about 20,000 people with an average age of 45, and keeps its people for most of their working life. Its attrition rate is less than 0.2 per cent—'better than Japanese companies,' as one manager commented. It operates ATMs across the country, provides telephone banking, and now has a flourishing Internet banking channel. In some ways, its profile would make it a vulnerable target for a direct bank, such as the SkandiaBanken model, in its market.

However, this profile is all that is traditional about BBV. Over the last 10 years, BBV has turned most of its branches into customer sales offices, rather than traditional transaction-oriented branches, by centralizing all back office IT systems and moving customers to direct channels like ATMs and telephone banking for high volume, low return banking transactions. It has split its customers into eight segments—versus two for traditional banks—and has tied its product and cross-selling strategies to the customer segmentation.

To link its product offers to customer segments and to provide seamless and knowledgeable service wherever a customer chooses to bank with BBV—either through a branch or direct channels—the bank has created an unusual mix of information capabilities centred around its branches, its people and excellent information about customers and products.

Training and Rewarding People for Sharing and the Proactive Use of Information

In the 1990s, BBV set up a formal training programme for branch employees to teach them how to be proactive in product cross-selling to customers and in customer service. Every new employee goes through the same training, which shows him or her how to collect, process and use customer and product information at every point of contact with the customer. All employee evaluations include how proactive people have been in sensing and collecting accurate customer information, and rewards, including stock options, are provided on an individual and team basis.

The bank also trains its employees about sharing information. Managers realized early on the importance of information sharing for the effective performance of people in the bank. To improve and track how well employees are sharing information among themselves about products, services and customers, the bank employs 'mystery shoppers'—usually retired former employees—to check that information is being shared among employees within and across branches. Similarly, all levels of managers are encouraged to share information between home office functions and branches. 'The managers who are more prone to share information are the bank's most respected employees,' commented the head of the retail bank. The senior manager for business development also observed, 'We realize quickly when information-sharing within a branch does not occur the way we expect. For example, if a branch does not share, it starts under-performing. When problems occur in a branch, we take the necessary precautions and ensure that information is shared at all times. We might, for instance, increase teamwork training for all branch employees and agree on a recovery plan with the branch manager.'

This combination of teamwork and information sharing is the bank's most important value in its strategy of growth and customer service. Senior managers understand that both these values create a more proactive use of information within the workforce which, in turn, increases the abilities of employees to sense and anticipate what is happening in their business environment.

Telescoping Good Information Management and Selling Products into One Act

During the 1990s, BBV invested significantly in building a simple, but elegant, IT system that could merge the activities of greeting, servicing and cross-selling to customers in one act. It gave this leading edge IT system a rather straightforward name—the customer sales support system. As we noted in Chapter 1, when a customer entered any branch, the process of greeting the customer allowed the branch representative to call up the customer account. The account provides the following information: demographics (i.e., customer socio-economic profile), product usage, segment profile and all previous interactions with the bank, regardless of the channels used. Any acceptance or rejection of a product offer was also recorded, with branch representative comments on the conversation with the customer. In addition, the system automatically compared the customer's products and services to the segment profile.

This comparison presented the branch representative with cross-selling opportunities on his screen and enabled him to be proactive in making an offer to a customer in a focused and intelligent manner. Such aggressive, yet focused, use of information places great pressure on the branches to have up-to-date and continually refreshed information about products and customers on a daily basis. Information maintenance is vital, since branch representatives should not offer the same product to a person two or three times, because this would undermine the bank's reputation with customers.

Excellent information management in operational and business process support systems provides the platform for using IT for managerial support as well. For example, branch managers meet with regional managers each month to discuss future sales opportunities. In preparation for these meetings, the managers analyse the branch sales activities in detail, focusing on sales to new customers and cross-sales to existing customers. During the meetings, branch managers agree on sales objectives for their branches for the following month—and sometimes on a weekly or daily basis for less successful branches. Thus BBV managers are able not only to use IT for enabling good information behaviours and information practices at the branch level, but also to exploit IT systems for supporting managerial analysis and decisions.

What has BBV done? It has capitalized on the IO interaction effect. It has turned each branch into a fine-tuned sensing centre by explicitly training for proactive behaviours to support real-time sensing of customer trends and by providing an IT system capable of analysing customer information to improve decisions related to cross-selling goals and improving business performance.

Lessons Learned: Attaining High IO Makes Your Company a Winner in an Established Market

BBV presents the case of a company that grows and creates customer value even in a crowded, saturated retail banking market like Spain's. It beats its rivals with high IO and excellent execution every day. It quietly leverages first-class information capabilities to win new customers and sell more to existing customers through branches whose reason for existence is simultaneous high-touch personal service and cross-selling of products. It exploits every direct channel, such as the Internet, and links them seamlessly through its IT systems to its people-centric view of financial services. In short, it does what most traditional banks cannot do and what most direct banks fear—it retains loyal customers and increases margins on product cross-selling and efficient use of direct channels, while attracting more high-value, high-margin new customers through highly personal and informed services.

Key Cross-Capability Characteristics of High IO Companies

What have we seen from our three case studies? That companies with high IO not only build the maturity of each individual information capability, but concentrate on creating and improving synergies across the three information capabilities. By aiming to improve proactiveness, sensing, IT for management support, and processing dimensions, these companies enhance their information effectiveness through the IO inter-action effect. Managers who encourage a proactive work force that thinks about how to use information for innovation and improvements to prod-ucts, and acts on this information, will create an environment where sensing information on changes in the competitive environment becomes an integral part of everyone's job. A proactive work force sensitive to the importance of monitoring competitive changes will recognize and exploit the power of IT, not just for operational purposes, but for management support to provide better information for strategic business decisions. They will also demand new IT applications to address their own decision needs and those of their colleagues. Improved IT for management sup-port, in turn, encourages proactive information behaviour by providing faster access to critical information. Finally, a proactive work force, armed with IT tools to gather and help analyse business information, will be able to improve their processing ability for more effective decision-making involving critical business decisions. This powerful cross-capability inter-action leads a company to use information effectively for greater business performance.

HOW DOES YOUR COMPANY SHAPE UP?

Our three case studies have shown how increasing IO maturity in a company is a function of improving each of the three information capabilities through actively managing a company's improvement journey. Each of these com-panies has been able to create powerful interactive effects by tying together information behaviours and values, information management practices and IT practices. The linkages, if properly leveraged with appropriate company business strategies, lead to superior business performance.

The key learning points from these three cases are as follows. First, building information capabilities takes time. This means that senior man-agers must be persistent and focused in improving information capabil-ities that improve business performance. There are no shortcuts or six-month crash programmes for moving from low to high IO.

Second, these three companies did not fragment improvement efforts for their information capabilities. Rather, senior managers pursued im-provements in information capabilities holistically and sought to build information capabilities concurrently, not sequentially.

Third, managers did not view the attainment of IO maturity as stop-ping at one point in time or levelling off. In each company, there is a palpable sense of urgency among managers and staff that they can do even better. These are companies in which managers and employees think aggressively and proactively about their business. They view IO maturity as 'temporary' and in need of continual refinement and improvement. Knowing more about their business can never stop, so long as business conditions remain turbulent and potentially disruptive. Each company recognizes that it must have well-developed information capabilities not only to run the business well today, but also to anticipate the future at the same time—it must have a dual approach to managing information capabilities.

Look at Figure 3.2 (see p. 60). Can you identify where on the IO maturity model your company or business unit performs well or poorly? Are there examples in business units or functions in your company where the IO interaction effect occurs on an ongoing basis? What are the constraints or weaknesses that keep the IO interaction effect from happening company-wide?

Companies can use the IO dashboard to obtain a reading of their current stage of IO maturity and the strengths or weaknesses in their information capabilities. As we have already stated, a company must be good at all three information capabilities to have high IO and business performance.

This is a starting point for evaluating your company's information capabilities and potential improvements. We will now look at the three case scenarios presented in Figure 3.3 of how companies facing different challenges improve their information capabilities to increase IO and business performance.

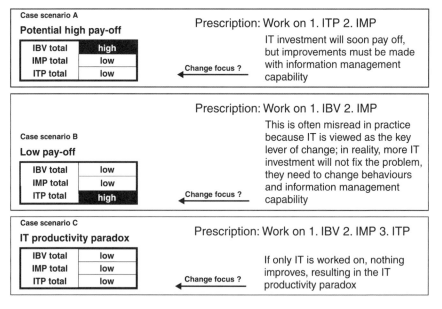

Figure 3.3: Scenarios of IO strengths and weaknesses

Case Scenario A: Fast-growing European Retailer of Eyeglass Lenses and Frames

This company started as a small, entrepreneurial concern in France in the early 1980s. The first waves of expansion in the 1980s resulted from internal growth and the acquisition of small competitors, which were integrated into their business model of delivering lenses and frames to customers in one hour or less. The company is intensely focused on service quality and a store-level style of employee empowerment and responsibility. This emphasizes person-to-person relationships and informal information use over more formal information management and IT support practices.

People Make the Business

The senior managers place great personal energy and emphasis on employee development, behaviour and motivation. Each employee is hired first and foremost for the right attitude, rather than specific skills. In-depth training is provided at the beginning and throughout a person's career, which instils the company values and behaviours across the company.

Employees understand that customer loyalty is the key to a service business and to company performance. Each store manager and employee is expected to place the utmost emphasis on customer service to guarantee satisfied, repeat customers in the future. Every interaction in the store is geared towards making the customer feel special—so special that his or her need for high-quality and fashion-oriented frames and lenses is anticipated. This requires every employee to listen carefully to customer requests and discuss these with other employees, including store managers and marketing staff.

For example, the original spectacle brand started by serving relatively affluent customer segments. Later, a second, lower cost brand was developed to serve more price-sensitive customers. The successful, new brand was born out of closely listening to customers and being attentive to other segments of the market. All of the company's employees are motivated to listen to customers and share information about special needs or potential new product ideas with their store managers.

A Large Acquisition Brings Rapid European and Global Expansion

In 1997, the French company acquired a large UK competitor that doubled its number of employees to 8,000 and increased its number of stores from

200 to 700. The merged company was now operating in 17 countries compared with 4 countries before the acquisition.

This sudden and significant regional and international expansion concerned the chief financial officer (CFO). Sustaining company profitability might be difficult, since no standardized business processes or information systems were in place to ensure day-to-day operational and financial controls within and across countries. Moreover, the informal and personal style of management by senior executives was now under strain, since the management team had to manage a geographically dispersed company with different store types, operating styles and cultures.

The management style of the CEO, who is one of the two original founders of the company, focuses, as one manager commented, on 'management by walking around—based on pure instinct and relying heavily on personal relationships.' This approach has worked well in developing an intense, store-level customer focus and service quality culture, but is not sufficient to run a large, diverse retail chain across Europe and internationally.

At the time, the CEO was adamant in his opinion about the incompatibility of IT and the company's 'people' culture: 'IT is not in the genes of this company!' As a result, IT systems, even e-mail, had been developed on an *ad hoc* basis, and customer information remained either in the heads of store managers and employees or in informal, local store systems and paper files. In 1998, the company began experiencing supply chain management problems in purchasing and managing spectacle frame inventories in Europe. Pressures were building to regionalize the supply chain and to define shared processes and IT systems at the store and brand levels across countries.

Learning about IO and Business Performance

It was during the acquisition period that the company's senior management teams participated in our study survey. Analysis of their results indicates that the company scores relatively high on information behaviours and values, but low on information management and IT practices as the IO dashboard in Figure 3.4 suggests. Due to its service focus, people culture and entrepreneurial growth, this company has the potential for high performance pay-offs, if appropriate IT and information practices are significantly improved in line with its regional and global expansion. Currently, this company is only marginally benefiting from the IO interaction effect due to weaknesses in these two information capabilities.

The company has already established strong information behaviours and values at the store and country levels. People use information proactively in stores and are willing to respond constructively to customer or operational problems, errors or mistakes. Store management is

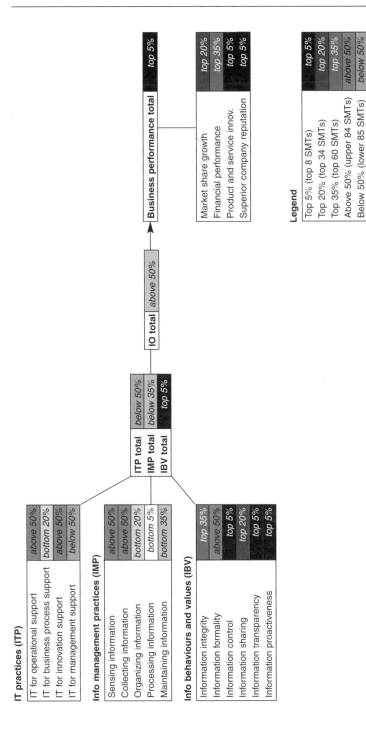

IT practices (ITP)

IT for operational support	*above 50%*
IT for business process support	*bottom 20%*
IT for innovation support	*above 50%*
IT for management support	*below 50%*

Info management practices (IMP)

Sensing information	*above 50%*
Collecting information	*above 50%*
Organizing information	*bottom 20%*
Processing information	*bottom 5%*
Maintaining information	*bottom 35%*

Info behaviours and values (IBV)

Information integrity	*top 35%*
Information formality	*above 50%*
Information control	*top 5%*
Information sharing	*top 20%*
Information transparency	*top 5%*
Information proactiveness	*top 5%*

ITP total	*below 50%*
IMP total	*below 35%*
IBV total	*top 5%*

| **IO total** | *above 50%* |

| **Business performance total** | *top 5%* |

Market share growth	*top 20%*
Financial performance	*top 35%*
Product and service innov.	*top 5%*
Superior company reputation	*top 5%*

Legend

Top 5% (top 8 SMTs)	*top 5%*
Top 20% (top 34 SMTs)	*top 20%*
Top 35% (top 60 SMTs)	*top 35%*
Above 50% (upper 84 SMTs)	*above 50%*
Below 50% (lower 85 SMTs)	*below 50%*
Bottom 35% (lower 60 SMTs)	*bottom 35%*
Bottom 20% (lower 34 SMTs)	*bottom 20%*
Bottom 5% (lowest 8 SMTs)	*bottom 5%*

Figure 3.4: The IO dashboard of a European retailer of eyeglass lenses and frames

willing to share best practices across stores and brands. Store manages share operating results with employees and across functions.

While information management practices in this retail business are relatively clear and simple for employees and store managers, they tend to be more informal at the store and country levels and between brand organizations. However, with the rapid expansion, senior managers see the value of achieving operating synergies and cost savings from regional supply chain processes and IT for operational and business process support. To respond to the new regional supply chain strategy, however, managers will have to begin to encourage more formal use of information within individual stores to support the new centralized information initiatives envisioned by senior management.

This company is ready to address regional growth challenges and is aware of the need to establish shared processes and IT systems across the region and internationally. It now has to examine the missing links in information management and IT practices, and work out how to plan the transition of its information behaviours and values across a large international retail business. The company has the clear potential to reap significant business benefits from using IT to manage its supply chain and its finances across the region. Using the IO maturity model in Figure 3.2, we can see that this company must first work on improving its IT for business process support before it can successfully implement strategic-level management systems for this new regional business model. It must also strengthen its IT for operational support across all stores to fully capitalize on this new strategy. Although the company is fairly good at sensing and collecting information on a local basis, it will need to set up standard ways of organizing and maintaining this information for use outside of individual stores. It can substantially improve the informal information practices across the stores by adopting more standard point-of-sale, customer profiling and account management systems. Once these systems are in place, it will have to spend considerable time training its employees to process the information accurately or hiring people with higher analytical skills to make better business decisions.

Case Scenario B: A Leading American Retailer of Athletic Shoes and Apparel

This US company was founded by two entrepreneurs in 1980. Noticing that many local young athletes in their home state did not have access to high-quality sports shoes, the duo bought $7,000 worth of athletic footwear and visited every high school and local athletics field within a 50-mile radius of their hometown. In 1984, the company developed an athletic shoe and clothing catalogue carrying the latest products from top-name brands such as Nike, Reebok, Converse and Adidas. By the late 1990s, the company had grown into a worldwide leader in direct marketing of athletics footwear, clothing, equipment and licensed or private label products.

Building a Business around Expertise and Excellent Information

The company's success centred on building strong relationships with high school coaches and 'technical athletes' between the ages of 12 and 22. The catalogue offered a deep product line of approximately 17,000 items and also specialized in hard-to-find sizes.

By 1997, a specialized information call centre was developed to support the specific information needs of both customers and call centre representatives. In addition to a detailed customer database, a product database provided representatives with information not only about real-time inventory in the warehouse, but also about product-specific information that might assist customers in making informed choices.

For example, a call centre representative could tell a customer if a specific shoe came in big or small sizes, or narrow and wide fittings. If a customer indicated what sport he or she participated in, the rep could also make suggestions on best-selling items or those items with long track records. Although the company had the ability to cross-sell to customers, this telephone selling technique was discouraged because of the nature of the main customers—12 to 18-year-olds who bought items with their parents' credit cards, based on parental approval of specific purchases. Young people were recruited from local communities to handle the telephones during peak times for this customer segment—after school and on weekends. A clear, standardized incentive and performance goal scale was based on the ability of the call centre representative to handle different levels of product information.

Sales increases were encouraged through a detailed customer database that tracked customer sales by sport segment and product line. A sophisticated IT-supported catalogue production system and well-run production processes allowed the catalogue group to create customized editions of the main print catalogue with ease. These editions targeted specific customer segments several times per year.

The Negative Impacts of Being Acquired

In 1997, the owners of the company sold it to a large US retail group, which was looking to acquire a direct marketing operation to support its athletic footwear and apparel retail stores.

The company was immediately placed under the new group management and, over the next few years, inconsistent and unclear business strategies negatively affected the company's behaviours and performance. Integrity, transparency and sharing were the hardest hit behaviours as the company's managers and people struggled to interpret and move the company in different directions to address new customer segments and product lines. Messages and strategic objectives communicated, and often mandated, by the group management were often not seen as credible by the company managers.

The company's top managers viewed a new group venture, E Group, created in March 1999, as lacking in credibility, even though the company would be the operational backbone for all the new E Group web sites.

Acquisitions Can Impact on Information Behaviours First and Often Negatively

The result of the post-acquisition process, as reflected in the IO dashboard in Figure 3.5, was that while information management and IT practices were both high overall, information behaviours and values ranked lower, in the bottom 35 per cent of the benchmark. The erosion of behaviours and values among the company's managers and employees in the post-acquisition period created a debilitating link in the company's efforts to achieve high IO. If group and company managers interpret the deficiency as one requiring more IT investment, then the situation may deteriorate. If the group managers and company managers acknowledge the erosion in information behaviours and values and work at them over the next few years, then the IO levels of the company may improve, and with them the business pay-off from very good information management and IT capabilities.

The good news is that proactiveness remains a main characteristic of people in this company, despite the negative effects of the merger. However, if the company fails to address the main behavioural problems—notably integrity, transparency and sharing—we would expect a rapid decrease in the proactiveness of its staff. Where should this company start to make meaningful changes in the near future? The IO maturity model in Figure 3.2 indicates that senior management should first address their integrity problem, followed by a concerted effort to formalize information and diminish the potential negative effects of information dissemination through the rumour mill.

Companies that Are Low on All Information Capabilities

In the previous case scenarios, we discussed companies that were good in one or two information capabilities, but low on the third. But

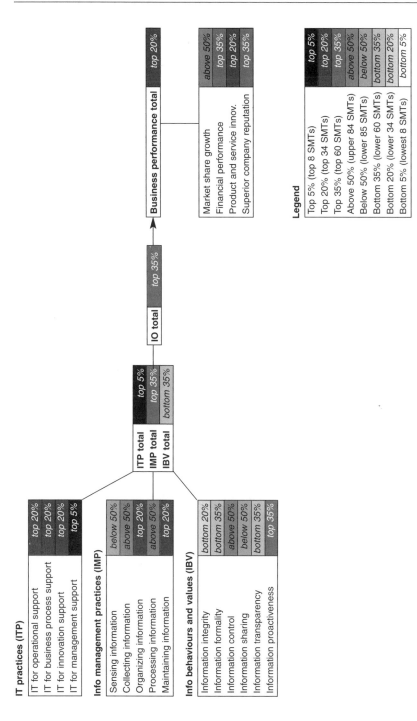

Figure 3.5: The IO dashboard of a US athletic shoes and apparel retailer

what if a company is low on all information capabilities? Where do you start?

Senior managers might choose to invest in IT, thinking that this is a way of improving information management practices and maybe even changing behaviours. If they did, their company might experience the IT productivity paradox—increasing investment in IT without a corresponding link to improved business performance.

The phrase 'IT productivity paradox' was coined as a result of economic and business studies in the 1980s and 1990s, which could not show a correlation between the vastly increased investments in IT in American companies—estimated at $1 trillion during the 1980s—and higher economic productivity or company profitability. This news was dismal for individual companies—higher investments in IT did not lead to higher profits. In many industries, researchers argued, IT could not create competitive advantage, but had become a competitive necessity. It was necessary to use IT, since everyone in the industry did so in more or less the same way. More recent research supports the view that, while IT does improve company efficiency and increase company output of goods and services, IT use intensifies industry competition by lowering barriers to entry, which in turn lowers prices. Cost savings are then reaped by customers, and not by individual companies.

Thus managers who believe that IT leads to competitive advantage, or is somehow a 'quick fix', may need to rethink the improvement challenge, especially if their companies are low on all three information capabilities.

Case Scenario C: European Retail Bank

Over the last five years this bank has gone through repeated restructuring and downsizing, as well as the acquisition of a competitor. These initiatives have wreaked havoc on the bank's IT systems, as one senior manager noted:

> One of the main problems that we have had is that of an old and expensive IT infrastructure. During the last five years, the focus of IT was to integrate systems inherited as a result of our acquisition of a competitor. This was well done, but no one looked forward to future applications and development of our IT systems. We now need a major modernization of our IT systems.

At the same time, the information management practices of the bank had deteriorated at the managerial and service levels. Managers and employees experienced either information overload or information neglect. Managers continued to receive voluminous reports on day-to-day operations, while employees could not reconcile customer accounts without the customer identifying his or her specific account numbers.

Information behaviours have also deteriorated through multiple downsizing and restructuring. No one trusts formal performance reports. People live in fear of redundancy and do not share information across departments. Information transparency and integrity are low, since no one wants to report customer or operational problems. Managers are reluctant to respond constructively to more bad news.

In this scenario, the company is low on all three information capabilities. If it invests in IT, it will see little performance improvement. As the case study illustrates, there is a danger that managers perceive the information problems in their company as IT practice issues, which can be corrected with better IT systems for operations and business process support. Managers know that IT has been consciously neglected over the past five years, and it is the subject of constant complaints by employees and customers alike. Poor information management may be seen as an outcome of poor IT practices, rather than as an outcome of fundamental weaknesses in behaviours and values among managers and employees.

We believe that the company should start working on information behaviours and values by following the paths prescribed in the IO maturity model, and then address changes in information management and IT practices. However, without a company-wide measure of effective information use like IO to test for improvements in information behaviours over time, senior managers may be tempted to reach for visible improvements in IT—thinking that at least they are removing the most obvious source of business performance deficiencies. This approach would address the symptoms, but leave untouched the root causes of their low IO score.

CONCLUSION

This chapter introduced the concept of IO maturity. We have recommended that, on their journeys to build information capabilities, companies focus on being good at all three to reap the substantial benefits from cross-capability interactions involving using information proactively, sensing and processing information appropriately, and deploying IT for management support. Our intent is to provide you with a clear roadmap to manage information capabilities for maximum business impact. In the next three chapters we will show you how to use the roadmap to improve each of the three information capabilities.

NOTE

1. For more detailed information about this analysis, refer to Marchand, D.A., Kettinger, W.J. and Rollins, J.D. (2001) *Information Orientation: The Link to Business Performance*, UK: Oxford University Press.

CHANGING PEOPLE'S INFORMATION BEHAVIOURS

Every company tries to promote a set of behaviours and values (that is, create a culture) that managers believe will improve business performance. However, not every company understands which specific behaviours and values will best promote effective information use.

Changing people's behaviours and values is a constant challenge for managers, for several reasons:

- Company cultures work because they are consistent and absorbed by employees over time. Changing behaviours and values in a company requires gradual adaptation and acceptance by people over months and years, not days and weeks.
- Before behaviours change, people must change their mind-sets. The more important the value or behaviour, the more people hesitate before redefining it to take on new beliefs.
- Changed mind-sets are no guarantee that people will behave consistently with their new beliefs. You may want to lose weight and eat more nutritious food, but you are unable to act consistently on your own beliefs.
- Before company employees adopt new behaviours or mind-sets, they will look to managers for cues. If managers talk about new mind-sets, values and behaviours, but fail to practice them, employees will quickly decide that they, too, should talk, but not act, differently.

In this chapter, we take a closer look at how information behaviours and values lead to greater IO maturity, and what actions managers can take to instil and influence these behaviours among their staff.

MAKING INFORMATION BEHAVIOURS AND VALUES (IBV) VISIBLE

Hilti Corporation

Hilti managers have recognized, since the very beginning of the business, that people and their behaviours are critical to making a company that relies on a direct sales force successful. The strong reliance on each employee's integrity has been a hallmark of the company since its inception. The high level of integrity at Hilti contributed to a high level of trust in the formal information sources about products, customers and operations in the company. As one manager commented: 'In our 1998 employee survey, our people said, "Not only do we get the information we need, we even believe it." This shows that if you give people the right information on, let's say, performance, this increases their trust in other information as well.' Another manager looked at the situation in a more practical way: 'Our community—here in Liechtenstein—is so small our information has to be trustworthy because it can be verified at night over a glass of beer.'

However, this high degree of information-sharing and trust in formal sources of information was not always present in Hilti. In the early 1990s, the company's employees had complained that they lacked information about key business issues, among them individual performance criteria and corresponding compensation approaches at various levels. To address these concerns, Hilti's senior managers started a company-wide initiative called the Hilti Information Management (HIM) Programme to share performance-based criteria and measures with employees. Managers and employees started to define the key information needs and terminology to clarify their common language and understanding of performance-based information throughout the company. Then they developed 'cockpit charts' with eight or nine key measurements per work unit or department. They taught employees at all levels to read these charts and to understand how to relate their own performance to that of their team or unit. They added graphic representation in the form of 'thermometers' to the charts to facilitate reading the results. Over time, they posted these charts in all work areas and on the internal IT network so people could see the charts from work teams and units across the company.

As this process advanced, employees became more confident in treating operational mistakes, errors and even occasional failures as opportunities to learn. Managers in the company continued to develop their ability to be open and transparent about mistakes, errors and failures. In fact, *not* admitting them before they were discovered by others, was viewed by managers and employees alike as a negative in annual evaluations.

During the 1990s, the process of sharing information about company and work unit performance built up a high level of trust among Hilti employees in teams and business units and across functions. However, as in most large companies, building a high-trust culture is a challenge when people work all over the world and are often reluctant to share information with someone they have never met. To facilitate information-sharing among the market organizations and business units, managers organized experience-sharing workshops and best practice forums where managers could meet each other, exchange information, socialize and develop trust for sharing information and ideas in the future. One senior manager noted: 'People who know each other are more willing to share information—that's just a natural phenomenon, I guess.' By the late 1990s, the CEO remarked:

> We have so much information in so many locations. To get all of that through the line [direct sales force in the market organizations] is a major challenge. The [information] technology is easy. It's not even the issue. It's more the attitude of the people that counts, and their willingness to bring this information, to release it.

A sign that this commitment to building trust and sharing information across the company is working are the recent stories circulating in Hilti about employee initiatives to voluntarily share information with others, despite the lack of personal contact and the geographic or cultural differences among them. One of Hilti's trainers, for example, has initiated an intranet forum for the over 200 trainers in Hilti to share information on what practices work or do not work.

At Hilti, senior managers continue to focus on new ways to make the workforce proactive in using information around the world. And, as a result of hard work on all sides, the company's information behaviours and values now reflect a bottom-up commitment by employees and managers to achieve the same ends.

CREATING PROACTIVE INFORMATION USE: THE IBV MATURITY MODEL

As discussed in Chapter 3, proactiveness is a key cross-capability needed to create the IO interaction effect in mature IO companies. These companies know that they can effectively create, and sustain, proactive information behaviours by putting in place the necessary building blocks. If your company is not where it needs to be in proactive information use among its employees and managers—unlike Hilti, BBV or SkandiaBanken—what steps can you take to improve your company's information behaviours and values?

Companies with mature IO know that certain relationships, or linkages, exist between six specific behaviours and values—integrity, formality, control, transparency, sharing and proactiveness. Figure 4.1 shows the results of statistical path analysis indicating where there exist causal relationships between dimensions of the information behaviours and values capability, and in which direction these relationships exist. The arrows in Figure 4.1 create a clear visual path of these relationships, moving from the bottom of the model upwards towards information proactiveness.

Following this path, we can see in Figure 4.1 that improvements to integrity, for example, will have a positive effect on both formal information use and transparency. Improvements to formal information use will likewise have a direct impact on the ability of a company to provide information control. Information control has a central role in the model: it not only directly affects information transparency, but also information sharing and proactiveness. Transparency has a direct effect on sharing, and sharing has a direct effect on proactiveness. Negative effects can occur along the same paths.

Companies with IBV maturity, therefore, have actively managed this path upwards, using dimensions on the lower end of the model as a base on which to build proactive information use—the most dependent dimension of the IBV maturity model.

Below we discuss each of the six dimensions of information behaviours and values presented in Figure 4.1, and describe the relationships between them. To help you see clearly these relationships, we have used The Bank (a low IO company) as a contrasting example to Hilti, a high IO company. The managers of this leading retail bank would like to be more proactive in using information to improve business performance but, over the last five years, they have largely failed to improve information behaviours and values. It may be useful to keep these contrasting cases in mind as you consider how to improve IBV maturity in your company or business unit. Figure 4.2 shows the contrast between the dimensions of information behaviours and values in the IO dashboards of these two companies.

The Bank

The Bank is one of Europe's largest banking groups. In 1993, The Bank merged with another large national bank and became an important financial services institution, offering retail, private and investment banking products. A series of post-merger restructuring, downsizing and cost-cutting programmes ensued, to increase profitability and shareholder value.

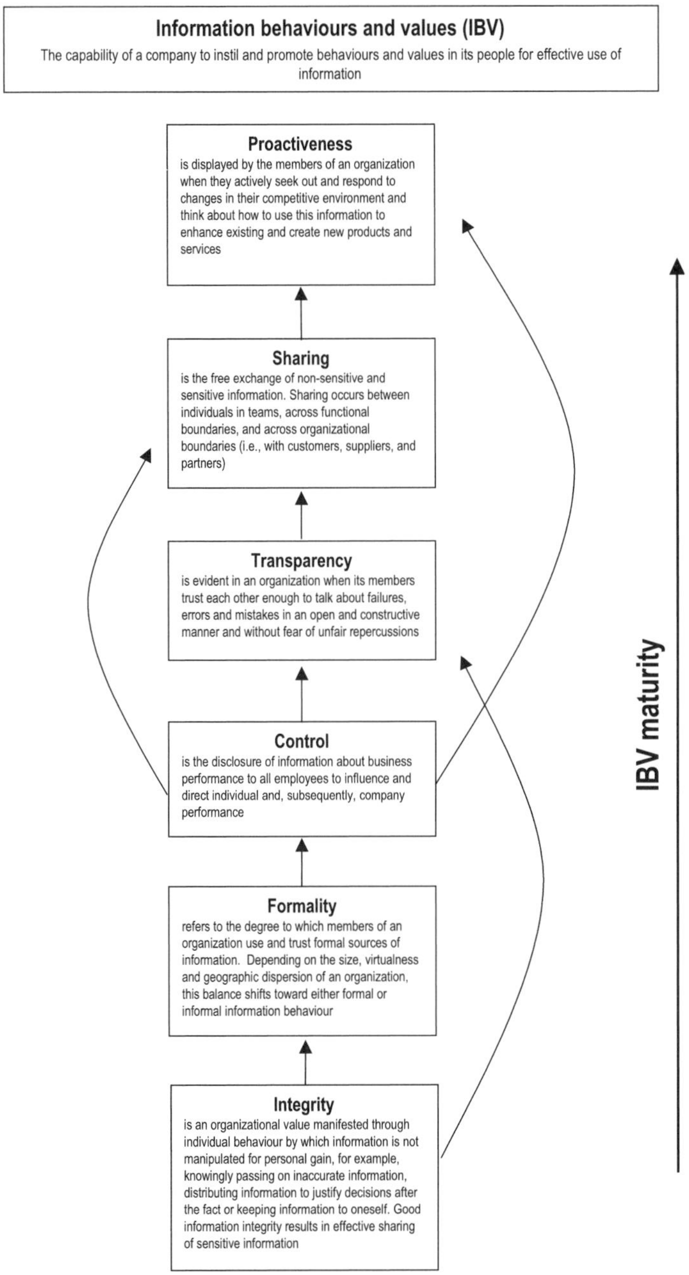

Information behaviours and values (IBV)

The capability of a company to instil and promote behaviours and values in its people for effective use of information

Proactiveness

is displayed by the members of an organization when they actively seek out and respond to changes in their competitive environment and think about how to use this information to enhance existing and create new products and services

Sharing

is the free exchange of non-sensitive and sensitive information. Sharing occurs between individuals in teams, across functional boundaries, and across organizational boundaries (i.e., with customers, suppliers, and partners)

Transparency

is evident in an organization when its members trust each other enough to talk about failures, errors and mistakes in an open and constructive manner and without fear of unfair repercussions

Control

is the disclosure of information about business performance to all employees to influence and direct individual and, subsequently, company performance

Formality

refers to the degree to which members of an organization use and trust formal sources of information. Depending on the size, virtualness and geographic dispersion of an organization, this balance shifts toward either formal or informal information behaviour

Integrity

is an organizational value manifested through individual behaviour by which information is not manipulated for personal gain, for example, knowingly passing on inaccurate information, distributing information to justify decisions after the fact or keeping information to oneself. Good information integrity results in effective sharing of sensitive information

IBV maturity

Figure 4.1: The IBV maturity model

Hilti's IO dashboard

Info behaviours and values (IBV)

Information integrity	top 35%
Information formality	top 20%
Information control	top 5%
Information sharing	top 20%
Information transparency	top 5%
Information proactiveness	top 20%

The Bank's IO dashboard

Info behaviours and values (IBV)

Information integrity	bottom 35%
Information formality	below 50%
Information control	below 50%
Information sharing	above 50%
Information transparency	below 50%
Information proactiveness	above 50%

Legend

Top 5% (top 8 SMTs)	top 5%
Top 20% (top 34 SMTs)	top 20%
Top 35% (top 60 SMTs)	top 35%
Above 50% (upper 84 SMTs)	above 50%
Below 50% (lower 85 SMTs)	below 50%
Bottom 35% (lower 60 SMTs)	bottom 35%
Bottom 20% (lower 34 SMTs)	bottom 20%
Bottom 5% (lowest 8 SMTs)	bottom 5%

Figure 4.2: Comparing information behaviours and values at Hilti Corporation and The Bank

During the past 10 years, retail banking in Europe has experienced several phenomena: mergers have generated large players; new currencies, like the euro, have opened up new opportunities; small start-ups have entered the market and conquered important market niches; insurance, investment and equity trading companies have started to break into the traditional retail bank market. In 1997, UBS and SBS of Switzerland merged and created the world's largest bank. The euro, introduced in 1999, opened up competition between pan-European groups, with German banks, for example, competing in France. At the same time, small start-ups, especially Internet-based ones, started to erode the market share of larger players. The blurring of boundaries between traditional banks and insurance and equity trading companies has expanded cross-selling opportunities and intensified competition in the same marketplace.

It is in the context of new opportunities—and new threats—that The Bank is attempting to build viable retail banking capable of offering broader financial services in a more competitive marketplace. The Bank has a culture based on hierarchy and strict reporting procedures. Local branches report to regional offices, which report to four central units. Furthermore, there are strict control mechanisms, which require transaction verification and authorization by top management. This creates highly structured, but often complicated, internal procedures.

Between 1994 and 1999, The Bank went through several restructuring projects. These projects resulted in lay-offs and cost-cutting, which have affected employee morale and openness. The Bank's employees generally keep sensitive information to themselves because they are afraid it might be counterproductive and hurt their career. Employees do not release more information than necessary.

As a result, The Bank experiences low integrity and employees tend to mistrust formal information. 'Our bank's formal information is either un-available, inaccurate or wrong,' said The Bank's chief controller.

Functional and leadership training are provided through a centralized human resources group. The Bank rewards individual achievements and leadership rather than team performance. In addition to management and functional training, The Bank organizes training in assessment centres, where managers meet for a week to be tested on their general and functional skills. Often, the results of the assessment centre training are used to select the best candidates for vacant positions and promotions. As the director of human resources pointed out, 'During training pro-grammes people feel tested and compete with each other.'

The Bank's procedural culture also undermines its information trans-parency and trust among employees. As a senior manager commented: 'We need a greater amount of trust among people in this company to get away from this "authorization mind-set and culture", which slows down work flow and creates an enormous administrative burden.' Information sharing occurs only along prescribed reporting lines within and among departments and is supported by an outdated network and e-mail system. Customer information is seen primarily as belonging to and the respon-sibility of each branch, with little cross-branch information sharing.

In the past, The Bank has not paid much attention to developing or rewarding proactive behaviours among its sales force. A product manager, mentioning The Bank's future challenges, pointed out: 'We are traditionally a conservative bank. We typically allow market pressures to dictate our changes. We have basically had a cost reduction strategy over the last five years. But now our strategy is to be more proactive with our product line. Yet we are faced with longer reaction times in branches, where cultural biases against aggressive sales strategies have slowed some of the more recent offensive product sales strategies. To help direct our sales force in the desired direction, we had to incrementally set higher sales targets, supported by some marketing measures, to change people's behaviour toward more offensive sales strategies.' The non-proactive behaviour is also reflected in the activities of The Bank's customer representatives. According to a senior customer manager, 'Our customer representatives spend only about 25 per cent of their time selling our products while they spend 75 per cent following up on administrative tasks.' The Bank also faces similar problems in attempting to develop a quality telephone sales force for their direct channel.

The Bank is a company with low information behaviours and values. Hierarchical structures, lack of trust among employees and low integrity create a cycle that is hard to change. Given the actions taken by management over the last five years, The Bank faces the significant challenge of changing information behaviours and values in order to be capable of competing in a changing marketplace in which cross-selling opportunities, absolute customer focus, and excellent information management and IT practices are paramount for competing successfully.

Information Integrity

Information integrity is an organizational value reflected in the individual behaviour of managers and employees. Those with integrity do not manipulate information for personal gain, such as knowingly passing on inaccurate information that will negatively affect another department, distributing information to justify decisions after the fact, or keeping important information to themselves. Good information integrity results in people being willing to share 'sensitive' information within a company to improve individual, team and company performance. Information integrity sets clear boundaries between purely personal and organizational uses of information and people's knowledge. At Hilti, for example, integrity is considered fundamental to ethical human interactions and cannot be negotiated under any circumstances, as the CEO emphasized: 'The fastest way out of this place is playing games with integrity.'

Information integrity also has a direct influence on two other behaviours. First, it enables the formal use of information sources and content by creating trust that such information is accurate, undistorted and will not be used in an inappropriate manner. People in a company trust that the reports and records that they access about customers, products and operations are 'trustworthy', since they believe that others in the company have collected and organized this information in as honest and responsible a manner as can be expected.

Second, information integrity promotes transparency about discovering and using information about mistakes, errors and failures in the company, since high levels of personal and organizational integrity are required for being candid about bad news and 'surprises' inside a company or with customers, suppliers and other outsiders. When people are afraid of losing face, or concerned about their job security or potential penalties, they are unwilling to disclose information that could make them look bad. After five years of restructuring and downsizing, The Bank's staff are understandably fearful about how information about customer and operational errors and mistakes will affect their jobs and their careers.

Information integrity defines both the boundaries beyond which people in an organization should not go in using information and the 'space' in which people can trust their colleagues to do with information what they would do themselves.

Information Formality

Information formality is the degree to which members of a company use and trust formal sources of information over purely informal sources of information. Do sales people in a company trust the customer or product information in their customer sales support system or do they replace it with informal intelligence, since they doubt the accuracy or credibility of data in the system? Although all companies rely on both types of information to operate and to establish social networks among people, generally companies seek to rely on formal sources and processes of information use because they are more stable, efficient and predictable over time than informal sources and processes.

Information formality is an important behaviour, since it enables the company to establish formal processes and information flows to manufacture high-quality products or deliver consistent services to customers. Managers and employees tend to use formal information sources and IT systems to promote efficiency in operations and process management. They also, to some extent, rely on formal information uses for management decision-making and innovation, if they believe that the information is valid, relevant and trustworthy.

Information formality improves control by providing accurate, trustworthy and consistent performance information throughout a company. Trust in formal sources of information will add credibility to this information, improving the influence of individual performance criteria tied to that of the company.

However, people in companies may supplement formal information for decision-making with informal sources inside and outside the company, if they doubt the reliability and veracity of the formal information. Companies with low levels of integrity among their staff experience lower reliance on formal information sources and systems, since people do not trust the information that they are receiving or using. In such companies, like The Bank, employees and managers may use informal networks and sources of information rather than formal sources, since they believe that these are more reliable, trustworthy and efficient.

Information Control

Information control is the use of information about business performance among managers and employees to clarify the relationship between individual and work unit responsibilities and company operations. It is also associated with the ability to cascade performance criteria and measures to all levels of the company and to communicate the relationships between individual and work unit performance to company performance and compensation/rewards.

The result of high information control is threefold. First, it can stimulate the emergence of new ideas and learning by improving performance at all levels and by reacting constructively to mistakes, errors and failures to improve transparency. Second, the sharing of sensitive performance information encourages the sharing of other types of sensitive, and nonsensitive, information. Third, it can motivate, monitor and reward the achievement of specific results at individual, work unit and company levels, directly improving proactive behaviours.

In companies with low levels of information control, performance information is tightly guarded among a small group of managers and is only shared with employees on a 'need to know' basis. People may know what their responsibilities are in this company, but will not necessarily know why they are doing the work for which they are responsible or what their contribution is to work unit and company performance. This impacts how transparent a company is with its information. It also undermines the willingness, or capacity, of people to share information with others in the company—how can I identify and share information appropriate for others when I don't understand what it is for? And finally, it decreases staff incentive to be proactive with information—to think about how to use information to improve products and services. For example, before the 1990s, Hilti managers were reluctant to share performance information with other departments in the company, since they felt that such information was too sensitive and should be kept within a small group of key players. During the 1990s, however, Hilti managers realized: 'People who are informed about the business and understand it are clearly motivated to go after common goals. Sharing numbers with your people and setting targets is really an incentive. If they see that they made 90 per cent, they will, of course, try to make it 100 per cent.'

The Bank's managers, by contrast, only share information about individual performance with employees. This practice leads to competition among individuals, which can enhance individual performance, but undermine team and company performance.

In companies with high levels of information formality and integrity—and, therefore, control—providing information about performance facilitates the setting of consistent performance criteria and measures in business units and teams and across functions. In these companies, the focus is always on making sure that people know what is expected of them as well as where they stand.

Information Transparency

Information transparency is evident when members of an organization trust each other enough to talk about failures, mistakes and errors in an open and constructive manner without fear of unfair repercussions. Information transparency permits employees and managers to learn from their mistakes and to engage in continuous feedback. The faster and more effective people are in identifying problems and responding constructively to them, the better they can modify their intended strategy and implementation approach to take into account new and emergent learning from inside and outside the company.

At Hilti, for example, learning does not only result from good training and sharing best practices, but also from discussing errors and mistakes—one's own and those of others. 'In our culture,' the CEO explained, 'we don't even talk about mistakes. Instead, we talk about opportunities to learn, about experiences.'

In contrast, since the degree of integrity and trust in The Bank is minimal, employees do not reveal information about mistakes and errors. This lack of transparency blocks learning about operational problems with customers and their accounts, which further undermines business performance.

In addition, information transparency is facilitated by information control—a high-trust environment among employees is nurtured by the willingness of senior managers to display and communicate performance-based information. As we noted earlier, Hilti managers discuss performance-based information on a regular basis with all their staff during meetings that are part of the normal planning process to set performance targets. They inform everyone down to the shop-floor workers. The meetings take place every two months; in the meantime, the numbers and 'cockpit charts' are always available through the company's intranet and e-mail system.

Information Sharing

Information sharing is the free exchange of non-sensitive and sensitive information. Sharing occurs between individuals in teams, as well as across functions and organizational boundaries. Sharing is a key behaviour often supported by managers. Information transparency facilitates sharing by allowing errors, mistakes and failures to be treated as constructive learning opportunities that build trust for the sharing of all types of company information. Information control also creates incentives that enable the sharing of information within teams and across functions in the company. This creates a form of 'enlightened self-interest', which promotes the attitude that people share information because it is in their best interests to do so.

At Hilti, we can see that sharing performance-based information from senior managers on down has led employees at all levels to engage in information exchanges. For example, market organizations and business units are now more effective at sharing information than in the past. Individuals who have never met before now provide each other with helpful information by e-mail.

Senior managers continue to promote greater information exchanges by sponsoring programmes and forums for sharing experiences. Encouraged by the lead of senior managers, employees initiate information exchanges proactively to leverage their own and the company's extensive information resources.

At The Bank, however, the centralized structure and hierarchy inhibit information-sharing among individuals and across functions. Knowledge residing with people and information resources cannot be fully exploited, since they are compartmentalized in the hierarchy of command and control, need to know, and poor information and IT practices.

Information Proactiveness

Proactive use of information is the critical behaviour that people in companies must display to actively seek out information about changes in the company's business environment and respond quickly to them. It also means that people will anticipate customer needs and respond by enhancing or creating new products and services. Proactiveness depends on information control and sharing, since both these behaviours build a powerful context in which to search for new information and ideas and to respond to them quickly by sharing the new information wherever it is needed in the company—for both company and individual benefit.

Hilti's managers continually challenge their existing assumptions and business realities to develop awareness among their employees about what information about markets, customers and competitors is useful for continued business success. Each member of the executive board spends a minimum of one to two days per month with customers on their sites to enable Hilti to better anticipate their needs and pick up new information about business conditions. The board members also exchange ideas with their employees to test new concepts and seek new information. As one senior executive noted: 'I ask my people a lot of questions, for example, "Why do we have a certain problem?" That way, I get a lot of information and it involves the people. And if they are involved, they come with their own energy and drive.'

Conversely, The Bank's most recent emphasis on developing more proactive information practices among its branch employees to cross-sell products and be more customer-focused has been difficult to implement. The Bank lacks strength in other key information behaviours—such as information formality, control and transparency—necessary to improve the proactive use of information. Thus, with low information behaviours and values, The Bank is not in a position to improve its IO maturity. Bank managers may wish to be more proactive, but their employees do not have the correct mind-sets, beliefs and actions in order to follow through.

The IBV Maturity Model

The path to mature information behaviours and values is summed up in the IBV maturity model shown in Figure 4.1. This model allows managers to quickly identify the most efficient way of building IBV maturity. Companies wishing to improve their information behaviours and values should begin to work at the bottom of the model by improving integrity, since this dimension has a direct and indirect influence on all other behaviours and values. By understanding these relationships and following the prescribed paths, managers can begin to build a solid foundation to support proactive information use in their company. We know that companies with high IO scores understand how to instil these behaviours and values in their employees. Senior managers continually and explicitly promote these values by personal example and, at every opportunity, recognize good behaviour and discourage bad. They also know how to derive the most value from the way these behaviours work together to make a company proactive in innovation and using information to respond to business changes.

A company with low IO may instil some but not all the behaviours and values. These gaps in people's mind-sets, values and behaviours—when coupled with potential deficiencies in information management practices and IT practices—will result in lower business performance. There are no shortcuts to building these behavioural practices, since they must all be present to a high degree for a company to achieve IO maturity. For this reason, we believe that companies like Hilti, BBV and SkandiaBanken, that exhibit high levels of these six information behaviours and values, have a potential competitive advantage over a company like The Bank. Companies like The Bank must transform their behaviours and values over several years to reach the position that these high-performing companies are at today.

MANAGING INFORMATION BEHAVIOURS AND VALUES (IBV)

If a company is not as mature or good in information behaviours and values as it needs to be, what corrective steps can managers in that company take? In this section, we explain ten ways that managers can improve the information behaviours and values of people in their company.

Guideline 1:   Do not compromise on integrity

Integrity entails telling the truth and establishing trust. Telling the truth involves honesty or avoiding deceit; it means representing reality as accurately as possible. People with integrity will present what they know about reality candidly and fairly by not hiding bad news or glossing over important facts or concerns that are difficult to present to others.

In organizations, integrity develops trust among people by defining boundaries within which they can legitimately use power and influence. In an organization characterized by integrity, people believe in and share a set of key principles that outline appropriate conduct in the company— they feel they have a duty to act within the accepted boundaries of ethical and appropriate behaviour.

At Hilti, for example, employees trust the integrity of managers, and managers in turn expect their employees to act with integrity. This reciprocal obligation to act with integrity is a fundamental part of the company's culture. Managers are well aware that integrity and mutual trust are preconditions for promoting open communication and information-sharing at all levels of the company. In the words of the CEO: 'We would rather tolerate mediocre performance by an employee or manager (which can be rectified) than lack of integrity.'

This uncompromising stance on acting with integrity in the company is required if people at all levels are to trust each other enough to share sensitive information about performance or errors.

Guideline 2:   Use integrity to build faith in formal information

If people in a company believe that others will collect and report information truthfully and accurately, they will trust formal information about customers, products, performance, finances and operations. Trust in formal information has three benefits:

- it cuts down time wasted re-collecting or reanalysing information received;
- it speeds up information use;
- it reduces people's reliance on informal information to double-check formal reports.

Let's consider an example of what happens in a company when low integrity leads to a distrust of formal information sources.

International Freight Forwarding: A Business in Need of Integrity

Established over fifty years ago, this international freight forwarding company developed into an industry leader in the 1980s and 1990s, offering integrated freight forwarding around the world by land, sea and air. Historically, country managers in the company had been given a lot of freedom to boost sales around the world.

Freight forwarding as an industry, however, had an 'integrity' problem as the CEO put it:

> Until recently, freight forwarders were considered the highway robbers of the industry. Our industry was dominated by obscure forwarding agents, unreliable transportation services, sloppy handling of merchandise and unwilling customs officials. As a result of this, customers could never be sure whether forwarded goods would reach their destination or not.

Within this very decentralized company, trust and integrity were equally underdeveloped. Budgets and profitability ratios were basically unreliable; no performance-related information was shared on a company-wide basis.

A change to a more centralized organizational structure and new senior management leadership had improved information-sharing about financial performance across the company. But, given the nature of the industry and the company's lack of integrity in the past, managers still did not trust performance-based information. One senior manager explained: 'If I get performance data for a particular country, I re-enter all the numbers in my own spreadsheets, as I have no idea how most of the numbers are calculated.' When a multinational customer wanted to know the sum total of his company's business with the freight forwarder, managers had to collect the numbers by phone, e-mail and fax from each individual country operation around the world. Again, no one knew whether the data was correct or not.

Contrast this example of low integrity and low trust in formal information with a leading Spanish manufacturer of toiletries and cosmetics with extremely high integrity and high trust in formal information used within the company.

Antonio Puig S.A.: From Family to Company Integrity

The Catalan Antonio Puig founded his company in 1914. By the mid-1960s, the company had expanded internationally and opened a subsidiary in the United States; it later expanded to other countries in Europe and south-east Asia. Operated as a family business, the company was managed by the founder's four sons following his death in 1979; now members of the third generation of the family have replaced their fathers in leading the company.

Antonio Puig had always encouraged his sons 'to stay together. Your unity will be your strength.' He understood that strong company values coupled with solid family values—especially high integrity—would ensure the company's long-term success. He even formalized his values for the family and company in two books:

- The *Family Handbook*—containing the family beliefs in integrity, trust and openness, and
- The *Family Protocol*—a series of rules for family members to follow in running the company.

The company's employees also recognize the high value placed on integrity by managers. 'The family cares very much about employee integrity and does not tolerate any behaviour that would go against those principles. We demand integrity among our employees, and we are absolutely honest with our customers and consumers,' commented the HR director.

For example, during the launch of a new product, some managers proposed describing the product as 'weight-reducing'. The senior managers refused to label it as such, knowing that the statement was not true. As one manager noted: 'In a family business, a lot of information shared with our employees is sensitive, because it is not available to the public. The integrity of our employees enables effective sharing of such information.' Puig managers and employees know that, if they make sensitive information known in the company and share it, the information will be used in an appropriate way.

Moreover, high integrity and honesty create trust in formal information at Puig. One senior manager noted:

> We have different levels of formality in our company's processes: recruiting at the management level is very informal, but monthly reporting of manufacturing data is very formal. I normally trust the formal information and do not need additional informal information to support my decisions in the factories. In our company, if data is not honest and accurate, it is not produced.

High integrity creates high trust in formal information use in these companies.

Guideline 3:   Make performance information explicit

As we noted earlier, Hilti's drive to make performance information explicit through detailed 'cockpit charts' that link individual and team performance to company performance helps employees to understand the relationship between their job and company objectives. Making performance information explicit sends a strong message to employees that managers believe in their contribution and are willing to share performance criteria and measures honestly with them.

An example of the lengths to which managers in some companies will go to make performance information explicit is captured by a division director of a leading global manufacturer of specialty chemicals.

Specialty Chemical Manufacturer

In the early 1980s, the UK division of the company had to reduce its workforce from 1,400 to 700 during a major economic downturn. The practices adopted then have been developed and nurtured throughout the company ever since. As the director commented:

> We realized that we owed our people a real explanation. We wanted them to understand why we had to do this. So we compared running a business—any business—to running a household . . . with only so much to spend before incurring debts. We also told them about product costing, some basic accounting, and what each employee costs.
>
> After that, we decided to introduce a performance-based bonus to reward our people in good times, but prevent the company from being hurt in bad economic times. We told our people how it would function and made sure that they all understood it. The unions were of great help in this instance, since they realized that we did this for the benefit of the whole company and each employee. In years when no bonus was paid, people were dissatisfied when they had to work so hard for no additional gain. So the guys

> from the unions explained to them that making new investments was a way
> of creating and saving jobs in the future.
>
> From then on, around the mid-1980s, our relationship with our people
> really changed. This was the result of increased communication with them.
> You have to be clear, make sure everybody understands you, and then stick
> to what you've said. That's crucial. You have to be consistent. Then they
> begin to see that you are not out to get them, but that they can rely on what
> you say. They begin to trust you. So, as a consequence of all this, our people
> have developed a very high trust in managers' integrity.

The company's commitment to making performance information explicit, even to employees who were later made redundant, had a long-lasting effect on the company.

Imagine if the company had dealt with the same situation in a different way. What if the managers had chosen not to communicate about the performance of their division with employees? Informal communications would have taken over in the form of gossip and rumours, which could damage employee motivation and the capability of the company to respond to the situation quickly and effectively. In this case, managers would have lost control of employees through the erosion of trust and credibility.

Guideline 4:   Cascade performance information throughout your company

Companies must not only make performance-based information explicit, but they must also cascade it through all levels. The process of cascading performance information articulates and links the relationship between performance criteria/measures and the business strategy, as well as tying employee rewards to company performance. With such programmes, a company improves feedback and learning about what works and does not work in implementing its business strategy.

The specialty chemical company mentioned earlier also has experience of the cascading process, as described by the head of the pigments division.

Specialty Chemical Manufacturer

The manager told the following story:

> Many years ago, when we started giving people more information about the
> business, I realized that we were not all talking the same language. I was
> talking to a group of workers about competitors, the industry, and 'selling
> pigments in the marketplace'. After a while, one of the workers said that he

had never seen pigments being sold in the marketplace and wondered where they were being sold. It took me a while to realize that he was talking about the local produce marketplace in the city centre, because that was the only marketplace he knew. Since that day, I have been very careful in my choice and explanation of words, no matter who I am talking to.

We need to give everyone in our company the business context, whether he or she mops the floors or shovels pigments. I always take time to explain to people how their own work fits into what we produce, and how this product is eventually used by our customers—and their customers as well. How do I do that with floor moppers? Well, of course you can't take the tediousness out of their work, but you can give them a sense of pride in what they are doing by explaining how they and their work contribute to the success of the company—and that they are part of this winning team.

By going to the trouble of cascading performance information to the floor mopper level, this manager not only builds company awareness and a sense of common purpose among employees, but also promotes the search for innovation. If given the opportunity, people will find innovative ways to improve their own jobs and those of others as well.

Guideline 5:   Use formal performance information to build openness

Sharing sensitive performance information throughout a company creates openness among managers and employees—a precondition for transparency. Transparency requires people to be open to the thoughts and concerns of others, especially when the news is not good. By being open, people can express, share and learn from their mistakes and those of others.

SkandiaBanken is a good example of a company that fosters an open working environment by sharing performance-based information with everyone. Information formality is a value supported by the bank's senior managers. The CEO insists that people get rid of paper on their desk and enter appropriate information into the IT system so that others in the bank can access and make use of it. Among other things, this belief in formality improves the ability of the bank to share performance-based information within each of the bank's call centre teams.

An IT system monitors employee efficiency in responding to phone calls, keeps a record of time, and calculates individual and team responsiveness. The system can be accessed by employees and managers at any time. The goal of this performance system is to make all work as transparent as possible.

'Everyone knows who is doing what. Everyone knows his or her targets and calculations for revenues and costs,' explained the CEO. 'We want to be as transparent as possible since we believe that it is critical for our direct business model,' noted the CIO. The CEO added: 'There must be a sense of openness that is shared among employees, and the information that is shared must be presented in a simple, understandable form.'

Guideline 6:   Develop team-based performance information to create openness

Another way that companies foster openness and transparency is by focusing on team, rather than—or in addition to—individual performance. Let's compare these approaches to creating openness by contrasting BBV with The Bank.

BBV rewards its employees for their contribution to their team, especially at the branch level. The Bank focuses entirely on individual performance and rewards.

At BBV, every employee is trained and rewarded as a team player. As we mentioned in the Introduction, team commitment was one of BBV's three main objectives in its first and second 1,000-day Programmes, designed to boost growth. Employees' contributions are valued in so far as they help teams achieve their goals. Any behaviour that undermines team commitment and trust within the bank's teams is not tolerated.

This attention to rewarding and training team performance fosters an atmosphere of openness in which employees trust each other and, as the head of HR noted, 'Employees believe that team success comes before individual success.' BBV is so convinced that team performance makes a difference in its business that it encourages 'fair' competition among teams. Every year the bank organizes a contest among all its branches for the best branch. The winner is awarded a special prize and bonuses are paid to all its employees. BBV managers are careful, though, that competition among branches does not hinder the bank's overall success.

In contrast, The Bank trains and rewards its employees based on individual performance. What is the result? People compete with each other and do not trust each other. Training sessions are competitive, since employees are fighting for advancement to a smaller number of positions. Information-sharing and openness are not rewarded. It is up to individuals to decide what information to share. Because employees are mainly focused on their individual goals and rewards, the result is a lack of transparency and cooperation among employees which, in turn, hurts business performance.

Guideline 7:   Use every mistake as an opportunity to learn

Transparency is essential to individual and organizational learning. People learn by trying things out, by doing new things. And when people learn by doing, they inevitably make mistakes, or sometimes even fail. People must feel free to examine the reasons for their mistakes, and learn key lessons so that they won't happen again. For this learning to occur in companies, managers must reveal, share and treat 'failures' openly and fairly, without blame or embarrassment. Only in this way can they create trust.

Even the 'best' companies will not be absolutely perfect in their implementation of strategies, processes and services. Mistakes with customers, errors in product quality and failures in new improvement programmes inevitably occur. If managers believe that no 'bad news is good news', assume that their efforts to implement strategies will not fail, or take for granted that defects in products and services are always 'someone's fault', the company will live in the shadow of its ignorance. When errors occur, no one will report them for fear of sanction. Thus they will not be corrected or avoided in the future. Over time, managers in the 'see no evil, hear no evil, speak no evil' company under-perform. Thus the essential business rationale for high transparency gets back to our original premise: companies inevitably make mistakes or fail at certain initiatives. The more quickly companies detect these problems and respond effectively, the better they will perform in the long run.

To bring home this important point, let's look at how Ritz-Carlton Hotels, a chain in the competitive luxury segment of hotels in the United States, have made the occurrence of customer and service errors a positive learning opportunity that makes good business sense.

Ritz-Carlton Hotels[1]

Personalized service toward its guests is the hallmark of Ritz-Carlton. From its beginnings in 1985, the company has been inspired by a clear service credo and set of values. Its managers aim at building consistent, customer-driven service processes and systems to assist the hotel's employees anticipate a guest's needs and preferences on each visit to a hotel in the chain and, at the same time, help people react instantly to satisfy a need, resolve a complaint or respond to a service error. In addition to careful screening of potential employees for a service-oriented profile, the hotel also gives all employees extensive training. A Ritz-Carlton employee participates in more than 100 hours of service quality education designed to reinforce service commitment, problem solving, idea generation and a can-do attitude.

The Ritz-Carlton devotion to selection and training is complemented by an appreciation of the power of employee empowerment. In the words of one manager:

Empowerment reinforces company values and makes training all the more effective. When you give people freedom, they have much more energy and commitment. We tell our people that if they see something going wrong, we want them to jump in and own the problem. And, once they are involved, they know they have the freedom to do what it takes to make things right. They can buy our guests dinner, or clothes—or adjust the bill. Staff throughout the hotel know that they have the power to compensate a disappointed guest for an amount as high as $2,000.

The key is Ritz-Carlton's ability to transform each incident into an opportunity to learn internally and restore the guest's faith in the company and its people. Such incidents—for example, a particular room is not ready upon a guest's arrival—are written up in a special 'instant action report' and are retained in a Ritz-Carlton database to make certain that such a service failure will not happen again to the particular guest at another Ritz-Carlton hotel. Over time, Ritz-Carlton Hotels benefit in two ways:

- they identify and respond to service problems quickly and learn from them, and
- they understand how service issues affect specific guests and make sure that they do not occur to the same person again—thereby increasing customer loyalty through better customer information about service experiences with the hotels in the chain.

Guideline 8:   Increase information sharing through better information control and transparency

Sharing appears to be a voluntary act, but in many circumstances we are asked, encouraged or urged to share our toys with siblings, our knowledge or information with team members or managers, and our time with spouses and children. What appears to be a simple and voluntary act is actually a more complex behaviour. Why?

Sharing depends on a set of preconditions—a common language, the existence of a prior relationship, and trust that the shared information will not be used against the sharer, or to the other person's advantage (and the sharer's disadvantage). A shared purpose or common stake in outcomes, or ownership of results, must be apparent. The sharing of information—including some understanding of what information people are supposed to share or not share—must be part of the company's culture. Thus sharing information is a complex business act that requires active encouragement and management in a company.

Banco Bilbao Vizcaya (BBV)

BBV, for example, uses a non-conventional practice to monitor and encourage information-sharing about customers and products within and across branches.

Typically, mystery shoppers are used in retailing to evaluate service quality—the nature of the contacts and interactions between a customer and a store clerk in offering products and services. At BBV, mystery shoppers are also used in this way in branches, but they are asked to evaluate a lot more than their customer experience.

A mystery shopper opens an account, for example, in Branch A and checks that all procedures are followed and that the experience is satisfactory for the customer. Then the mystery shopper goes to Branch B and performs a more complex act, such as buying an investment fund. While carrying out this second transaction, the mystery shopper checks the information about himself or herself, as a customer moving from branch A to B. The mystery shopper also checks that the branch representatives follow the cross-selling practices described earlier and record remarks related to the nature of the customer contact.

As retired employees, the BBV mystery shoppers understand the bank procedures and IT systems well and know what branch employees are expected to do with information within and across branches. The shoppers report to bank managers on information-sharing between branches as part of their service quality and cross-selling checks. 'We have a very open relationship with our mystery shoppers and they provide a valuable contribution to improving the bank's information sharing,' notes BBV's head of retail banking.

What might appear to be an auditing procedure in some companies is employed in BBV as a constructive way of learning about how employees use IT systems and are motivated to collect and store information about customer interactions that other branch employees will use in future customer contacts. By having high levels of transparency and constructive use of performance-based information across branches, BBV employees recognize that sharing information promotes not just their branch's success, but also the performance of the bank as a whole. Thus mystery shoppers are viewed as constructive opportunities for branch representatives to show what they can do, rather than as auditors of company procedures.

Guideline 9:   People who understand the business and are informed will be proactive

The process of openly sharing performance-based information inside a company, coupled with high levels of transparency, creates a powerful context for employees and managers to act proactively—to seek new ideas and information or apply information in new ways. As we noted in Chapter 3, proactive behaviour does not come about by accident. Mature IO companies build it up systematically over years by reinforcing the behaviours and values that lead to (or create) this proactive disposition in people. Moreover, mature IO companies can rely on the fact that employees with this disposition will act to create business value every day in many small—and not so small—ways, rather than depending on the occasional heroic efforts of a few.

IKEA: Swedish Furniture Retailer[2]

The culture of IKEA is described in a booklet that each new employee receives:

> It's all about people, about our relationship with each other and the world around us, about thrift, hard work, humility, and willpower. Our culture allows no barriers between different categories of personnel . . . The true IKEA spirit is founded on our enthusiasm, on our constant will to renew, on our cost-consciousness, on our willingness to assume responsibility.

To create this enthusiasm among employees, performance-based information is shared openly in the company and individual initiative is promoted. If an employee wants to initiate a project, create a new product line, or make changes, it is the employee's responsibility to present a project plan and budget that justifies the cost and time involved.

One such employee is Per Tovas, a general maintenance worker in a US branch of IKEA. In the early 1990s, IKEA had agreed to retrofit 90 per cent of its facilities with fluorescent lighting to comply, by 1997, with the US Environmental Protection Agency's Green Lights Programme. Tovas had volunteered to head the initiative for his store in Plymouth, Pennsylvania. After reviewing reports by several consultants, he realized that their analyses were conflicting and that they did not understand IKEA's needs for retail light levels and lighting quality.

Therefore, he undertook the retrofitting and energy audit for the entire store himself. The results of his analysis were striking. IKEA's controllers preferred a two-year payback on all major investments. At a cost of $151,000, Tovas calculated that the total savings at the store for electricity, maintenance and energy generation would be $85,322 a year—an undiscounted payback period of 1.78 years.

As a consequence, IKEA retrofitted all US stores with Tovas's recommended lighting system. When asked why he initially took on such a large project, Tovas replied: 'Sometimes you see something that you have to do . . . [yet] there are still a lot of areas needing improvement.

This incident is a good example of the thousands of celebrated—and not so celebrated—actions people will undertake on their own initiative if they understand their role and what is expected of them in terms of performance, as well as having access to useful information. Companies like IKEA and Hilti find ways of leveraging the power of their employees to seek information and act proactively to solve problems and generate ideas at a faster rate than their competitors. These abilities provide significant leverage in marketplaces that are turbulent, not forgiving and rapidly changing.

Guideline 10:   Good localized information behaviours do not add up to leveraging information company-wide

Throughout our research, we have seen many highly decentralized companies with good localized information behaviours. These firms have developed these behaviours in their stores, sales forces, country operations or business units. As we saw with the European retailer of eyeglass lenses and frames in Chapter 3, the senior managers of these companies celebrate the entrepreneurial, empowered, and proactive behaviours of their employees. In many ways, they believe that localized initiative and appropriate information behaviours and values make their employees more effective in serving local markets. And they are correct—partly.

At the same time, these same managers do not see or know a good deal about their company outside of the local contexts in which they function. As such companies grow, they do not know how many customers they lose because information about them is not shared between stores; or because sales people do not share information about customers they do not like and so stop calling on them; or the company does not achieve lower costs of operations because it has neither the supply chain processes nor the information systems to manage operations and business processes efficiently across stores, sales territories, countries and business units. Not only do localized information behaviours and values mask information needs across such a company, they may also inhibit information sharing and use company-wide.

Therefore, it is not good enough for companies to develop appropriate information behaviours and values locally, unless the company improves those behaviours and values company-wide and at all levels. This is a striking difference between companies. The European retailer of spectacle lenses and frames has good local behaviours, but no information management practices and IT systems to leverage information behaviours and values company-wide across brands, across countries and globally. In contrast, Hilti has systematically developed its information behaviours as well as its information management and IT practices on a company-wide basis across market organizations, business units, regions and globally at all levels during the 1990s.

Two Managerial Caveats When Changing Information Behaviours and Values

The ten guidelines presented in this chapter for improving your company's information behaviours and values are the starting points on the journey that your company must take to consistently and systematically instil and build these capabilities in your people and managers. However, as you launch yourself on the journey, keep two caveats in mind:

Caveat 1:   Managers can influence some behaviours more easily than others

Some behaviours and values, such as integrity and transparency, are more rooted in the individual person than others, such as control, sharing and formality. Managers must be aware that not all behaviours can or will change at the same time just because managers think that they have taken appropriate steps.

This phenomenon can be seen in the following example of a turnaround programme undertaken to improve information behaviours and values in a major business unit of a large financial company facing declining market share and customer dissatisfaction.

US Division of an International Financial Services Company

Senior managers realized that over several years the field force selling to business customers was not as effective as it could be. After evaluating its 120 sales representatives, senior managers decided to effect change through a new approach to performance criteria, rewards and information sharing. These new performance criteria and measures would be simple to understand, shared across the group, and link individual performance to market share, end of day volume, and end of day growth rate in developing customer business.

These managers also sought to formalize and improve the quality of the product and customer account information that had previously been provided to the sales force. For example, all presentations and customer selling points were made available to everyone to improve the quality of sales efforts. A new IT network linked the sales force to one another and to the home office to share information within the business unit.

In addition, senior managers developed a company-wide information sharing initiative to influence all employees, especially the sales force. A strong culture of 'these are my numbers and I own the customer' pervaded the entire business unit. To show their commitment to information-sharing, senior managers encouraged sharing of customer information at all levels in the business unit—a step that represented a major mind-set shift in the business unit.

Two years after beginning these initiatives, substantial improvements had been made in the business unit's information behaviours and values. However, the results of the business unit's IO dashboard in Figure 4.3 indicate that two of the behaviours—integrity and transparency—continued to lag behind the others. A senior manager commented: 'Trust still does not fully exist. People continue to use information for their own benefit to position themselves and their department. We still have a long way to go.'

Info behaviours and values (IBV)

Information integrity	bottom 35%
Information formality	above 50%
Information control	above 50%
Information sharing	top 35%
Information transparency	bottom 35%
Information proactiveness	above 50%

Legend

Top 5% (top 8 SMTs)	top 5%
Top 20% (top 34 SMTs)	top 20%
Top 35% (top 60 SMTs)	top 35%
Above 50% (upper 84 SMTs)	above 50%
Below 50% (lower 85 SMTs)	below 50%
Bottom 35% (lower 60 SMTs)	bottom 35%
Bottom 20% (lower 34 SMTs)	bottom 20%
Bottom 5% (lowest 8 SMTs)	bottom 5%

Figure 4.3: The information behaviours and values of the US Division of a leading financial services company

As we noted at the beginning of the chapter, changing mind-sets, behaviours, and values is never easy. Building integrity, transparency and trust requires not only managerial action, but also employee acceptance. Many companies will need months and years of focused efforts before all information behaviours and values have been turned around.

Caveat 2:   Poor managerial behaviours and values take years to overcome

Some managers may be in the fortunate position of starting a new business unit or company. They may be able to develop information behaviours and values right from the start. In established companies, however, changing behaviours is more difficult. You may be in a company or business unit with a history of poor information behaviours and values. Or you may be a new manager in a business unit where cultural tales of a past CEO or other senior managers with poor information behaviours and values still circulate as if they happened yesterday. In either case, overcoming the legacy of poor information behaviours and values may take considerable time and effort.

This lesson is poignantly told through the experiences of a major US financial services company, which had experienced very poor information behaviours and values by several CEOs over ten years before we interviewed the current CEO and his senior management team.

US Financial Services Company

For many years, this company was managed in a command and control style by CEOs and their senior managers. Information was hoarded inside departments and only given on a need to know basis. Managers feared retribution for wrong decisions, and employees lived in fear of making mistakes and errors.

Performance information was closely held by the CEOs to keep the people who reported directly to them under their control. 'Divide and conquer' was the water cooler comment about executive committee politics. Not surprisingly, executive committee members did not receive all the performance information from CEOs. Integrity problems plagued all levels of the company, since people were encouraged to pursue their career and departmental advantage at the expense of others. One CEO in the 1980s was asked to resign following a discovery by the board of directors that he had presented falsified data on company performance. 'There was a strong sense among senior managers that information would be filtered and used selectively,' commented one senior manager. 'This was the nature of their personalities—to use power to keep others in the dark and keep control.'

Over a decade later, the company is still struggling with the legacy of the old corporate culture and ways of using information. Not only are the impacts of this bygone era still fresh in people's minds, but they also make steps to improve the management style and information behaviours and values difficult to implement. Young employees absorb the old and new values and are unsure about how to act. Old employees remember the old era and wonder whether the more recent steps by senior managers to improve behaviours and values are genuine.

There are many established companies and business units whose legacy of information behaviours and values is poor at best. In these companies, senior managers who pursue significant improvements in the information behaviours of their employees must confront the credibility gaps and legacy of the old ways of doing business. They will have to overcome the private doubts and often unexpressed concerns of employees. They will have to persuade the doubters that their steps toward improving information behaviours and values are genuine and will take hold over time in the company's ways of doing business.

CONCLUSION

In this chapter we have shown you how to improve the information behaviours of your company and business unit by following the paths prescribed in the IBV maturity model. We have identified the six behaviours and values—within one of the three information capabilities—that are critical to high IO and business performance and discussed the sequence in which managers should pursue improvements. In the next chapter we will examine how to leverage the power of your information management practices (IMP).

NOTES

1. Klein, N.W., Sasser, E. and Jones, T.O. (1995) 'The Ritz-Carlton: Using Information Systems to Better Serve the Customer,' Boston: Harvard Business School Publishing. Case Study 9-395-064. May.
2. Reichart, J. and Larson, A. (1998) 'IKEA and The Natural Step,' Charlottesville: Darden Graduate School of Business Administration, University of Virginia. Case Study UVA-G-0501.

5

UNDERSTANDING THE POWER OF INFORMATION MANAGEMENT

Information in a business is more than just 'data' about customers and their transactions. The information about a customer is what the people in a company will act on. The representation of the customer in company customer records, orders and transactions is the content sales representatives or managers use to make decisions about customers—how to sell to them, meet their needs and satisfy them with new products. If the content is a true reflection of the customer's history and behaviour with the company, then company employees will treat the customer right. If the content only partially reflects the customer's buying behaviours, past purchases and complaints, company representatives will act on what the company's records show.

The power of information management depends on the ability of a company's managers and employees to sense, collect, organize, process and maintain the 'right' information about customers, products, operations and business conditions and to act effectively on this information. Companies with high IO make their knowledge explicit, that is, they formalize their people's knowledge so others can use it. Their information practices also make it possible to use the information wherever and whenever their employees need to make decisions about customers, products, operations and changing business conditions.

In contrast, companies that have low IO do not understand how to use the knowledge that is in their employees' heads explicitly and consistently. Managers in these companies do not know what information creates value for their business and how to exploit it. Their employees complain about having too little of the right information to do their job and too much of the wrong information. Since managers and people do not trust the information that is available for them to use, they do not spend their time and attention continually improving information management practices. They rely on gut feelings, or what is in their head or the heads of others, but not on the formal processes in place for managing their company's information resources. People in low IO companies lose touch with the realities of their business internally and externally, since information about their customers, products, operations and business conditions cannot be trusted or relied on when it comes to managing and changing their business.

In this chapter we will take a closer look at how good information management practices lead to higher IO and what actions managers can take to create effective information practices in their company.

MAKING INFORMATION MANAGEMENT PRACTICES (IMP) VISIBLE

Banco Bilbao Vizcaya (BBV)

BBV's head of retail banking understands the importance of managing information in achieving business success:

> Information is a key enabler of our business day to day, and our branch activities revolve around sensing, processing and maintaining customer, product and financial information. We collect information every time we speak with customers. We analyse the information on a continuous basis to identify opportunities for better customer service and cross-selling of our products.

The recent history of BBV reveals constant attention to creating the business tools and training people to sense, collect, organize, process and maintain information as linked procedures around customers, products and performance-based information. As we noted in Chapter 2, the bank has a well-defined customer segmentation strategy based on eight categories of customers. How does the bank refine its knowledge of these segments and appropriate products for each?

Mining Information Value from the Branches

The centre of the bank's customer information management strategy is the use of the branch as a proactive sales and customer service outlet that integrates all customer contacts with the bank whether through direct channels such as ATMs, telephone banking and the Internet or through the branches. The bank builds on the information collected and organized through all its customer contacts and refines its customer and product knowledge using several different approaches.

For example, product developers within the bank's home office use data mining techniques to process and refresh customer information and knowledge of the eight customer segments. Recently, a Spanish law provided tax incentives on a specific type of pension fund. Seeing this change as a good business opportunity, bank analysts identified specific customer segments that would be most interested in this new type of pension fund and designed its own product offer to target those segments. Several weeks after the new product was introduced, the analysts employed data mining techniques to review the product targeting with customer feedback. They concluded that two additional customer segments could be offered the new pension fund product if the bank's representatives offered the product along with a life insurance policy. They revised the product promotion information in the customer sales support system for all the branches and sales of the new product increased dramatically. In addition, branch managers immediately introduced this new product information and how to sell it to specific customer segments in the bank's on-site training programmes.

Seeking Business Intelligence Around the World

As well as responding rapidly to internal customer information and external opportunities to sell new financial products, BBV's managers leave no stone unturned in the continuous quest to learn about new business practices, competitor moves and market shifts in their home market and around the world. The bank has a specific commercial development department, whose staff travel around the world selecting 'interesting companies' to visit both within and outside the financial services industry. 'We just visited a partner bank in Finland,' commented the head of the department, 'which had particularly innovative ATM practices. We think that we will present our findings to our top management and propose some changes in our ATM approach.'

Having sensed new business practices externally, BBV managers schedule regular and frequent sessions each year to share leading edge practices internally. Each fall, all branch managers are invited to a conference where they share practices about all aspects of branch management as well as gaining exposure to new external business practices. A senior manager and former branch manager commented:

> During one of those sharing events, I identified who in the bank had effectively sold specific life insurance policies. Thanks to these sessions, I built a

successful plan and implemented it in my branch, resulting in a major improvement in sales of those products. The manager who helped me become the bank's expert on selling life insurance was also recognized for his contribution throughout the bank and later promoted as well.

Continuous Training of Employees in Good Information Practices

Not only is the bank good at analysing internal information and sensing new information externally, but it also pays special attention to training its employees on how to use the information about customers, products and performance available to them. The controlling department in the bank employs 10 full-time people dedicated to training and supporting BBV's employees in the use of new product, financial and operational information.

The department head observed: When we introduce a new product, a variable rate mortgage, for example, our employees need to know how to interpret the calculations on rates given by the IT system and how to sell the new product to the customers. My staff help the bank's employees to use the new product information and collect feedback on what information should be revised and improved.

These examples of information management practices at BBV highlight the bank's understanding that superior performance in today's financial services industry depends on excellent information use by everyone in the bank. All employees and managers must comprehend their responsibilities for sensing, collecting, organizing, processing and maintaining information and execute them well every day. Moreover, since business conditions are constantly changing, the bank engages in aggressive sensing of external ideas and best practices; it then shares this information as rapidly as possible among managers and trains employees to adapt current practices accordingly. In this way, the bank is constantly testing today's ideas and practices against emerging external realities that will change the bank's practices tomorrow.

KNOWING HOW TO USE INFORMATION TO CREATE VALUE: THE IMP MATURITY MODEL

If you ask managers in companies with high IO what information creates direct business value, they can readily identify the key categories of specific information. They can also discuss the information management practices required to enhance the effective use of the targeted information by their employees. If you pose the same question to managers in companies with low IO, their answers usually focus on why it is difficult to provide their employees with good-quality information or why their staff cannot leverage the information they already get. Managers in low IO companies sense that they are weak in information management practices, but there are always good business reasons for not focusing their attention and resources on improving these practices.

If these lapses in managerial attention to information management practices go on long enough in a low business performer, the gap between it and a high business performer can take years to close, if it closes at all. A key reason is because a company with high IO is actively managing and is good at all five information management practices, not just one or two. In this section, we show you how to move towards higher IO by better understanding and improving all five information management practices, or dimensions, through the IMP maturity model.

Companies with mature IO know that certain relationships, or linkages, exist between the five specific information management practice dimensions—sensing, collecting, organizing, processing and maintaining. Figure 5.1 shows the results of statistical path analysis indicating where there exist causal relationships between these dimensions, and in which direction these relationships exist. The arrows in Figure 5.1 create a clear visual path of these relationships, beginning with sensing, and moving in a circle from collecting to maintaining. We refer to these relationships as the information life cycle.

Following this path, we can see in Figure 5.1 that improvements to sensing, for example, will have a positive effect on the way information is collected. Improved collecting practices will improve the way information is organized. More effective ways of organizing information, consequently, have a positive influence on the processing of information for business decisions. Better processing abilities create improvements to information maintenance. Finally, improved maintenance of information directly affects the collection of information, saving on the need to recollect the same information over and over again, and closing the path of the information life cycle. Companies with IMP maturity, therefore, have put in place business processes to deal with all practices together to best manage the cyclical nature of information management.

Below we discuss each of the five dimensions of information management shown in Figure 5.1, and describe the relationships between them. We continue to follow the example of The Bank, begun in Chapter 4, contrasting its poor information management practices (see p. 88) with the good ones of BBV. In Figure 5.2, we note the benchmark rankings for information management practices from the IO dashboards of both banks to emphasize their differences.

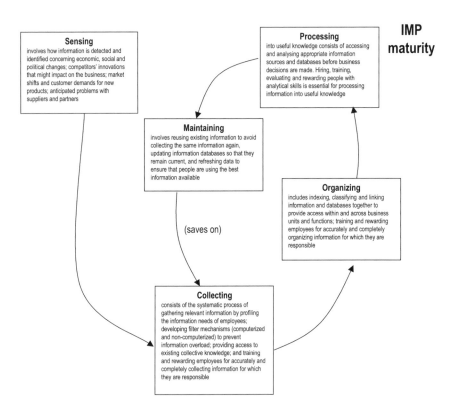

Figure 5.1:   The IMP maturity model

The Bank's information management practices

Customer information management

The Bank's customer information management is based on a customer segmentation of three segments: corporate customers (CCs), private individual customers (PICs)—including those customers with more than 20,000 euros in their account—and mass individual customers (MICs)—including those customers with less than 20,000 euros in their account. While all types of customers have access to direct banking channels such as

BBV's IO dashboard

Info management practices (IMP)

Sensing information	top 35%
Collecting information	top 20%
Organizing information	top 20%
Processing information	top 5%
Maintaining information	top 35%

The Bank's IO dashboard

Info management practices (IMP)

Sensing information	top 35%
Collecting information	below 50%
Organizing information	top 35%
Processing information	below 50%
Maintaining information	below 50%

Legend

Top 5% (top 8 SMTs)	top 5%
Top 20% (top 34 SMTs)	top 20%
Top 35% (top 60 SMTs)	top 35%
Above 50% (upper 84 SMTs)	above 50%
Below 50% (lower 85 SMTs)	below 50%
Bottom 35% (lower 60 SMTs)	bottom 35%
Bottom 20% (lower 34 SMTs)	bottom 20%
Bottom 5% (lowest 8 SMTs)	bottom 5%

Figure 5.2:   Comparing information practices at BBV and The Bank

telephone and Internet, PICs and CCs were assigned a customer relationship manager at their local branch.

When a mass individual customer enters a branch, the branch representative is unable to identify the customer's profile, since the IT system does not provide on-line data on the customer's behaviour or product holdings. If the customer has opened his or her account at another branch, or is using other channels such as telephone or Internet banking, the branch representative cannot access the customer's account.

When a private individual customer enters a branch, he has the option of dealing with his relationship manager. However, the customer information other than transaction information acquired by the relationship manager about the customer is not collected or shared with anyone else in the branch. Each relationship manager is responsible for an average of 850 customers. Customer transaction reports, new customer profiles and asset targets are distributed to each manager on a quarterly basis. A centralized customer management accounting system can be accessed daily, but it only records sales volumes and customer/sales ratios. As a marketing senior manager pointed out, 'With such a large number of customers, it is impossible for our relationship managers to establish personal relationships with all customers. The three month lag is too long to give the sales staff the adequate information to follow up on sales leads.'

Product information management

An unfocused product strategy has resulted in a deep product line with too many product offerings. Without access to updated customer profiles and historical product information, product managers and product developers find themselves frustrated. 'Our product information is in a state of chaos,' said a senior product manager. 'We have information available, but none of it is linked or organized in a way that is easy to find. If you know the product number, you might be able to find some information in the system. But on the whole it is very difficult to find what you need in terms of product information.'

A senior marketing manager added: 'Despite the fact that we know what kind of product information we would like to have, we do not have a management information system in place to deliver the necessary information. For example, we cannot determine product profitability because we do not have the correct measurements.' According to one senior product manager, 'The problem is that there is too much information available, so you have to sift through so much unimportant information to find pertinent information. Another problem is that each department is responsible for updating its own information, and no one has time to do it. No one views it as a priority.'

Every month I receive two full binders of new product suggestions,' added the head of the retail banking unit. 'I am overloaded with complex information that I do not have time to analyse adequately. As a result, I end up making quick and dirty decisions.'

The company's chief controller summed up The Bank's information management practices: 'Our management accounting systems still lack information about our channels, products and customers—information that is essential to improving the profitability and effectiveness of our business.'

Sensing Information

Sensing is the phase of the information life cycle in which people detect and identify information concerning: economic, social and political changes; competitors' innovations; market shifts and customer demands for new products or services; and anticipated problems with the company's suppliers and partners. Sensing information is essential to high IO, since companies must continuously identify events, trends and changes in business conditions and make sense out of them to collect appropriate information, develop new strategies, or make decisions.

Although it is one of the most difficult dimensions to develop because it depends on the reasoning and judgement of individuals, sensing is the point of particular management attention in companies with high IO. Good sensing practices ensure that a company stays in touch with its environment as a precondition for responding appropriately to change. Good sensing practices ensure that people look for, evaluate and choose the right information. At BBV, for example, developing knowledge about new market trends and customer preferences is critical for new product development and for refining customer segmentation strategies for cross-selling. The Bank, too, shows above-average rankings for sensing on its IO dashboard. The benefits of this practice are not realized in this low IO company, however, because of the poor management of information collecting, processing and maintaining processes. This severely limits the effect good sensing practices can have company-wide. For example, new information sensed about customer preferences by individual customer relationship managers remain, for the most part, in the files or heads of these managers since no formal processes have been instituted to collect and capture this information. In addition, information sensing has a direct influence on the information a company collects. How a company's employees become aware of changes in business conditions that impact on their current mind-set and ways of doing business is critical to understanding what types of information to collect—not just to run the company today, but also to prepare it for making changes in information management practices tomorrow. Managers and employees of a company must continuously perform reality checks, appraising perceived business opportunities, threats and risks and what new information they should explicitly collect and use.

Collecting Information

Collecting information is the practice of systematically gathering relevant information, as changes are detected in business conditions or in customer, partner, competitor and supplier behaviours. Although information technology has significantly advanced the ability to collect more data and to make it available more broadly—with powerful computers and networks such as the Internet—the critical management concerns still revolve around the collection of appropriate and relevant information. There are several points to consider:

- Managers need to understand the information responsibilities and needs of other managers and of employees at various levels and for various tasks. In most companies, the organizational structure and lines of authority provide the initial definition of the information responsibilities and reporting requirements of managers and employees. This is important because individual users evaluate the relevance of collected information and determine whether the benefits of collecting the information outweigh its costs. Without a clear understanding of the information needs of other managers and functions, information valuable to others can be lost.

- The right type and amount of information need to be collected to avoid information overload when the information is organized and prepared for use. Poorly managed companies tend either to collect too much of the wrong types of information or too little of the right types.

- Knowledge residing in a company's employees and existing information resources must be identified. The opportunity cost of not identifying available information and expertise means that people must collect what has already been gathered before, or they must do without the information and expertise that the company already possesses, but cannot locate.

- It is not enough to assume that people will collect information accurately and completely, since collecting information that people may not directly use, but on which others depend, is often perceived as a low priority part of the job. Instilling a sense of responsibility for the collection of information requires careful attention to training and rewarding employees.

BBV managers, for example, have defined clear practices for collecting customer information. They have evaluated their customer segments and focused people's information collection practices on these segments. They also train branch employees and managers to collect customer information effectively—and reward them, too. They provide employees with well-developed IT tools, such as the customer sales support system, to execute their information responsibilities consistently and easily.

In contrast, at The Bank, few managers know what information is relevant. Marketing managers receive lots of data in monthly binders but cannot use the data efficiently. Employees are not trained to collect customer and operational information and, as a result, a good deal of customer information is unavailable for branch operations and new product development.

Since collecting information influences how information is organized, poor information collection usually results in poor information organization in companies with poor information management practices.

Organizing Information

Organizing information focuses on indexing, classifying and linking information and databases together to provide access within and across business units and functions. This phase depends heavily on decisions made during the sensing and collecting phases. Moreover, ensuring that information and databases are properly organized and linked requires managerial attention to the training and rewards that employees require to effectively implement this phase of information management.

Organizing information involves important decisions that managers and employees must make and revisit on an ongoing basis:

- It is necessary to know what categories to use in organizing information. Whose purposes will be served through the categorization scheme? In many companies, databases are organized by function or department. This may work well at the local level, but can create confusion on a company-wide basis. In today's more integrated business enterprise, other departments and functions—or even suppliers and customers—may have to share these databases across linked business processes.
- Making information available through networks and databases does not necessarily make it usable, unless managers and employees can agree on shared language, terminology and classification schemes for organizing information sources. For example, different departments may use the same terms, such as customer, order, shipment and payment, but with different meanings.
- Organizing information, like other work responsibilities, requires appropriate skills, expertise and work habits. People responsible for this practice evaluate and make choices about how to organize information that determines whether or not it can be easily accessed and used.

At BBV, the customer sales support system provides a standardized approach to organizing and using both customer and product information. This permits universal access and sharing of information across—not just within—functions and branches.

At The Bank, product and customer information is organized into databases by department and function. Although information is fairly well organized for those managers within the department, managers outside the department or function have no common way of indexing and classifying information about products and customers. If a manager in The Bank does not have the exact product number, for example, product information in the bank's IT systems cannot be found. Managers at The Bank complain that there is too much information and that it is not adequately filtered, indicating a problem in the way information is collected, processed and maintained. Effective organizing of information facilitates the processing of information, since it permits people to access and analyse appropriate information sources and databases before making decisions.

Processing Information

Processing information involves turning information into useful knowledge by analysing appropriate information sources and databases. Analysis is a critical step in information processing since individuals evaluate available information and choose which information is appropriate for business decisions. The purpose of analysis is to translate information into specific knowledge that can be used by members of an organization to achieve the objectives of the business unit or company. Analysis in most companies is an ongoing responsibility of managers and employees, not just for special occasions or big decisions. Since most work today involves 'knowledge work' by people who are specialists, processing information into useful knowledge becomes a responsibility of most, if not all, managers and employees. Moreover, since knowledge work is difficult to observe and measure, managers must pay special attention to the hiring, ongoing training, evaluation and rewarding of employees to ensure that they have hired the right people to process information into knowledge in their company.

BBV, for example, has a highly developed approach to converting information into useful knowledge within every branch and the home office. Managers develop sophisticated product cross-selling strategies through detailed analyses of customer accounts and profiles. Based on their product strategies and customer segmentation, branch representatives are prompted by the customer sales support system to cross-sell specific products to individual customers—removing more *ad hoc* or gut feeling decision-making from the front lines.

At The Bank, decision-making about cross-selling to existing customers is not really based on the analysis of customer specific information. Only if The Bank's relationship manager has informal knowledge of specific customers can he or she cross-sell products to them. However, these managers each handle between 700 and 1,000 customers, so it is not possible to be effective at cross-selling in this organization.

We also know that processing information influences maintaining information by creating a business context in which managers and employees can be clear about what information needs to be maintained and why.

Maintaining Information

Maintaining information involves reusing existing information to avoid collecting the same information again, updating information databases so they remain current and refreshing information to ensure that people are using the best information possible.

Reusing information to avoid collecting, organizing and processing it all over again is often advocated by managers, but these suggestions are more often ignored than supported. There are several reasons why reuse is difficult to practice.

1. There is a natural human tendency to go out and seek new information and assume that information already collected is stale or not useful.
2. Managers and employees may not be aware that information has been already collected in one part of the company, so they start gathering it again in their own department or business unit.
3. Managers may inadvertently encourage new searches for information by redefining the decisions and problems that they face just enough for previous efforts at collecting, organizing and processing information to look different, when they may basically be the same.
4. The information previously collected may not be easily accessible due to the way in which it has been categorized or automated.
5. People in a company may be reluctant to reuse information that they do not 'own'. Reuse in some companies is constrained, since people are not encouraged to share information that they have already collected, organized and processed.

Thus, reuse must be actively encouraged by managers. For many companies, it requires deliberate decisions by people to be aware of what information the company has already collected, organized and processed, and to avoid collecting new information if existing information is good enough for decision-making.

In contrast to the barriers facing reuse, many companies have developed sophisticated processes to make sure that their operational systems and databases are updated continuously. Processes and procedures for updating can be built into the way automated systems operate for order fulfilment, payment processing and purchasing. For most types of operational and process support systems, companies have learned over the last ten years to design these systems with continuous updating in mind. Not updating information can seriously delay decisions, degrade services and lead to poorer business performance.

Continuously refreshing information is the newest aspect of maintaining information. Increasingly, managers and employees work in teams on projects and special assignments, and make deals on a regional and global basis across time zones. Software tools such as Lotus Notes employ features such as 'replication', which permit team members to know when documents have been modified, and by whom, each time they are accessed. The need to continuously refresh information in documents and files that are used by different teams during diverse working hours becomes critical to the speed and quality of their work.

At BBV, employees are urged to reuse customer information and profiles. They are obliged to update these records every time they have a customer conversation. While back-office systems automatically update customer accounts with transactions made through all banking channels, managers and employees are focused on proactive maintenance of critical product and customer information in the bank. When BBV organizes new product promotions, it reuses the available product and customer information by integrating new products into its customer segments and cross-selling strategies—thereby avoiding having to re-collect customer information all over again.

In contrast, The Bank's managers point out that 'maintaining information is not a key priority of The Bank'. Since people do not trust the accuracy of the information available, when they have to make a decision, they try to look for new information, which they normally cannot find!

The IMP Maturity Model

As discussed in Chapter 3, both sensing and processing are key cross-capability dimensions needed to create the IO interaction effect in mature IO companies. These dimensions represent the two most critical points at which people evaluate the relevance and importance of information to their decision needs. Sensing is critical because it is at this point that people evaluate and choose which new information they will collect for their own benefit, and for that of the company. Similarly, when processing information to make business decisions, people will evaluate the relevance and usefulness of the information available to them for these decisions. A choice at this point determines whether or not the information will be maintained, or deleted, in the future.

The IMP maturity model in Figure 5.1 is very different from the behaviour model presented in Chapter 4. Because the relationships between the information management practices form a circle, we cannot tell where the circle begins or ends. This implies that a step-by-step or linear approach may not be the most effective way of improving information management practices.

The circular model also shows that both strong and weak individual information management practices can have a multiplying effect because of the recursive nature of the model. A company that is very inward looking, for example, does not monitor changes occurring in the marketplace very well. This results in poor sensing practices where little new information is collected for the benefit of the company. Although the information collected and used to make appropriate business decisions is outdated, this information continues to circulate, being maintained for the next decision or problem. In the worst case, the company fails to detect important changes occurring in the competitive environment. This company is caught in a vicious circle of poor information management that will continue to reinforce itself unless changes are made to information quality.

Thus, IMP maturity demands a holistic approach to managing all five dimensions simultaneously. Managers who ignore any one of these practices will fail to create the information management maturity needed to produce world-class performance in their companies.

Figure 5.1 also shows that while sensing plays an integral role in the IMP capability, it lies outside the circle and is not directly affected by any of the other dimensions. Sensing demands special attention by managers and may require new ways of thinking to effectively manage.

Companies high in IO address each phase of the information life cycle to improve information use. They also understand how each of the information management phases sharpens the company's focus on learning which information and information practices create the most business value.

A company with high IO improves all five dimensions of information management practices on an ongoing basis. A company with low IO focuses only on a few dimensions, most often on collecting and organizing information than on sensing, processing and maintaining the right information for its business. There are no shortcuts to building good information management practices, since they must all be present to a high degree to achieve high IO.

MANAGING INFORMATION PRACTICES

In this section, we present ten guidelines that your company can use to develop effective information management practices and increase IO maturity.

Guideline 1: Managers and employees must develop an explicit and focused view of the critical information necessary to run the business

Good information management should constantly focus on the decision contexts of managers and employees. It is people, primarily, who use information; so thinking about information needs is, or should be, part of everyone's job. Leaving the responsibility for good information management to information specialists or IT staff may give temporary peace of mind. However, it invites confusion about how people put information to work and can raise doubts as to whether people are motivated to treat their 'information responsibilities' as carefully as their other work responsibilities. In short, information responsibility should mean information accountability. Companies should keep information as close as possible to where the actual work is done.

Hilti Corporation: Sales Force Automation Project

In Chapter I we discussed how Hilti developed its sales force automation project. The IT department had attempted—fruitlessly—to deploy this IT system in several countries before senior managers gave the project team a deadline to either achieve sales increases or terminate the project. What went wrong with earlier attempts to implement this project?

Very simply, the users of the IT system—Hilti's direct sales force—had not been asked enough for their input. The IT project team had defined the information requirements of the new system with little reference to the actual information needs and uses of the sales force. Thus the early system's design specifications not only did not address the needs of the users, but also created additional work for the sales reps with no immediate benefit to them. Sales reps were required to collect and enter data that was not relevant to their job and which did not help them produce any increase in sales.

In this case, senior managers intervened to refocus the project on the needs of the sales force or terminate the project. The IT department changed its approach and carefully examined sales force behaviours and processes to understand the right concerns regarding information use. They profiled the needs and behaviours of individual sales people. They also mapped and validated the information behaviours and practices that constituted a successful sales person and discussed what role IT could play to support this.

During this process, the project team also identified the relevant information needs of marketing, customer support and new product development staff. This established ways to capture suggestions from customers about service and product improvements that could be shared with these groups. Finally, the team suggested changes in the training and rewards that the sales force needed in order to change information behaviours and information management practices. This was necessary to ensure support of the new IT tools and to increase sales—a business outcome critical to each member of the sales force and to the company as a whole.

Although it may sound obvious that people need to 'own' their information responsibilities and be accountable for the information they use at work, many managers and their employees take no time to understand their information needs and address them directly. Information specialists and IT staff drive projects with little reference to how these projects will influence information behaviours and change fundamental information management practices of employees and managers. In such cases, senior managers do not work proactively to clarify which information is critical to running and transforming the company, and managers and employees receive the information 'that they deserve' even if it stops them from reaching their business goals.

Guideline 2:   When people do not understand the business, they cannot sense the right information to change the business

In companies with high IO, as a precondition for making effective decisions, managers and employees constantly search their external environment. By sensing the right new information, the company's managers and employees observe:

- changes between their current perceptions and associated ways of collecting and using information inside the company, and
- changes in business conditions that require the reinterpretation of opportunities, threats and risks as well as the ways in which information is collected and used.

Managers and employees can only sense information effectively when they understand what drives a company's business performance and know the factors that might influence it. Without this understanding and a managerial focus on its importance, managers and employees will be 'blind and confused' (see Figure 2.4); they will fail to sense key changes in the company's marketplace or wider business environment.

Companies with high IO, like Hilti, BBV and SkandiaBanken, constantly inform and educate their managers and employees about the external forces and factors that influence business performance. Therefore, they know how their own performance is linked to the need for a better understanding of these forces in their job and for the company as a whole. Senior managers in these companies are constantly alert to changes in the outside world that may affect the success of their company. Moreover, they expect their employees to be equally aware of external changes that may affect their success locally and their company's overall position.

In contrast, in companies with low IO, like The Bank, employees are preoccupied with internal practices and procedures. External changes in business conditions are the responsibility of senior managers, who alone must sense and respond to changes with little formal support from the workforce. While such companies may appear temporarily secure from outside forces and in charge of their future, this appearance is illusory. In reality, they 'don't know what they don't know' and therefore exist in a fragile state subject to unexpected shocks and events that could adversely affect them.

Guideline 3:   Carry out sensing face to face with people who have primary knowledge of the business context

Because the essence of good sensing is testing your perceptions and interpretation of the constantly changing outside world, it is best done—according to high IO companies—face to face. Testing involves having conversations with people who have varying perspectives. These conversations shape your perceptions of the outside world and your conclusions about what may influence your business. Moreover, a company that takes advantage of the sensing of its workforce by distilling the changes in perceptions and information that may alter its decisions is better equipped to manage its future. This personal sensing, however, should not happen second-hand or through intermediaries. The essence of good sensing is evaluating and choosing key sources for information sensing—ones that can lead to new, useful insights and information.

European Business Electronics Company

Within a business unit of a global business electronics company, headquartered in Europe, there is a need for constant sensing of new technologies that might influence future fax products. This 500-person unit is responsible for product development, international marketing, production and distribution of fax machines worldwide. It is among the world's leading manufacturers of fax machines. Since product life cycles in the computer, electronics and telecommunications industries are so short—three to six months—companies can no longer rely on annual forecasts and trend analyses. Moreover, many of its leading competitors are based in California or Asia Pacific.

About ten senior managers constantly travel from Europe to key locations around the world to talk to and benchmark customers and competitors. They also attend industrial fairs to exhibit their products, see what competitors are up to, and listen to customers and suppliers. For their major customers—the five or six top trade firms like MediaMarkt in Germany and Staples in the United States—they organize what are called dealer councils. In these structured sessions, the senior managers present new product ideas and prototypes, test reactions and discuss modifications to future product concepts. The top buyers provide feedback on existing and new products—what sells and doesn't sell, and what customers may require in the future. Managers collect and distil this information to share with their colleagues and employees back home.

The sensing process is also reviewed for its effectiveness in deriving new insights and usable information for the business unit. It is designed not only to generate new perceptions, but also to facilitate the systematic sharing of information in conversations and briefings with other managers and employees across the business unit. Over time, the business unit has developed clear criteria for evaluating its information sources for sensing new information and perceptions inside and outside the industry and for translating this market intelligence into successful new products.

Guideline 4: Collecting the right information takes ingenuity and hard work by employees and managers

Collecting the right information about your customers and products is difficult. In our research we discovered that many companies suffer from two information problems at the same time.

First, many people in the company have poor access to the information they need to carry out their responsibilities. Although IT staff may have designed the latest formal information systems to tap employees' actual and perceived information needs, business conditions and processes are constantly changing—and so are information management practices. As a result, IT-supported information systems quickly become outdated. Because they are 'programmed systems', they continue to routinely produce the same types and volumes of information, even if the information has become irrelevant. Conversely, the absence of relevant information often goes undetected—companies often fail to realize that their information is no longer relevant, so they do not collect valuable new information.

Second, although employees may know exactly what information they need to collect, because of structural and industry barriers they may not be able to collect it. Companies may not be able to collect information about customers because other companies own it; or they may be cut off from information about the use of their products since the downstream partners who actually sell the product to end users neither collect nor share information.

From a customer perspective, this problem is frequently encountered in day to day life. Almost anyone who has travelled on an aeroplane, for example, can relate to the following scenario.

Airline Catering

You are a frequent traveller and are tired of the standard meals of your favourite airline. So you ask for a special vegetarian meal, hoping that the new meal will offer some variety and perhaps even be better for you. After three or four flights with the 'veggie' option, you are unimpressed with the bland servings and strange, 'healthy', drinks like soya milk. You mention to the flight attendant that the veggie meal does not look good and tastes worse. The flight attendant even agrees with you, and nearby business passengers say their meal is not much better. Yet, after several more flights, nothing changes. The same meals, the same agreement from the flight attendants that they are awful, the same comments from nearby business travellers resigned to their standard meals. Nothing changes.

What you may not know is that this feeling of frustration about your veggie meal, and your dissatisfaction is shared by the senior managers of the airline catering service. Here is how the senior vice president of one of the world's leading airline catering services views the frustration of collecting information about customers' reactions to their in-flight meals:

> In the past, the catering service was a fully integrated part of the entire airline structure. When the catering service was separated from other operations as a stand-alone company, a new type of customer–vendor relationship developed within our company. While we now consider the airline as our customer, we are struggling with how to get closer to our customer's customers—the passengers who consume our products. This can be tricky, and we have not figured out how to effectively manage this aspect of our business.
>
> In order for our company to grow, we need to know how the customers of our customers like our meal services and how we can improve them. We would like to move into customization of our meal services. But the knowledge that resides in the airline about the customer is not currently transferred to us, so there is an information gap.

The immediate result of this information gap is that the information management life cycle is broken, resulting in inadequate organizing and processing of customer information in the catering company due to poor sensing and collecting processes between the airline and the catering service. The result? The catering service is unaware of customer reactions to the vegetarian meals.

What can the catering company do in this situation? It needs to create an information management process with its partner airlines to systematically capture and organize customer reactions to meal options. A major campaign by the catering service company may be necessary to persuade airline flight attendants to record and report customer comments about meals or to examine what customers have left on their meal trays when the trays are collected. Inter-company information management practices may require the training and rewarding of airline personnel for collecting customer reactions and complaints and passing them on to the catering service. In short, these structural barriers between companies may have to be removed by senior managers of both the catering service and the airlines in order for customer meal services to improve.

Guideline 5:   Profiling, classifying, indexing and linking information are essential for its effective use

People are generally motivated to collect and organize information they will use immediately. Problems arise in companies when collecting information is separated from organizing, processing and using it. People in various departments or units may carry out these activities, using different information systems. In such cases, employees who collect information, or information and IT specialists, need to understand how other people will use the information to make decisions.

Some companies appoint people as knowledge domain managers. They are responsible for identifying reliable sources of information for specific subject areas in the company. They assign value to the information according to who needs it and make sure that it is shared with those who need it most. These new positions are appearing in professional service companies, such as management consultancies, where information about clients and client engagements is often unavailable to people in the firm who later need it for other purposes, such as marketing and research.

Ernst & Young[1]

In 1997, Ernst & Young, the fourth largest accounting and consulting company in the world, created a Centre for Business Knowledge to improve the management of information and knowledge inside the firm. Ralph Poole, the centre's director, described the profiling, classifying and indexing activities of the centre:

> After removing client-sensitive information, we develop 'knowledge objects' by pulling relevant information such as interview guides, work schedules, benchmark data and market segmentation analyses out of documents and store them in the computer system for people to use. This approach allows many people to search for and retrieve codified information without having

to contact the person who originally developed it. That way information can
be used more efficiently and effectively.

Some companies may require knowledge domain managers to profile,
classify, index and link information. Other companies may need to train
operational people—sales representatives, for example—to recognize the
best way to organize the information they collect about product use and
customers for marketing and product development units to use.

In companies with high IO, such as Hilti, BBV and SkandiaBanken,
every employee regularly collects information for later use by employees
in other departments. In turn, such companies evaluate their line employees on the quality of the information they collect and organize for
later use. These companies understand that information management
practices are not discrete activities unconnected from the work of others,
but are linked processes on which many others in the company depend
for their information effectiveness.

**Guideline 6:   Training people to collect and organize information,
and rewarding them for it, is vital to the performance of both
tasks**

Although collecting and organizing are closely linked information management practices, they will be ineffective unless companies specifically
train their employees to carry them out, and reward them for doing so.
In companies we visited with low IO, managers seem to assume that
collecting and organizing information is part of everyone's job and,
therefore, that people do not require special training or rewards for
doing these tasks. Collecting and organizing information is considered
to be embedded in people's work responsibilities and should not be
singled out for specific training and rewards. The irony is that these are
the companies whose managers rate as being low on IO and business
performance.

In high IO organizations, senior managers are convinced that only
when they train employees to collect and organize information
effectively—and reward them—will they do these tasks faithfully each
day. Although these managers also believe that information management is everyone's responsibility, they focus on making the collection
and organization of information explicit for all employees and managers. Since these companies place high trust in and rely on formal
information sources and systems about customers, products and operations, they also focus on training their people to collect and organize
information continuously, in a careful and effective manner. Managers

in companies with high IO make themselves accountable for the quality of the information required to ensure superior business performance. Information management is simply too important in these companies to be left to chance.

Guideline 7:   Speak the same language to use the same information

Organizing information properly requires a company to define a common vocabulary for business information and also categories around which to collect and organize the information. Various departments and functions may use different definitions of common terms such as customer, order, shipment or payment, so managers and employees must figure out which definitions the company will use and which categories of information it will program into IT systems.

US Division of an International Financial Services Company

In 1997, the US division of a large financial services company launched a major initiative, as part of a restructuring, to improve the information management and IT capabilities of its sales force in order to increase sales and profitability. The president of the division described the difficulty of achieving a shared language that his people could all agree on:

> In the past, information collecting and reporting was a 'boy scout' system. We had more data than we wanted. We had processing capabilities, but could not make them come to life under our existing systems, structure and style of management. We had a database, but it was old and outdated, difficult to hook up to and to use. The information definitions did not reflect our business and, therefore, we never got to the point where we could act on information provided by the system. The quality of the information was so poor that it could not be used to make decisions.

By bringing together a group of people with expertise in database management, marketing and finance, the division set out to define and customize not only the IT system, but also the language that would be used by the entire sales force in the division. This common language became the basis for defining all information categories in the database. In addition, the shared language also allowed the sales force to quickly find, interpret and analyse the information in the new IT system. In short, information effectiveness improved because people in the division had finally agreed on a shared language and definitions for their business.

Guideline 8: Richer definition of information requirements results in better analysis and decisions

Defining information requirements enables appropriate analysis and decisions. Analysis translates information into usable knowledge, which enables managers and employees to make effective decisions. Thus defining information requirements carefully, in line with decision-making and analytical needs, should influence the information a company collects and how it is organized.

At BBV, for example, customer segment analysis and product cross-selling strategies drive information management practices both for branch representatives and for the bank's managers and headquarters. The information that bank representatives collect and organize for the customer sales support system is defined by the bank's understanding of customer behaviour in its segments and by product strategies relative to those segments and cross-selling.

In contrast, at The Bank, information collecting and organizing is out of touch with information processing needs. 'We have too much information, and do not know how to use it,' complained one marketing manager. The Bank's information collection and organization reflect a past era of doing business, rather than current and future needs for analysis and decision-making. In addition, The Bank suffers from overly simplistic customer segments on the one hand and very complex product lines on the other—a typical case of too little relevant information about customers and too much irrelevant information about products that people in The Bank do not understand.

Guideline 9: Scenario-based training can facilitate information processing

Scenario-based training is another way for companies to improve the processing abilities of their employees.

US Financial Services Company

In the US division of the financial services company discussed under Guideline 7, the 1997 restructuring programme exposed the sales force to scenario-based training to expand their analytical abilities and options in dealing with corporate clients.

As the head of US operations noted:

Before 1997, we had an unfocused field force whose only goal was to establish relationships with any corporate customer they could find. Our field force was working, but no one knew exactly which corporate customers were providing the most revenue. We had to stop making emotional decisions (about customers we liked, but who gave poor returns) and start making decisions based on economic realities.

The company developed scenarios that offered alternative business cases in relation to their corporate customers. The financial models required reps to enter specific data about customers and then helped to calculate the business case using explicit assumptions. The business cases were then reviewed, which assisted the reps in measuring best return scenarios in relation to specific corporate customers. The process improved the decision-making and analytical abilities of the reps—moving them toward fact-based decisions, rather than gut feeling.

Guideline 10:   If you don't maintain information well, you lose business

Companies with high IO maintain information well. To deal with business changes more rapidly, they continuously refresh, update and reuse information. They maintain it primarily to support their agility with customers and markets, rather than to minimize risks and reduce costs. Poor maintenance of information, conversely, can upset customers and may cause business losses. Two examples from the experiences of our research team come to mind:

Case Scenario A: Austrian Retail Bank

One of our research team members was a client of an Austrian bank that promoted special savings accounts for financing future home purchases by urging its reps to offer these new products every time a customer entered the branch. Every time this client visited a branch of the bank, he was asked whether he would be interested in opening such an account. After several similar occurrences, he began to wonder: Had the bank reps not recorded that he had been asked this question several times? Hadn't they looked into their IT system to see that he already had such an account? Didn't they update account status in their files?

Why was this happening? The building society that had secured these accounts with the bank typically paid a high commission to bank employees to sell these accounts. This policy obviously conflicted with good information maintenance practices. After sending a letter of complaint to the manager of the customer services centre and receiving no reply, our client decided to switch banks.

Several months later, he learned that the bank managers had changed their practices by making sure that branch reps did not cross-sell this product without checking to see if the customer had already opened such an account or had been offered the account earlier. Who knows how many customers switched banks before this change was instituted?

Case Scenario B: Boston Luxury Hotel

A second member of our team had been using the same luxury hotel in Boston, Massachusetts, for several years for business trips and personal trips with his family. After five years and more than twenty stays, this customer assumed that the hotel had clear records of his room preferences and other needs at the hotel. The hotel was known for its excellent service, good restaurant and seaside location. After arriving from Switzerland with his family on one trip, the customer learned that the reservation had been changed. Instead of two rooms reserved for his family as on previous visits, only one room was available with an extra bed. The customer inquired why the change had been made and the reception clerk did not know. So he asked for the reception manager and asked the same question. The manager indicated that the hotel had switched to a new customer reservation system. In order to save money, no previous records of loyal customers had been entered into the new system.

The result: After an hour's discussion, the customer's family was given a second room as originally requested, but the family decided not to stay at the hotel again since neither customer loyalty nor accurate reservation records were priorities for the hotel. A few years later, he learned that archived customer records had been included in the new customer reservation system, and that loyal customers would be given special preferences—a belated turnaround by the hotel managers, in the face of customer losses.

Companies with poor organizational memories lose customers and business. The good news is that people in companies generally act on the information that is available to them. The bad news is that this information is often incomplete or inaccurate. Thus, without careful attention to the ways information is updated, reused, and refreshed, companies with low IO may be losing customers every day without knowing it. Unlike our customers who write letters or personally complain, most customers just walk away from companies who cannot remember what business they have done with their loyal customers.

CONCLUSION

In this chapter we have shown you how to leverage the power of information management practices in your company or business unit. We have identified the five information practices that are important in achieving high IO and ten guidelines to improve these practices. Now that we have addressed the second capability leading to high IO, in the next chapter we will examine how IT practices can be developed to enable the right information behaviours and information management practices to improve business performance.

NOTE

1. Sarvary, M. and Chard, A. (1997) 'Knowledge Management at Ernst and Young,' Stanford: Stanford University. Case Study # M 291.

6

BOOSTING THE IT
PAY-OFF

Managers are constantly bombarded with news and advertising about the latest, newest and fastest IT developments and how they will make their companies more efficient, more innovative and more competitive. As the intensity of competition increases in every industry, companies employ IT to improve the output of goods and services, to lower prices and to benefit more demanding customers. New entrants in the same industry sectors use IT to overcome the barriers to entry and to position themselves in the industry's value chain to 'pirate' the margins and customer relationships of established companies.

With IT and e-business, the race gets faster, keener and more demanding for all companies, yet managers suspect that IT accelerates the pace of running but gives no firm a sustainable competitive lead. Thus companies spend more on IT for competitive necessity than for competitive advantage. Each company must run in the race with IT and e-business investments, but IT practices alone will not lead to superior company performance. For many managers and companies, therefore, the link between IT investments and practices and improving business performance remains elusive.

Companies with low IO run faster in their industry and spend a lot on IT, but do not get much, if any, improvement on the bottom line. They focus on automating today's operations and business processes, with little emphasis on developing IT practices that enable their managers and employees to use information proactively to meet tomorrow's business challenges and be faster and more innovative in generating new ideas and products. Senior managers in these companies see IT as a cost and always look to keep their commitments in IT focused on the basics—on what is necessary to operate the business or essential to enable them to run with their competitors in the industry. Many of these companies have chief information officers (CIOs), but their main task is to manage the IT infrastructure and be the intermediary between the business units and the suppliers of IT services and products. While the CIO's role is necessary to run the business, senior managers often doubt the CIO's abilities to create value for the business. In companies with low IO, senior managers often get the IT that they deserve.

In contrast, companies with high IO recognize that IT practices must focus on doing well what is competitively necessary—deploying IT to manage business processes and operations effectively. But these companies also target their investments on uses of IT that:

- prepare their managers and employees for tomorrow's information-based competition, and
- help them to be more innovative in developing new products and services in their industry.

Companies with high IO recognize that being good at IT practices is not good enough. To get the full business value from IT, they must improve their information management practices, information behaviours and values of their employees. In high IO companies, IT can enable superior business performance by contributing to effective information use. CIOs in high IO companies understand that to support today's operations and business processes IT practices must be defined and shaped by business decisions about information use. At the same time, IT practices must position the company to develop distinctive abilities for using information to create future business value.

Since the senior managers in companies with high IO appreciate the links between high performance and IT practices, information management practices, and people's behaviours and values, IT employees and CIOs are fully contributing members of the senior management team. Managers view IT and the CIO not as functionally separate from the real business, but instead as part of the fabric of a successful company.

In this chapter we examine how good IT practices lead to high IO, and what managers can do to boost the business pay-offs from IT in their company.

IMPLEMENTING EFFECTIVE IT PRACTICES (ITP)

SkandiaBanken

The success of SkandiaBanken's direct banking model depends on the company's ability to develop IT practices that meet the existing and emerging needs of a rapidly changing business. IT practices in the company are driven by three main business objectives:

- Seamless integration of information about customers and products;
- A unified interface with the customer, no matter what direct channel the customer employs; and
- Direct and flexible access to the financial services industry IT infrastructure in Sweden and globally.

With these business needs, the bank's CIO concluded: 'We had to present one face to the customer, which meant total channel and information integration.'

Keeping IT Practices Simple, Practical and Creative

Rather than embarking on complex and risky process redesign and IT projects—as other companies in the same situation might have done—managers at SkandiaBanken believed that simplicity and practicality should dominate their approach to deploying the bank's IT systems. As a result, IT projects are deliberately kept small and as simple as possible. 'It is difficult to create easy, small solutions—it is much easier to complicate things,' noted the bank's CIO.

To get away from a technological view of business IT projects, project teams design IT systems around employee routines, customer needs and product integration, stressing process over technology concerns. Technical people are excluded from design discussions to encourage creativity. In the words of the CIO: 'It is difficult for people to understand that it is not the technical people that make the system work—it is the people who use the system that are the real developers. They may not know exactly how the technology works, but they know what they want to be able to do with it.'

One View of Customer-based Unified Business Information

At SkandiaBanken, IT for operational support is based on a unified system and infrastructure across all employees, business units and customers. Databases about customers and products are integrated to provide one view of the customer across all business units. In addition, all direct channels—call centre, telephone and Internet—for interacting with a customer are integrated for easy access to account and new product information.

To ensure that the less skilled employees in the bank's three call centres can perform consistently, SkandiaBanken was the first bank in Europe to develop an application link for telephone-activated pop-up screens. These screens provide customer, product and cross-selling information to call centre employees as soon as the customer rings. The voice-activated system is designed to improve performance efficiency and monitoring of call centre activities. A sophisticated telephone monitoring application allows both employees and managers to measure ring times, average length of phone calls, and time not spent on customer calls on an individual and team basis. The director of remote banking observed that:

> Several years ago, we found that call centre employees were spending 50 per cent of their time performing administrative tasks, and only 30 per cent of their time on the phone with customers. The new monitoring application has helped us to more than double our phone time to 65 per cent by giving many of the administrative tasks to support staff. It also allowed us to increase our telephone pick-up times—now 90 per cent of our calls are picked up within three rings. This represents an extremely high service level.

In addition, the bank's IT systems support business processes by tying the systems to a unified database, rather than functional databases. 'We wanted all information in the company to come from one customer database and one product database,' noted the CIO. 'We were not concerned about owning all of the databases, but instead about how to blend elements of the business to make the business model work.' The company found the solution through the development of an electronic 'switchboard' application, which can flexibly link internal and external databases and IT systems. Customer views can be customized for each of the four different businesses, depending on specific information needs, so SkandiaBanken can interface directly with the financial services industry IT infrastructure in Sweden and globally. This application also facilitates new business development, since new databases and services can be linked easily and old ones removed.

Internet Banking and Good Information for Management Require a Solid IT Platform

Well-integrated business process information and a flexible IT infrastructure provide the platform for using IT for business innovation and new product development. For example, in 1996, SkandiaBanken launched its new Internet banking site, which was also linked directly with the existing call centre and telephone banking systems. Customers can use the same pin number for interacting with all three channels. Customers can also transfer their funds between accounts, whereas other Swedish banks permit only limited fund transfers. The Internet site has also permitted

SkandiaBanken to launch new products and to work with its sister company, Skandia Insurance, to cross-sell insurance products.

A strong platform for using IT to operate key business processes also enables the bank to use its systems for management support and decision-making. Since the bank depends on balancing deposit growth with interest rates on savings that are 1–3 percentage points above banking industry rates in Sweden, IT systems must carefully monitor the performance of all business units. Scenario tools are used by managers in areas such as credit risk management, preferred payment plans and car leasing, to identify high-risk customers and to take appropriate risk positions. Management information systems also permit managers to bypass customer segmentation policies and track customer behaviour in real time. 'We do not attempt to segment our customers until they have joined the bank and established a history with us,' explained the CIO. 'We then work with the customer individually to promote products directly to them.'

These examples highlight how SkandiaBanken uses IT to support all aspects of information use in the direct banking business. The bank is able to achieve competitive advantage in the Swedish banking market through the skilful integration of IT practices to run its day-to-day business and to use information for product innovation and decision-making by managers and employees about future business opportunities.

KNOWING HOW TO USE IT TO BOOST VALUE CREATION: THE ITP MATURITY MODEL

Companies with mature IO know that certain relationships, or links, exist between four IT practice dimensions—IT for operational support, IT for business process support, IT for innovation support and IT for management support. Figure 6.1 shows the results of statistical path analysis indicating where there exist causal relationships between these dimensions, and in which direction these relationships exist. Similar to the IBV maturity model, the arrows in Figure 6.1 create a clear visual path of these relationships, moving from the bottom of the model upwards towards IT for management support.

Beginning at the bottom of Figure 6.1 with IT for operational support we can follow the path upwards. Improvements to IT for operational support will have a positive effect on both IT for business process support and IT for innovation support. IT for business process support, while not linked to IT for innovation support, does directly influence IT for management support. IT for innovation support also influences IT for management support.

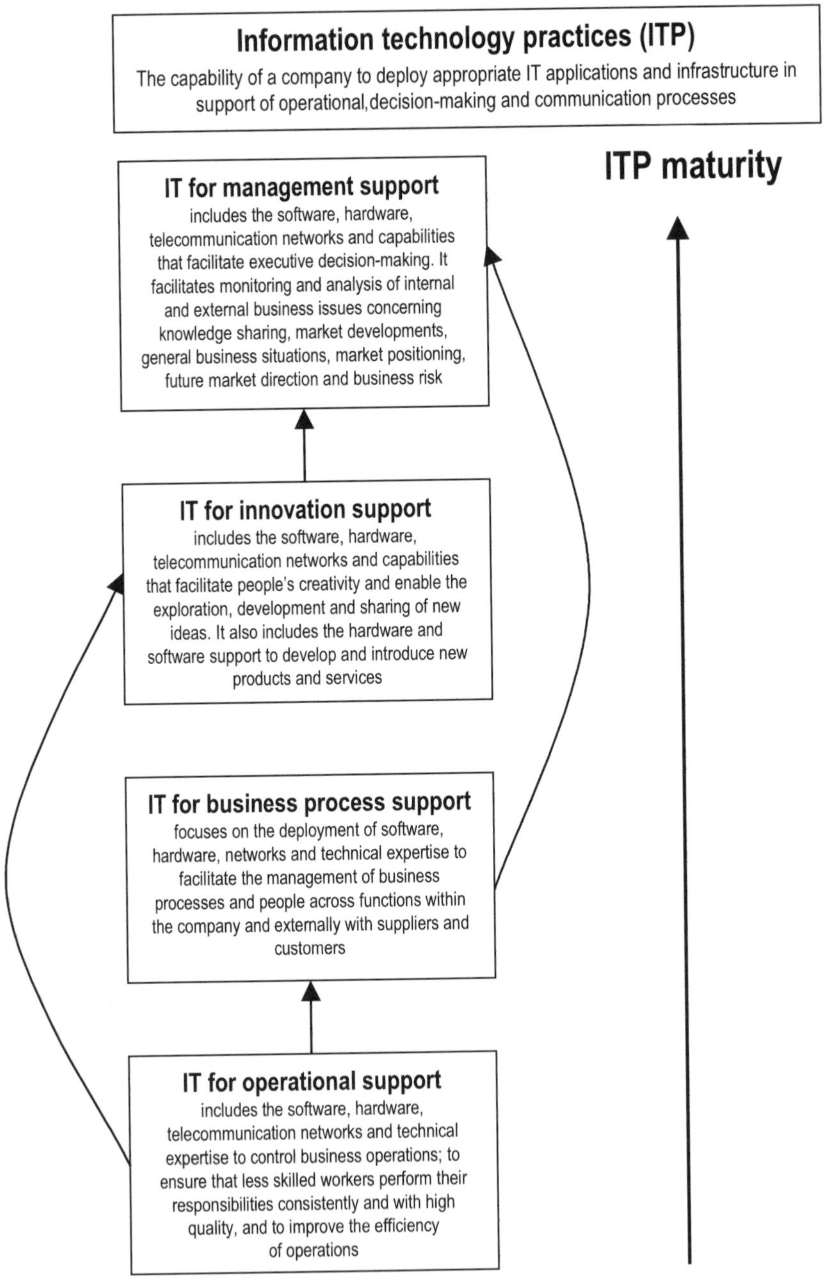

Figure 6.1: The IT practices maturity model

Companies with ITP maturity, therefore, have actively managed this path upwards, improving dimensions on the lower end of the model as a base on which to build effective IT for management support—the most dependent dimension of the ITP maturity model.

Below, we discuss how you can raise your company's IO maturity by improving all four dimensions of IT practices as suggested in Figure 6.1. To help emphasize the difference between low and high IT practices, we contrast the case of The Bank (see Chapters 3 and 4) with SkandiaBanken. Figure 6.2 illustrates IT practices scores for the two banks on the IO dashboard.

SkandiaBanken's IO dashboard

IT practices (ITP)

IT for operational support	top 35%
IT for business process support	top 5%
IT for innovation support	top 5%
IT for management support	top 20%

The Bank's IO dashboard

IT practices (ITP)

IT for operational support	bottom 35%
IT for business process support	top 35%
IT for innovation support	bottom 20%
IT for management support	below 50%

Legend

Top 5% (top 8 SMTs)	top 5%
Top 20% (top 34 SMTs)	top 20%
Top 35% (top 60 SMTs)	top 35%
Above 50% (upper 84 SMTs)	above 50%
Below 50% (lower 85 SMTs)	below 50%
Bottom 35% (lower 60 SMTs)	bottom 35%
Bottom 20% (lower 34 SMTs)	bottom 20%
Bottom 5% (lowest 8 SMTs)	bottom 5%

Figure 6.2: Comparing IT practices at SkandiaBanken and The Bank

The Bank's IT practices

The development of The Bank's IT systems has been negatively affected by multiple restructuring initiatives and by several attempts to integrate the systems of The Bank with those of a competitor they acquired in 1993. The CIO said:

> Until 1993, The Bank had very sound, well managed IT systems. To deal with the integration of the acquired bank, the IT department attempted to unify

the two systems by cloning The Bank's IBM platform and copying the system of the acquired bank onto this clone. Although this created a similar information set-up, because of different operations and products, the copied system could not be easily merged. Thus, instead of ending up with one merged system, we ended up with two separate platforms and data centres.

As a result, branch employees have to switch from one system to the other, depending on the bank with which the customer first opened an account. Six years later, in 1999, only 80 per cent of the two systems have been merged, with the remaining 20 per cent still being integrated.

In 1996, after another restructuring, The Bank decided to create two business units. This hindered progress on system integration: IT had to reflect the two separate business unit structures. Thus the data centres of the two banks were divided into two separate units (see Figure 6.3), creating further problems in the ability to share information between departments.

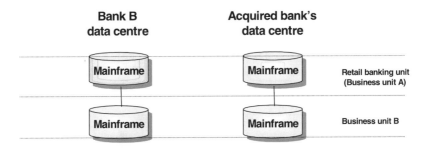

Figure 6.3:   The Bank's IT architecture

Another obstacle is the legacy system that provides interdepartmental links to information. One frustrated senior network manager pointed out: There is no search mechanism, so you can never find the information you need unless you know the exact product code or account number. If you do not know the code, you could spend hours trying to find the information.

'One of the main problems that we have is that of an old and expensive IT structure in need of modernization,' explained the CIO. 'During the 1990s, no one looked forward to future IT applications.'

In April 1998, The Bank decided against building an entirely new IT systems architecture, opting to redesign the current system by reducing complexity. 'This was a major decision. When we looked to the outside, we could not find one example of a company that had been successful at building an entirely new system.'

IT for Operational Support

Employing IT for operational support involves using software, hardware, telecommunications and technical expertise to control business transactions, to ensure that less skilled employees perform their responsibilities consistently, and to improve the efficiency of operations. These practices enable a company to improve productivity and boost output of goods and services by standardizing transaction processing and operations. IT practices also enable companies to monitor and control employee performance and behaviours linked to operational tasks and responsibilities. Information use is highly structured and well defined, either as a transaction or as feedback, for monitoring and recording employee actions. Application examples include payment systems, order processing systems, policy management systems, checking and credit card systems and accounting, payroll and personnel systems.

As we have seen, at SkandiaBanken IT for operational support provides less skilled employees with pop-up screens of customer and product information to ensure consistent customer interactions. An IT application monitors and controls call centre operations so managers and employees can speed up and deliver consistent customer services.

At The Bank, however, the IT department is still struggling after several years to integrate different systems following the merger with another bank. Employees have to switch back and forth between two systems to serve a customer, who they can only identify through account numbers. Similarly, product information is only accessible if employees remember product codes. At The Bank, IT for operational support often constrains, rather than promotes, efficiency and productivity.

IT for operational support is necessary, but not enough on its own for IT practices maturity. These IT practices provide the infrastructure and transaction knowledge on which IT for business process support can be built to link business processes, network employees across functions and interact on-line with suppliers, partners and customers. IT for operational support provides the platform and potential for connections so that managers and employees can use information to be more creative, share their knowledge and create new products and services.

IT for Business Process Support

Using IT for business process support means deploying software, computer hardware, networks and technical expertise to enable the management of business processes across functions within a company and with suppliers, distributors and customers. Over the last ten years, many manufacturing companies have installed new software and systems to operate their supply chains from product engineering and manufacturing to inventory management, distribution and logistics, and order processing. They have also implemented new financial control systems and human resource management systems. Collectively, these are called enterprise resource planning (ERP) systems and are sold by such companies as SAP, Oracle and PeopleSoft. In addition, service-oriented companies have also implemented systems to automate back-office transactions and to improve front-office sales and account management. In both manufacturing and service companies, there has been a clear shift from 'product push' to 'customer pull' approaches to managing information in business processes.

At SkandiaBanken, for example, the development of the switchboard application permits the bank to manage business processes seamlessly by connecting employees with customers. It ties internal databases with external databases to service customer needs for financial services in Sweden and globally. In contrast, at The Bank, because business processes and IT systems have still not been integrated with those of the merged bank, unified product and customer account information is not available. Employees often have to access two separate customer account files, one for each bank.

Good IT use for business process support also promotes effective IT for management support by providing information across business processes and from customers, suppliers and business partners. This lateral availability of information across functions and departments in a company provides a platform for using information for new product development, for business analysis and risk assessment regarding strategic decisions, and for planning new marketplace strategies for customers and against competitors.

IT for Innovation Support

IT for innovation support facilitates employee creativity and permits the exploration, development and sharing of new ideas and their application in a business. A number of software programs are available, including groupware such as:

- Lotus Notes, for collaborative teamwork
- computer-aided design for new product design
- graphical simulation tools to test products
- geographic information systems for improved target marketing.

Moreover, the explosive growth of the Internet, e-mail and broadband networking, as well as the digital integration of video, voice and data have also substantially increased the abilities of companies to easily develop, share and use documents for knowledge work.

At SkandiaBanken, the development of an Internet channel for customers has led to product and service innovations such as on-line self-assessments for customer credit clearance for loans and on-line mortgage approvals. At The Bank, an old and expensive IT infrastructure combined with poor IT for operational and business process support do not permit the use of information on product preferences and customer accounts to develop new products and services.

Good IT for innovation support also enhances IT use for management support by providing new internal and external information that helps managers and employees anticipate market and business changes and generate creative responses.

IT for Management Support

It is through good use of IT for management support that the positive interaction effects between the three information capabilities are achieved. IT for management support is directed at enabling strategic and managerial decision-making in a company. It facilitates monitoring and analysis of internal and external business conditions concerning the sharing and use of knowledge among people, market developments and positioning, and new business risks and opportunities. Companies with high IO have learned how to leverage IT tools and techniques to anticipate market trends, evaluate new business opportunities and exploit their market positions. Applications include:

- executive information systems
- decision support systems
- data mining
- database marketing
- on-line analytical processing
- group decision support systems
- risk management systems.

At SkandiaBanken, IT for management support provides on-line performance assessment tools for business units, such as risk scenarios and real-time customer behaviour analysis for new product development.

In contrast, at The Bank, the focus is on getting IT for operational support 'right'. However, this preoccupation with fixing existing systems directs scarce management attention and resources away from efforts to use IT for innovation support or management support. The Bank's managers are locked in a form of 'group think' that delays or postpones taking key decisions and making efforts to use IT for improving customer satisfaction and creating new business opportunities.

The ITP Maturity Model

The path to mature information technology practices is summed up in the ITP maturity model (see Figure 6.1 on p. 148). This model allows managers to quickly identify the most efficient way of building ITP maturity. Companies needing to improve their IT practices should begin working at the bottom of the model by improving their IT system for operational support, since this serves as a direct base on which to build effective IT for business process and innovation support, and has an indirect influence on IT for management support. We can see from the model that IT for business process support becomes a more prominent issue for companies facing globalized markets or those that want to provide superior IT for management and strategic-level decision-making. By understanding these relationships and following the prescribed paths, managers can begin to build a solid foundation to support the development of IT for management support—not surprisingly, the most difficult dimension to control and develop.

The ITP maturity model also indicates that companies with high IT investments, but low IT practices maturity, may be spending too much on IT to support basic operations. These companies fail to develop business and innovation applications that could provide them with more competitive advantage.

High IO companies know how to break out of this cycle. The break-out strategy depends on knowing how to use ITP across a range of applications and infrastructure that a company can only develop and implement over time.

Companies with high IO understand that, to retain their position among the industry leaders, they must use IT to effectively run today's operations and business processes. In the pursuit of competitive necessity, these companies get the most from their IT investments and practices, but they also build for the future. In contrast to companies with low IO, high IO companies have developed IT practices to improve their processing and use of information.

They have also taught their people to employ information and IT proactively and continuously to improve business performance.

An Investment Framework for Achieving IT Practices Maturity

We noted earlier that all too often companies focus their IT investments on increasing output and productivity instead of going for competitive advantage. Indeed, the IT productivity paradox suggests that if managers believe that IT investments can only make the company more efficient and reduce costs, then that is what they will do with IT. In one sense, the IT productivity paradox is a self-fulfilling prophecy.

Since a company needs high levels of information management practices and appropriate information behaviours and values, IT investments alone will not lead to IO maturity. All three information capabilities must be high and focused on whatever gives a company the unique business capabilities that eliminate the need to compete solely on price in their industry and differentiate them by creating value with customers and facilitating innovation. Thus the challenge for companies is not to invest in IT simply to stay in the race with the leaders in their industry: they must invest in IT to build distinctive information capabilities that provide high business returns on their use of information.

Figure 6.4 provides a framework for evaluating your IT investments in terms of ITP maturity and achieving high returns on effective information use in your company. We define 'return on effective information use' as the business value a company creates by using IT to build distinctive information capabilities—those that provide the company with competitive advantage and do not just serve competitive necessity.

In the right hand column of the chart are the IT practices necessary to run a business: IT investments for operational support (such as systems running payrolls, general ledgers, accounting, external financial reporting and payments). Most are required to operate a business competently in any industry, but provide little or no direct competitive or distinctive value. Being good at these systems is a basic requirement for operating a business today.

In the middle column are the IT practices that are essential for a company to compete among the leading companies in an industry. A company must be good enough at using IT for business process support to be perceived as a player in the industry. At best, the top five to ten companies in an industry will probably receive comparable benefits over time from using IT for business process support. For example, in the bulk chemicals industry, all the leading companies have implemented enterprise resource planning (ERP) systems such as SAP R3 for financial administration, process control, distribution and logistics. Senior managers in the industry believe that such systems are essential to control costs and manage information across the supply chain for timely deliveries, and that industrial customers expect their suppliers to operate this way.

In the left column are the IT practices that can lead a company to be distinctive in creating business value with information. Investing in IT for innovation support is critical for new product and services development, as well as for fostering creativity and knowledge sharing among people

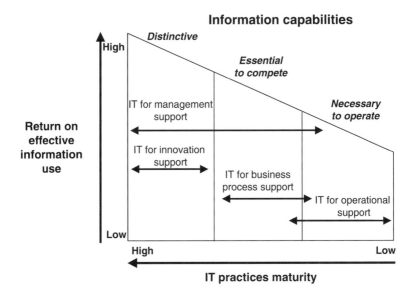

Figure 6.4: An investment framework for evaluating IT practices maturity

inside and outside the company. IT for management support is important not only for running the business today, but also—more significantly— for anticipating and responding to changes in business conditions tomorrow. Thus we can conclude that companies with low IO tend to spend too much on IT to:

- support basic operations that are necessary to run a business, and
- support business processes that provide information capabilities essential to being a player in the industry.

These companies get a low return on their IT investments.

In contrast, companies with high IO aim to invest enough in IT to operate basic systems and to use IT for business process support to compete with other leading companies in their industry. However, senior managers in these companies also try to exploit IT for innovation and management support, build distinctive information capabilities, and achieve higher returns on effective information use. To sum up, companies with ITP maturity have resolved the IT productivity paradox.

First, they have diversified their investments in IT across all four categories of IT practices. Second, they seek to build distinctive information capabilities to break out of the 'pack' of leading players in their industry and achieve superior returns on effective information use in their industry—a key concern that we address in more detail in Chapter 8.

MANAGING IT PRACTICES (ITP)

In this section, we present eight guidelines that your company can follow to improve its IT practices and increase its IO maturity. These steps can help your company to properly balance its IT investments across those information practices that are necessary, essential to compete and distinctive, as presented in Figure 6.4.

Guideline 1: Operational excellence is a competitive necessity

Although IT for operational support does not necessarily provide a high business return on effective information use, it is necessary in order to run a business efficiently. Since it provides the technical abilities and operational knowledge for deploying IT for innovation and management support, it must be executed well in order for a company to achieve high IO. Not being good at IT for operational support means that a company cannot manage basic operations credibly. It also means that a company will be unable to develop in its business and IT people the technical and operational knowledge they need to execute the IT practices that provide a much higher return on information use. Thus being good at IT for operational support is competitively necessary today as a building block to ITP maturity.

Let's look at an example of operational excellence at work.

Norwich Union

Norwich Union is one of the largest and best-known insurers in the United Kingdom, providing a full range of financial services to 7 million customers worldwide. With over £50 billion in funds under management, its operations extend to Europe, Australia, New Zealand, Canada and the Middle East.

Beginning in 1996, Norwich Union Direct began serving the general insurance needs of its customers in the United Kingdom over the phone. Shortly after its launch, it added the company's life and pension products to its insurance products and became known as Norwich Union Direct Financial Services. To deliver these more complex financial products, the company needed to integrate the activities of its 150-person call centre with its 150-person direct sales force so its operations would appear seamless to customers. The company began using Lotus Notes and its replication feature to link on-line the call centre interactions with customers and the appointment scheduling for its sales force to call on customers as rapidly as possible.[1]

When a customer requires a relatively simple insurance product, such as personal liability insurance, the call centre handles the sale over the telephone. However, when a customer inquires about more complex products, such as pension funds, Norwich Union has to complete a full fact-finding questionnaire regarding the customer's working history and financial profile. This is best achieved in a meeting with the customer so that the sales person can assess the customer's financial profile, review and anticipate his or her retirement expectations, and recommend the best product to fit his or her retirement needs.

Since each sales person has a laptop computer, customer calls for retirement products are registered in the call centre database. Every time a sales person dials into the database, all customer information is automatically replicated or updated in the sales rep's PC for use in the field to schedule appointments, provide further information after initial calls, and service the needs of the customer for related financial products. By operating in this way, Norwich Union is able to provide its sales force with continuously updated transaction and inquiry information on their customers.

Guideline 2:   IT for operational support can be strategically outsourced

Many companies selectively outsource IT for operational support, since they cannot or do not want to run all operations themselves.

SkandiaBanken

When SkandiaBanken defined its direct business approach, ownership of operational systems was specifically identified as a low priority if the bank could employ the external services of the financial services industry infrastructure in Sweden and globally. Unlike more traditional banks, SkandiaBanken did not want to develop its own systems or databases to process transactions such as paying bills, assessing credit risk, clearing payments, issuing credit cards or trading equities. In each case, senior managers evaluated the operations already functioning for traditional banks in Sweden and available for outside services. If existing operational systems could be leveraged to deliver competent services, the bank decided to make maximum use of these external services to help serve its customers and execute transactions.

For some time now, senior managers at SkandiaBanken have not viewed their future as that of a 'bank', but rather as that of a 'product delivery channel' for a broad range of financial services provided by fund managers and other companies in the Skandia Group. In the words of the CEO: 'As a product deliverer, we provide the branding, but not necessarily every single product. This gives us tremendous flexibility for the future.'

Many companies reach operational excellence by forming strategic partnerships with other companies that offer basic operational abilities and services, rather than developing these abilities for operations in-house. Such companies are able to use and manage the outsourcing process so that they receive the benefits of competent operational services without owning the operational knowledge and systems. As we suggest in Chapter 7, skilfully managing external relationships can help a company leverage its IT, information and people practices to build information capabilities without owning them. Companies can substitute and strategically employ other companies' information capabilities both to save on investing their own resources and to extend the depth and scope of their information capabilities.

Guideline 3: Effective operations provide an information platform for business innovations

Companies that are good at IT for operational support have the opportunity to build on their abilities and use IT for innovation as well. In the case of SkandiaBanken, we have seen how effective IT for operations provided a platform for using IT for new Internet banking. In fact, without effective product, customer and transactional information systems in place, the addition of Internet direct banking would have not been possible, since Internet banking requires fast, flexible and efficient operational systems to support the web site.

This link between IT for operations and IT for innovation is perhaps nowhere more evident than in Wal-Mart, which uses its supply chain systems to provide its suppliers with information about their product sales and promotions in Wal-Mart Stores.

Wal-Mart[2]

Wal-Mart Stores, Inc. operates more than 2,400 stores and 450 Sam's Clubs in the United States, with an additional 720 stores worldwide. Although Wal-Mart is already known as the world's leading retailer, with excellent supply chain systems that track every product sold in stores to replenish them automatically from warehouses and suppliers, it is constantly seeking ways to use IT for innovations in managing information with suppliers.

Wal-Mart initially developed a proprietary system called Retail Link for easy access to sales, inventory and shipping information about a supplier's products sold in Wal-Mart stores and Sam's Clubs. In recent years, Wal-Mart has turned Retail Link into a major platform for added collaboration with suppliers via the world wide web.

Suppliers access and share operational data over the Internet and work hand in hand with Wal-Mart buyers. In the past, suppliers were able to analyse five quarters of sales history. Now, they have access to up to two years of data—enhancing their ability to spot and react to long-term trends. As Wal-Mart's CIO noted: 'We have high expectations of our suppliers, and we provide a great amount in terms of business systems capability. Retail Link gives Wal-Mart buyers and suppliers the information that they need to treat each store as if it were the only one in the chain.'

The previous day's information (up to midnight) on over 10 million customer transactions is available for every store in every country before 4 a.m. the following day. Over 7,000 suppliers can access Retail Link and find answers to any question at any time. Wal-Mart averages about 120,000 queries per week to its data warehouse, which is twice as large as the next Fortune 500 company's data warehouse—101 terabytes.

This information strategy has become critical for analysing shifts in consumer preferences and permits the continuous monitoring of purchases down to the single product level. Suppliers see significant benefits in using the new Internet-based Retail Link. As the vice president for the Russ/Liz Claiborne team serving Wal-Mart observes:

> Retailing has become so information-intensive that it's critical that we are freely able to share information and have access to the same information that Wal-Mart buyers are analysing. The system helps Russ/Liz Claiborne understand where a product is working and where it's not, so that we can take action quickly. Having two years of sales data will allow us to see trends developing that can impact the way we merchandise an individual store.

Retail Link is perceived as a critical innovation for Wal-Mart buyers as well. The president of Wal-Mart's stores division noted: 'Our investment in this technology helps our supplier partners and Wal-Mart buyers provide customers with what they want—the right product in the right store at the right price.'

Thus excellence in using IT for operations provides leading companies like Wal-Mart with the means to leverage IT for continuous innovation—one of the building blocks for a company seeking high IO.

Guideline 4:   Use IT to synchronize different players and processes to achieve a seamless customer response

For many companies today, improving their internal supply chain with IT is not enough to satisfy customers. Companies must compete using a network of suppliers and partners, who also leverage their supplier and partner relationships effectively to respond to customer needs. Network competition requires that companies use IT to tie their suppliers and partners into their operations to achieve a seamless process of delivering products and services to customers.

Dell Europe's order to delivery process is an excellent example of how IT can be used to manage the network of suppliers, delivery companies and operations to produce a fast, seamless and effective customer response.

Dell Europe[3]

The Europe, Middle East and Africa Group of Dell Computers sells direct to companies and consumers in 18 countries in the region from a manufacturing and support base in Limerick, Ireland. Dell's competitive advantage is selling the newest technology direct to customers, building to a customer order of one, and delivering the highest quality product at the lowest cost. The Dell direct model offers smooth customer care from order placement to delivery, as well as after-sales support and service.

As soon as an individual order is received by Dell, the information about the order is disseminated throughout the company and to its suppliers and partners to orchestrate all parts of the supply chain network. This is critical, since the only inventory, or stock, is held in 'hubs', or warehouses, by suppliers waiting for orders to be processed by Dell. When an order is received, it triggers the flow of components from the suppliers through the hubs to Dell's assembly site.

Dell processes customer orders the way a baker makes bread; for Dell this means: 'Today's orders today'.

Dell downloads orders throughout the day, schedules them through the assembly line, completes the order and loads the finished product directly on to trucks for delivery. The trucks loaded with computers designated for a customer's country depart via the hub to collect monitors. Then the complete order is delivered to the customer's door within four days in Europe.

Dell Europe has over 200 suppliers for over 2,000 components. For each component, Dell selects a few high-performing companies and builds strategic alliances with them, using, for example, Intel processors, Sony monitors and Logitech mice. Dell shares order and inventory information freely with them as well as with its hub partner, Irish Express, by integrating computer systems and maintaining constant phone and personal communications.

Suppliers maintain predefined stock levels—usually for eight to ten days—in the hubs, based on Dell's sales forecasts. Suppliers own the inventory in the hub until it is transferred to the Dell assembly plant to fulfil a specific order. Suppliers find that real-time information-sharing allows them to manage inventory and production more effectively. In addition, Dell is often the first to communicate a component quality problem because it delivers within five days of assembly and gets reports of problems in the field directly from customers, instead of through retailers, distributors and wholesalers like Compaq or IBM.

For deliveries, Dell teams up with companies such as Walsh Express, UPS and others in Europe. These companies link their IT systems to Dell's customer support system to automatically track shipping status and estimated delivery dates. When a customer calls Dell's customer care department or checks the order status on the Internet, Dell can tell the customer where his order is and when it will be delivered, no matter which delivery company has physical possession of the product at the time.

For companies like Dell, each day's success in responding to customer orders is based on the real-time synchronization of all the suppliers, hub partner and delivery companies to make sure that every order is built to unique customer needs and delivered in 'customer time'. Seamlessly linking the IT systems of the Dell network of partners to fulfil an order from placement to delivery enables Dell to make its direct model work every day for customers.

Guideline 5:   Use IT to support effective processes at the customer end of the demand chain

Many companies use IT to support operations and business processes at the back end of the supply chain. Manufacturers have invested in IT to automate financial, manufacturing, inventory and distribution processes in their supply chain. Similarly, many service companies such as banks and insurance companies have used IT to speed up their back-office administrative processes and make them more efficient. These companies have given most of their IT investments and implementation time to the IT systems that are necessary to operate or essential to compete. In most cases, the same companies have deferred focusing on using IT at the customer end of the demand chain, where they could create distinctive information capabilities with customers or permit their supply chain to be run in a more customer-friendly and responsive manner. High IO companies, such as Antonio Puig S.A., which we discussed in Chapter 3, exemplify this approach.

Antonio Puig S.A.

In 1996, Antonio Puig re-engineered its order-to-invoice process and installed the appropriate IT applications (Ross systems) in support of the change. After this initial effort, the company decided to adopt more industry-wide standards for its ERP software and chose the German software company SAP; it also appointed an information systems (IS) director.

The IS director summarized the company's reasons for moving from Ross to SAP: 'When the Ross system was implemented, we knew that we would use it as a temporary solution. When we decided to implement SAP, we redefined our IT plan and adopted it as a long-term solution.' The IS director developed a three-year strategic plan based on three main objectives: flexibility, integration and communication. But, contrary to practice in many companies, the SAP roll-out started in sales, not manufacturing or finance. The CFO of the company explained the rationale for this decision:

> We decided to start implementing SAP in the sales area because we strongly believed in this initiative. We didn't feel the need to show quick successes to convince our top management—the family and the company were behind this initiative from day one.
> Since the initial SAP implementation, our information practices and the types of information available have improved significantly. Before, only account managers knew about their customers, and they were the only ones with customer information. Now anyone in the organization can get an understanding of single customers, channels and product volumes, for example.
> In our pre-SAP dealings with a leading French hypermarket chain, we were not aware of their perfume business—all we did was sell toiletries and other related products. With the new sales information from the SAP system, however, we are able to cross-sell perfumes in their stores. We even organize cross-promotional events with them. This capability has created many business opportunities.

Antonio Puig's managers focused on implementing ERP systems from the customer side first. Armed with this new sales system and information, they were then able to move toward setting up auto-replenishment systems for their customers' stores and moving stock directly from their factories to the customer sites—eliminating warehouses and buffer inventories. Moreover, Antonio Puig could exploit the business information benefits of implementing SAP software directly with their customers long before their competitors could. Their competitors had focused on automating the back end of the supply chain first and were years away from implementing their SAP systems for improved sales, order fulfilment and building relationships with customers.

Guideline 6:   Effective IT support for business processes provides an information platform for using IT for management support

For many companies with low IO, poor information for management support of strategic and tactical decisions is a direct result of poor information use for business processes. Senior managers in these companies complain about 'management information systems' that give them little useful management information or 'decision support systems' that offer little help in making decisions. In many ways, these managers have put the cart before the horse. Using IT for management support cannot work well unless the company has IT systems to support high-quality information use within and across its business processes. If manufacturing companies do not focus on improving their supply chain processes or facing their customers, they cannot expect to have IT systems that will process information for operational and management planning, financial management or longer term sensing and forecasting of customer demand. Similarly, service companies must integrate business processes using IT before they can use IT to support the high-quality information they need to make business decisions.

In companies with high IO, such as Hilti and BBV, we have seen how they have focused on getting IT support in place for key processes to manage customer and product information for sales support, cross-selling and customer service. From this base, they have developed sophisticated systems and databases for management support, product innovation and business strategy formulation.

A similar journey by Heineken's home market company, Heineken Netherlands B.V., illustrates how companies choose to improve key supply chain processes and IT systems first and then turn their attention to improving the quality of management and planning information.

Heineken Netherlands B.V.[4]

During the early 1990s, Heineken Netherlands embarked on a long-term journey to improve supply chain processes and IT systems facing its customers and subsequently to substantially transform the types and quality of management and planning information to manage its business. Following meetings in the early 1990s with Heineken's largest customer, the supermarket chain Albert Heijn, Heineken managers realized that the company needed to improve both the speed and flexibility of its beer deliveries to its customers.

To do so, Heineken embarked on a five-year journey to redesign its customer supply chain and redefine its approach to using IT in its business. The CFO of the company requested a benchmark of the company's IT operations at the time. The findings indicated that Heineken spent twice as much on IT as its competitors in return for half the effectiveness. Thus senior managers concluded that Heineken required a major transformation of its core IT systems supporting every aspect of its supply chain from brewing, packaging and distribution to order fulfilment and sales. To implement this new approach, the CFO appointed a new IT director promoted from within the business who redirected the basic mission of the IT function from implementing 'beautiful IT' to implementing IT that 'helps us sell more beer'.

The business-oriented IT director linked the new IT approach to evolving supply chain processes, which required more cross-functional sharing of order and product information. He froze the existing mainframe applications and support staff and outsourced the old IT systems and technical staff, while the company built a new business-oriented IT team and a more customer-focused approach to supporting supply chain processes. Over the next few years, Heineken's IT department gradually replaced old mainframe systems with new standard application packages that supported all the functions of the new supply chain approach, from brewing to selling more beer. The IT function was reconfigured from the old highly vertical, functional approach to a more team- and service-oriented approach, supporting horizontal flows of information and decision-making in the new supply chain.

As the new supply chain project neared completion, the company began to develop new decision support systems to plan and manage the new supply chain as well as forecast customer demand. One of senior management's goals for the use of management support systems was to have a 'new unity of data'. As the CFO put it: 'Having unity of data is crucial. Only a few years ago, we discovered some departments were using different unit volumes than we were in finance and accounting. And this just should not happen in any organization.'

The move to clarify definitions for shared information led managers to develop improved IT support for supply chain planning and monitoring. The company had been engaged in planning activities in functions such as production, logistics and order forecasting, but again there was no unity in the planning efforts or in the levels of planning from operational and

tactical to more strategic and long-range planning. Thus the company began to implement a decision support system that enabled planning across
the supply chain as well as across levels and time horizons. The company
also improved the information support for predicting demand by including
information on weather forecasting in the Netherlands and events such as
World Cup soccer matches, concerts and special social events.

As the IT director noted some years later, the second phase of
Heineken Netherlands' transformation of its supply chain for customers
was created on the back of the first phase 'to develop business possibilities! That is the second phase's most important feature.'

Guideline 7:   Focus your best IT resources on what makes you distinctive

In most companies, the time, attention and expertise of top-quality IT
people are in short supply. Too many IT business priorities are chasing
too few IT resources. Companies with high IO understand this. They
focus their best IT resources on information capabilities that make them
distinctive. They sub-optimize or outsource the rest. Because they know
that many of their competitors focus their best resources exclusively on IT
for operational and business process support, they try to take advantage
of IT for innovation and management support. The high IO company
knows that those who leverage IT to create new products and services
and improve management decision-making will reap the benefits of a
higher return on information.

In contrast, companies with low IO dissipate their best IT resources on
the functions that are necessary for it to operate, with little time, attention
or people expertise to do what is essential to compete well or make them
distinctive. For these companies, there never seems to be enough time or
IT people to devote to what is important, since the pressures to do what is
necessary always seem to be urgent.

For example, at BBV, the IT applications that are considered distinctive
and essential to compete are kept in-house and implemented by the most
talented and experienced IT staff. Applications that are necessary to operate, however, are either outsourced or performed according to the following rule—they implement the 80 per cent of these applications that are
most important and do not seek to allocate scarce resources to the remaining 20 per cent.

How do managers at BBV know how to allocate IT resources across
their business application portfolio? Each IT resource investment is
specifically sponsored and discussed across the bank's key business
areas. The managers in those areas decide together whether investments
are strategic or not. As the CIO observed: 'IT investments are always
justified by the business areas. The bank does not invest in IT for its own
sake. The process of approving the IT budget illustrates how IT and the

business areas work together. During the budgeting process, the business areas define the level of IT investments, based on their perception of what is strategic or not. Then the IT department gives its opinion and advises the business areas on the different solutions available. And at the end, the executive committee approves the budget justified by the business areas.

'Initiatives like Year 2000 and the euro—non-strategic applications— are totally under control. The IT people who deal with these issues are completely outsourced. The entire bank's internal IT resources are dedicated to developing applications that we consider strategic, like those that help support the integration of channels,' explained the CIO.

In contrast, The Bank has been trying to 'fix' its IT for operational support for several years. In addition, it has kept non-strategic IT issues in-house. This approach has left them with no IT resources to invest in more distinctive IT support for new product development or better management decision-making. Like other companies with low IO that we have seen, The Bank's managers focus on what is necessary to operate and lose sight of the information capabilities that could make them distinctive. In such companies, the best IT people often leave for more interesting work in companies where they work on IT practices and applications that directly support business value creation, that are more interesting and better for career advancement.

Guideline 8:   Good IT practices can uncover new business opportunities and lead to innovative management actions

A company with high IO obtains key benefits not simply from tying its IT practices closely to the way it creates business value today. It also benefits from new business opportunities and management initiatives that spring up from being able to do 'better things' with IT inside the company and for customers. As companies seek to transform their business with e-business projects, this synergy as a result of being good at IT support for operations, business processes, innovation and management support is critically important. A good example of how effective operations and business processes can provide a platform for new business ventures can be seen in the E Group, created in 1997 through the acquisition of the leading American athletics shoe and clothing retailer mentioned in Chapter 3.

E Group

Although the merger of the retailer with E Group at first raised some concerns about the levels of information behaviours and values in the retailer, E Group was able to leverage its direct marketing, as well as its operational and business processes, practices to exploit significant new e-business opportunities.

The American retailer had in the past developed superior IT for operational support to manage its call centre and warehouse operations. This system gave call centre reps on-line access to detailed customer information as well as product information about inventory levels and specific product features. In addition, a sophisticated IT-supported catalogue system allowed the retailer to easily create customized and specialized editions of the main print catalogue. These editions targeted specific customer segments several times over the course of a year.

These IT-supported business capabilities became the platform for winning new business opportunities. In 1999, E Group won the contract to become a major sport league's official catalogue and e-commerce retailer. The contract included designing, merchandising and fulfilling the league's official catalogue and web site. E Group was responsible for the back-end delivery of all catalogue and Internet-related merchandise. Because of its effective IT support for direct marketing, product information, call centre operations and fulfillment processes, the new product line could easily be integrated into the existing business model. Thus E Group captured new business opportunities and rapidly integrated them with its existing e-commerce business through leveraging the excellent IT practices of the merged athletics shoe and clothing retailer.

CONCLUSION

In this chapter we have shown how to improve and manage IT practices to build information capabilities that can differentiate your company from others in order to achieve superior business performance. Mastering the four IT practices, or dimensions, discussed in this chapter can add significantly to your company's or business unit's information orientation. Being good at IT practices, one of the information capabilities, is the third step toward achieving IO maturity and higher business performance. This chapter completes Part III, which aimed to show you how to improve each dimension within the three information capabilities, as well as tying these dimensions together to achieve higher IO and business performance.

In Part IV, we turn our attention from 'managing' to 'competing' with information capabilities. In the next three chapters, we focus on the crucial link between a company's business strategies and the information capabilities (IC) required to effectively implement these strategies; we discuss the IC maximization effect; and we look at competing with information capabilities on a global scale or across many business units.

NOTES

1. (1996) 'CTI award for Norwich Union Direct,' *Insurance Systems Bulletin*, November, 12:5.
2. Bradley, S.P., Ghemawat, P. and Foley, S. (1996), 'Wal-Mart Stores, Inc,' Boston: Harvard Business School Publishing. Case Study # 794024.
3. Marchand, D.A. and Boynton, A. (1999) 'Dell Direct in Europe: Delighting the Customer with Every Order,' Lausanne, Switzerland: International Institute for Management Development (IMD). Case study.
4. Marchand, D.A. and Vollmann, T.E. (1995) 'Heineken Netherlands B.V. (A): Customer-Driven Supply Chain Management Transformation,' Lausanne, Switzerland: IMD. Case study.

IV

STRATEGY AND COMPETING WITH INFORMATION CAPABILITIES

In Part IV we present important new findings from our two and a half year international research study that extend the IO maturity model and information orientation metric in three ways.

In Chapter 7, we present a comprehensive view of corporate strategy that encompasses the strategic priorities that companies hope to achieve. We relate a company's strategic priorities and the five business capabilities—organizational structure, processes, people, external relationships and information capabilities (IC). We then show how managers in successful companies relate their investments in IC relative to their overall business capability mixes to achieve their strategic priorities.

In Chapter 8, we examine the ways in which successful companies substitute investments in IC for the other four business capabilities and in doing so either cut costs or enhance services and products. We call these trade-offs between IC and the other capabilities the IC maximization effect. We explore how companies close the gaps between expectations for future strategic changes and their implementation. We explain how being an industry leader in competing with information allows a company to leverage the IC maximization effect.

Finally, in Chapter 9, we shift our discussion from managing and competing with IC in a single company or business unit to the context of a global company with multiple business units. We show that corporate managers of a global company must adopt a portfolio approach to managing information capabilities across their business units if they are to achieve superior business performance across the entire company.

7

BUSINESS STRATEGY, INFORMATION CAPABILITIES AND BUSINESS PERFORMANCE

What senior management team would not want to report that it has consistently created new business opportunities, delighted each and every customer, slashed excess costs and eliminated business risk to the greatest possible extent? This strategic formula for business success appears straightforward in principle, but is difficult to achieve. Constant pressure from ever-changing global markets as well as company resource and capability limitations force managers to fall short of achieving all four of these strategic priorities at the highest levels.

Within this context, managers are forced to make daily decisions that require them to deviate from planned, or 'deliberate', strategies in their pursuit of achieving superior business performance. This continual readjustment results in an emergent strategy, reflecting the actual strategic path senior managers have travelled. By examining the cumulative effects of these trade-offs over time and the business capabilities used by senior management teams, we have been able to understand more clearly the strategies followed by companies—and their relationship to business performance.

In this chapter we highlight the relationships between the strategic priorities senior management teams have realized, the way they have allocated company capabilities and the impacts of these decisions and actions on business performance. We demonstrate that specific combinations of strategic priorities, supported by appropriate investments in information capabilities, can lead a company to business success.[1]

THE EVOLUTION OF COMPANY STRATEGY

The Resource-based View of Strategy

Understanding which strategic choices create competitive advantage has been the focus of managers and strategy researchers alike. The traditional view of strategy development describes an activity in which a rationalized strategic plan is devised by top management and then implemented by middle managers. These managers tactically oversee resource allocations based on the company's development of certain business capabilities.

This resource-based approach acknowledges that external competitive forces, as well as the internal capabilities developed and deployed by companies over time, will both determine the success, or failure, of a company's competitive strategy.[2] Companies attempt to create 'mixes' of capabilities within their companies that are difficult for competitors to imitate in order to successfully achieve their strategic priorities.[3] The combination of strategic priorities and the business capability mix used to achieve these priorities make up a company's 'strategy'.

The model presented in Figure 7.1 shows the factors that managers must consider in developing strategy under the traditional resource-based view of strategy development. Managers first make a rational assessment of the competitive environment's opportunities and threats. Market trends, customer requirements, supplier relationships and competitor initiatives all factor in managers' assessments of their company's competitive situation. Based on this assessment, they frame specifically how they will achieve their strategic priorities at the highest levels.

Based on existing strategic definitions,[4] we have categorized four generic strategic priorities actively pursued by senior managers in leading their company toward success, as defined in Figure 7.2.

Strategic priority 1:   Creating new business opportunities (CBO)

Companies that emphasize this strategic priority often use a differentiation strategy that offers innovative or unique products or services to gain and sustain competitive advantage. Companies that proactively pursue this strategic priority strive for the constant creation and speedy development of new products, services, channels and markets. By creatively introducing new and better products and services, companies may create entirely new business realities.[5]

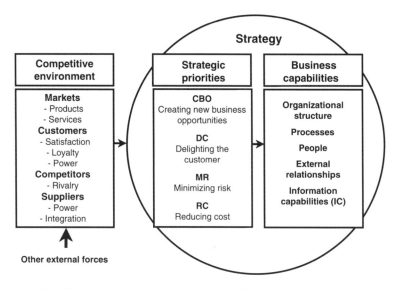

Figure 7.1:   Resource-based strategy model

Creating new business opportunities (CBO)

Companies that proactively pursue the CBO strategic priority strive for the constant creation and speedy development of new products, services, channels and markets. By creatively introducing new and better products and services, companies may create whole new business realities

---

Delighting the customer (DC)

Companies that proactively pursue the DC strategic priority strive to increase the loyalty of existing customers and gain new ones. This is typically accomplished by actively differentiating products and services, exceeding customers' expectations and offering superior customer service

---

Minimizing risk (MR)

Companies that proactively pursue the MR strategic priority strive to minimize risk through the detection and subsequent management of potential business losses or harm. Companies that compete on their ability to minimize risk are typically proactive in managing market risks, credit risks, operational risks and legal risks

---

Reducing cost (RC)

Companies that proactively pursue a RC strategic priority strive for a cost leadership position in their industry. Companies that compete on their ability to reduce and control costs typically concentrate on actively managing labour and other operating costs as well as carefully monitoring product and process efficiencies

Figure 7.2:   The strategic priorities

Strategic priority 2:   Delighting the customer (DC)

Managers understand the significant value of long-term or lifetime customers. Companies that emphasize this strategic priority believe in a
strong, direct link between customer satisfaction and business profit, and
they strive to increase the loyalty of existing customers and gain new
ones. These companies seek to exceed customers' expectations and offer
superior customer service. Over time, managers can orient the entire
organization toward delighting customers so they would never consider
buying similar products or services from competitors.[6]

Strategic priority 3:   Reducing cost (RC)

Many companies either by choice, or need, substantially reduce cost to
stay competitive. In its extreme, management theorists such as Hambrick
(1985) go as far to say that these companies become 'efficient misers' in
their pursuit of cost efficiency. Ways of reducing costs depend heavily on
industry dynamics and competitiveness. However, this strategy generally
has an internal orientation, with concentration on product efficiencies and
cost control towards the goal of becoming the lowest-cost producer in an
industry. Companies that pursue this strategic priority typically concentrate on actively managing labour and other operating costs, as well as
carefully monitoring product and process efficiencies.[7]

Strategic priority 4:   Minimizing risk (MR)

Traditional theories on strategy do not include the management of risk as
a distinct strategic priority. Yet managers know the importance of forecasting, managing and—ultimately—controlling risk in business strategy.
Companies, generally, seek to sense and manage four types of risks:

- Market—risk of loss due to adverse changes in the price of products or
  services or in the price of assets or contracts
- Credit—risk of another party defaulting on financial obligations
- Operational—risk of losses incurred by management failure, human
  error or inadequate processes or controls
- Legal—risk of loss resulting from legal or regulatory judgements.

Companies that proactively pursue this strategic priority strive to minimize risk through the detection and subsequent management of potential
business losses or harm.[8]

The resource-based view of strategy maintains that competitive advantage arises from the influence, use and combination of key business capabilities that cannot be easily imitated by competitors. As seen by the
arrow from strategic priorities to business capabilities in Figure 7.1, managers decide which key business capabilities can best be leveraged
toachieve their strategic priorities. Based on resource-based strategy, we
have identified five key business capabilities—organizational structure,

processes, people, external relationships and information capabilities (IC).[9] Figure 7.3 provides a definition of each capability.

Experienced managers need little introduction to why the right mix of business capabilities enables the achievement of strategic priorities. For example, business process re-design projects often occur across different organizational units or functions and may also include outside partners or suppliers. Managers also use restructuring initiatives to change organizational structures for improved reporting and responsibility within a company. Another way that managers attain strategic priorities within their organization is by investing in people and their competencies. Competency training for improving skills and expertise, development of corporate values and behavioural norms, and monetary and non-monetary motivation are just a few examples of how managers leverage the knowledge and energy of their people.

Business capabilities can also be built up through different forms of external relationships such as mergers and acquisitions, joint ventures, partnerships, alliances or more informal external relationships.[10] Strategic alliances and partnerships have become important in creating competitive advantage, especially in highly competitive industries and markets such as consumer electronics and personal computers.

We include information capabilities or 'IC' as the fifth key business capability in our strategy development model.[11] As we have discussed throughout this book, the effective management of the three information capabilities— information behaviours and values, information management practices and IT practices—and the interaction that occurs with IO maturity leads to higher IO. Companies that invest in the development of these capabilities can achieve high IO and improve their business performance. From a strategic viewpoint, therefore, the three information capabilities can be collectively viewed as one key business capability—'IC'—available to managers for achieving strategic priorities and increasing business results.[12]

Given resource limitations, managers often emphasize some of these business capabilities over others. In allocating a company's resources, managers make a trade-off among these five business capabilities to create what we call a 'business capability mix'. For example, a company that acquires another company may focus more on organizational structure or process to improve performance rather than on IC or people skills training.

Or, in another example, in attempting to open up new geographical markets, managers would develop the organization of the company to place greater local customer support personnel in the field while cutting corporate support staff. They would link their sales force to the Internet for sharing information with other company departments. They would enhance management control by implementing IT systems to monitor employee performance and provide on-line customer and product information.

Organizational structure

refers to the hierarchical and network relationships in organizations, including:

- spans of control
- allocation of decision rights
- degrees of job enlargement

Processes

refer to the sets of logically related tasks which are performed to achieve a defined business outcome. Processes can be:

- business processes or
- management processes

People

refers to the investment in human capital and the mix of shared values and behavioural norms exhibited by people over time in an organization, including:

- competencies (knowledge and skills)
- motivation and rewards
- manager selection
- communication networks

External relationships

to a company's activities to build competencies and capabilities outside organizational boundaries, including:

- mergers and acquisitions
- joint ventures
- partnerships
- alliances
- informal external relationships

Information capabilities (IC)

refer to the capabilities of a company to build

- information behaviours and values
- information management practices
- information technology practices

Figure 7.3:   The five key business capabilities

In this case, a strategic decision to open a new market leads to a higher allocation of business capabilities involving people, organizational structure and information capabilities. In other cases, managers may also need to implement a process improvement programme for the supply of products in the market and provide more training to the sales force in the use of new IT systems, or they may need to establish new external partnerships with other companies in the market, or improve the way the company uses information about products and customers to increase financial performance and delight customers.

Strategy development, therefore, is dependent both on strategic priorities and business capabilities. Ideally, a company intends to excel at all four of its strategic priorities—creating new business opportunities, delighting the customer, reducing cost and minimizing risk—which, combined with an allocated mix of business capabilities, will result in high business performance. What is intended, however, is most often not the strategy that is actually realized. Pressures from ever-changing global competitive environments constantly challenge managers' strategic decisions. In addition to a pool of limited resources, managers find themselves constrained by past development and the use of specific capabilities in their companies. Managers find that, despite good intentions, they fall short of achieving all four of these strategic priorities at the highest levels. What results is an emergent strategy.

Realizing Emergent Strategy

Traditional resource-based theory assumed relatively stable competitive environments and a static capabilities allocation matched specifically for that environment. Contrary to this, we believe that strategy development and implementation is a dynamic process, constantly being revised to respond to competitive pressures and resource limitations. Because of the dynamic nature of business environments, most managers realize that strategic priorities are more like moving targets than rigid directives. While strategic plans are used as tools to set strategic guidelines for the future, effective business strategy must remain dynamic and flexible to meet the reality of a global, hyper-competitive world. Within this context, a company must also be able to integrate, build and reconfigure internal and external competencies to respond to changing business conditions and to attain competitive advantage.[13]

As shown in the emergent strategy model in Figure 7.4, managers continuously evaluate the success of their strategies based on business performance results. Poor performance results in the re-evaluation of the capability mix used to achieve strategic priorities. The company's ability to attain all strategic priorities at the highest levels, however, is constrained by business capabilities, which cannot be easily disentangled from the company's past experience and overall skills and knowledge base.[14] Managers may have little influence over the capabilities available to them, and most find that they are unable to attain all four strategic priorities at the highest, or even equal, levels. This constant readjustment is illustrated in Figure 7.4 by the double arrows between strategic priorities and business capability mix.

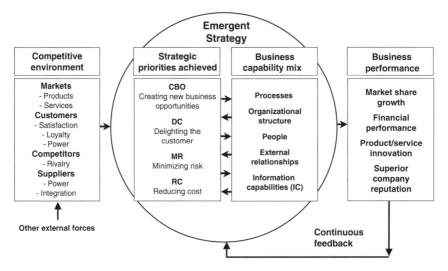

Figure 7.4: Dynamism of the emergent strategy model

Due to these constraints over time, the intended strategy of attaining all four strategic priorities at equally high levels gives way to an emergent strategy that reflects the strategic path that a company has actually taken.[15] The effectiveness of these emergent strategic priorities is gauged by how well they achieve business performance.

This dynamic and comprehensive model shown in Figure 7.4 allows us to represent the rich business context faced by senior managers while permitting us to focus later in the chapter on the unique role that information capabilities play in strategic development.

European Freight Forwarding Company

During the 1990s, this company shifted direction to emphasize external and customer-oriented strategic priorities more. A less than satisfactory financial performance underscored the need for change. In addition to serving customer needs better, senior managers hoped to create new business opportunities by landing long-term multinational accounts. The traditional role of the freight forwarder as 'agent only' had become outdated as customers demanded complete, point-to-point forwarding contracts.

Responsibility for the entire transport chain and an undertaking to guarantee quality required a subsequent shift in the company's capability mix—away from an organizational structure that emphasized decentralization and independent offices, toward business capabilities that would allow for sophisticated logistical services; namely, process integration and information capabilities. To tailor forwarding solutions for customer needs, the company embarked on an integrated IT programme to provide seamless support to create customer satisfaction. Senior managers expected that strategic priorities emphasizing customer delight and the creation of new business opportunities—combined with an increased emphasis on information capabilities to achieve these goals—would result in a strategy that would improve their business performance.

WHICH COMBINATION OF STRATEGIC PRIORITIES LEADS TO SUPERIOR BUSINESS PERFORMANCE?

Emergent strategy results from limitations in a company's capabilities relative to a changing business environment. For many years, researchers have also recognized that within these emergent strategies, companies often emphasize certain combinations of strategic priorities over others.[16]

The first of these combinations is based on strategies that are oriented toward influencing factors outside the organization, giving the company an external bias. This entrepreneurial approach towards creating business value and focusing on the customer has been called strategic 'proactivity'.[17] The second of these combinations is based on strategies that are oriented towards internal affairs, giving the company an inward-looking bias. This more conservative approach towards cost efficiency and risk containment has been called strategic 'reactivity'.[18]

Proactive strategies have been deemed more effective and successful than reactive strategies focusing only on internal affairs (such as cost-cutting and minimizing risk).[19]

Based on these definitions, we can classify combinations of strategic priorities as either having a proactive or reactive bias.[20] As Figure 7.5 shows, companies adopting a proactive bias emphasize the strategic priorities that focus on an external/market orientation. Thus companies with a proactive bias give more weight to creating new business opportunities and delighting customers than to minimizing risk and reducing cost. Companies adopting a reactive bias give more weight to strategic

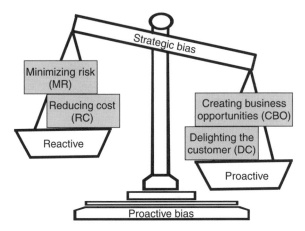

Figure 7.5: A competitive environment forces a company to adopt a strategic bias

priorities that focus on internal efficiencies such as reducing cost or minimizing risk. As the scale in the figure suggests, we assume that companies with a proactive strategic bias produce a higher pay-off than those with a reactive strategic bias.

Measuring Emergent Strategy

To determine if a certain strategy (strategic priority bias and business capability mix) results in higher business performance, we developed a measure of emergent strategy to be tested against a measure of business performance (see Figure 7.6).

We asked senior managers from 169 senior management teams to report, on a scale of 1 to 10, the extent to which they achieved each of the four strategic priorities—creating new business opportunities, delighting the customer, minimizing risk and reducing cost—over the past five years. Compared with the ideal or intended strategy of achieving a 10 for all four strategic priorities, we created a measure of the company's emergent strategic priorities. Scores from managers within each team were averaged to produce an aggregate senior management team score.

The strategic bias was then calculated based on the difference between the sum of creating new business opportunities and delighting the customer and the sum of minimizing risk and reducing cost: (CBO + DC) − (MR + RC). A positive number indicated a proactive bias, a negative number a reactive bias.

Senior managers were also asked to assign percentages to relative contributions of each of the five business capabilities, to make a total of 100

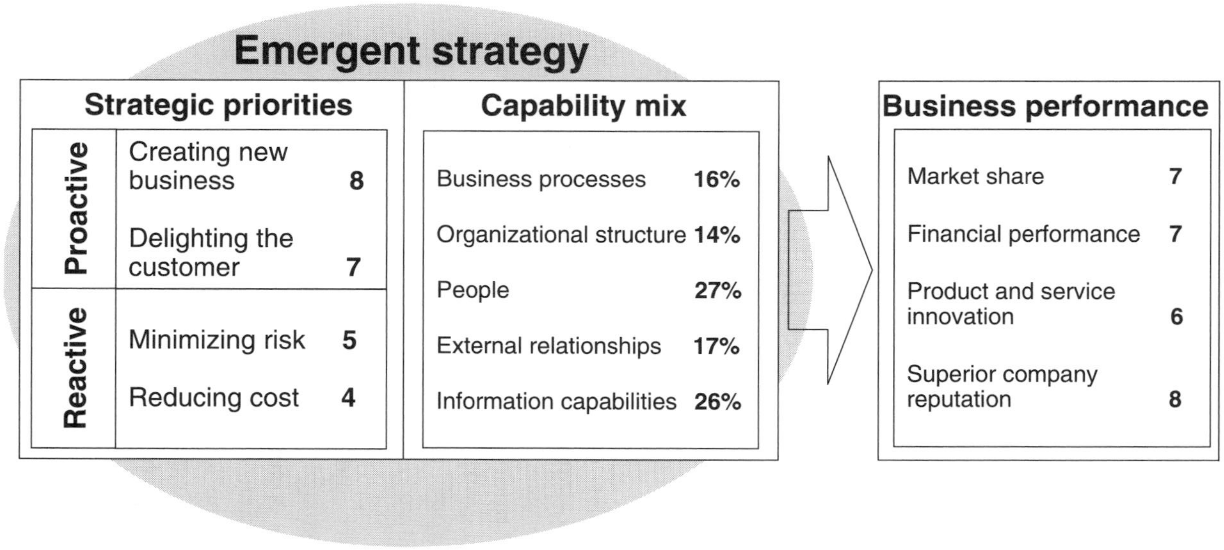

Emergent strategy

Strategic priorities

Proactive	Creating new business	8
	Delighting the customer	7
Reactive	Minimizing risk	5
	Reducing cost	4

Capability mix

Business processes	16%
Organizational structure	14%
People	27%
External relationships	17%
Information capabilities	26%

Business performance

Market share	7
Financial performance	7
Product and service innovation	6
Superior company reputation	8

Strategic priorities: 1 low to 10 high
Strategic bias (proactive and reactive): (CBO + DC) – (MR + RC)
Capability mix: Allocation of all capabilities equals 100%
Business performance: 1 low to 10 high

Figure 7.6: Measuring the strategic bias of emergent strategy

per cent. The business performance metric was based on a 1 to 10 rating of market share growth, financial performance, product and service innovation and superior company reputation.

Using this model, we were able to determine a company's emergent strategy, which reflects the strategic priority and capability mix of the company over the last five years. Figure 7.6 presents actual scores to illustrate the strategy of one company with a proactive bias. As we can see, the company has placed more emphasis on creating new business opportunities (with a score of 8) and delighting the customer (7) than on minimizing risk (5) and reducing cost (4); hence, they had a proactive bias (e.g., [8 + 7] – [5 + 4] = +6). Within its capability mix, the highest percentage allocation is on people (27 per cent), followed by information capabilities (26 per cent); external relationships (17 per cent) and business processes (16 per cent) are next in line, with organizational structure (14 per cent) last. The company also shows good business performance, with individual performance ratings all above a 6. Based on these descriptive scores, we can begin to see patterns in proactive and reactive emergent strategies.

Different Patterns of Strategic Priorities in Companies

We used a statistical cluster analysis technique to determine if there actually existed groups of companies among our senior management teams that use different patterns of strategic priorities. We suspected that either two or three strategic priority groupings existed.[21] The cluster analysis revealed three distinct groups of emergent strategic priorities among our senior management teams. Our research also found that companies do follow either a proactive or a reactive strategic bias in their emergent strategic priorities.

As Figure 7.7 shows, the Group 1 had the strongest proactive bias (almost +3)—senior management teams in this group chose to emphasize creating new business opportunities and delighting the customer over reducing cost and minimizing risk. We call this group Growers, since they have the greatest bias toward strategic priorities that stress an external, growth-oriented strategy.

The Group 3 had a reactive bias (< –1), choosing to emphasize reducing cost and minimizing risk rather than creating new business opportunities and delighting the customer. Because of its focus on internal matters and cost-cutting, we call this group Cutters.

The Group 2, between Cutters and Growers, appeared to be moving toward a more proactive bias, seeking to place more emphasis on creating new business opportunities and delighting the customer. We call this group Makeovers.[22]

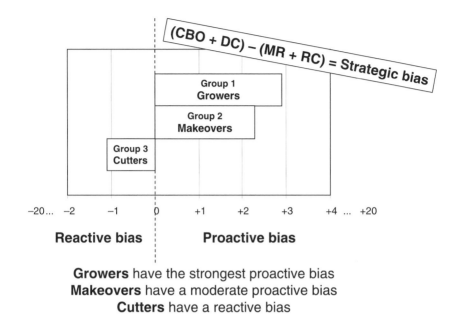

Growers have the strongest proactive bias
Makeovers have a moderate proactive bias
Cutters have a reactive bias

Figure 7.7:   Three groups of emergent strategic priorities

While distinguishing these three unique strategic priority groups is interesting, it is not of much practical value to managers unless we can establish that a particular approach to strategy leads to high business performance pay-offs.

Does a Certain Strategy Set Result in Improved Business Performance?

According to our research, the answer is yes. We found that companies that follow certain emergent strategic priorities do achieve better business performance. Growers, who have a proactive strategic bias in their strategic priorities, have significantly better business performance than Cutters, who have a reactive strategic bias.

Makeovers, however, did not achieve higher business performance than Cutters.[23] This finding indicates that a proactive strategic bias alone does not improve business performance. It also suggests that there may be a 'right' combination of strategic priorities and capabilities to increase business performance. Why did Makeovers, which followed a proactive strategic bias, not perform better than Cutters, which followed a reactive strategic bias? To answer this question we examined the business capability mixes of the three cluster groups.

Looking across the graph in Figure 7.8 at the three groups, we can see that the highest-performing group, Growers, allocated more to IC (> 25 per cent) than either Makeovers or Cutters.[24] Similarly, Growers allocated more to external relationships (> 15 per cent) than Makeovers and Cutters (both > 10 per cent).[25] Cutters, however, allocated more to organizational structural changes (> 15 per cent) than either Makeovers or Growers. Cutters and Makeovers also allocated a similar amount to processes, with Growers bringing up the rear.

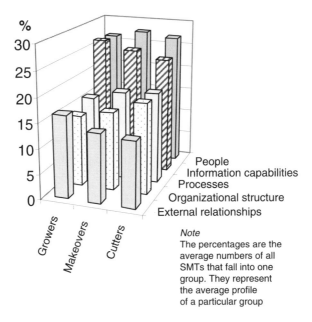

Figure 7.8: The capability mixes of Growers, Makeovers and Cutters emergent strategies

We can also see that Makeovers appear 'between' Growers and Cutters for every capability allocation except for that for people, where they lead.[26] We can see that, like Cutters, Makeovers allocate more to organizational structure and processes than Growers do. Their IC and external relationship allocations, however, are higher than Cutters' allocations for the two capabilities. Thus our capability mixes suggest that Makeovers are in transition, moving away from a Cutters' capability mix toward one that is beginning to resemble that of Growers, which places relatively more emphasis on IC and external relationships, and less on organizational structure. Makeovers share a proactive bias with the Growers. But, in the past five years, they have tried to implement their proactive strategic priorities with the 'wrong mix' of capabilities.

What we see among our Makeover group is that despite the desire for a more proactive Grower strategy, managers in this group are constrained by attributes of their business capability mix that prevents them from attaining this strategy. For example, sunk costs associated with the development of specific processes over time may prevent managers from addressing a new strategic direction. A hierarchical organizational structure with well-defined decision centres and ownership may be inflexible to change. Cultural norms developed over many years may hinder the development of a new strategic outlook. Change within this context is often a painful experience, and not easily implemented.

Do Companies with Superior Business Performance Invest More in Developing Their IC?

From Figure 7.8 we can see that the highest-performing group, Growers, not only allocates more to IC than do Makeovers and Cutters, but also allocates the most to IC (> 25 per cent) within its own capability mix. Grower companies use IC investment more than any other business capability to achieve proactive-biased strategies and, as a result, create superior business performance.

Company Strategy within a Real Case Context

What we have just seen is that the strategies that emerged as the most successful were those that had a proactive bias with a capability mix which emphasized IC and external relationships more, and organizational structure and processes less. The following case studies—from each of the three strategy groups—also illustrate the differences between successful strategies and less successful ones.

The Grower: Banco Bilbao Vizcaya (BBV)

BBV has used Grower strategies over the past five years to achieve superior business performance. Managers have developed and used the company's information capabilities—building appropriate information behaviours, effective information management systems and reliable IT support for sales representatives in the branches—as the primary way of achieving its strategic goals.

BBV has also focused on using external relationships to support the creation of new business opportunities. In 1996, the bank unveiled a plan to spend $2 billion over four years on developing retail banking activities in Latin America. Previously, BBV's presence in Latin America had been limited to a few representative offices, a subsidiary in Puerto Rico, and a 20.6 per cent stake in the Mexican financial group Probursa. As part of the plan, BBV raised its share in Probursa to 70 per cent, giving it management of the group, and it acquired controlling stakes in Banco Continental (Peru), Banco Ganadero (Colombia) and two small Mexican banks, Banco Cremi and Banco de Oriente. 'Our international policy has always been to enter markets where cultural affinities give us a competitive advantage, so Latin America is an obvious target and we believe our style of banking, which consists of small client-oriented branches, is particularly well adapted to Latin America,' commented one BBV executive. Chile, Argentina and Brazil topped BBV's list of target markets.

In 1998, BBV announced that it would invest an additional $3.5 billion over three years in Latin America, putting its position in the region on a par with that of Spanish rival, Banco Santander. 'Diversification of investment, as well as reinforcing efficiency and domestic market positions . . . are the way to compensate for a fall in margins that is causing a fall in profitability in European banking,' commented a BBV spokesperson. 'While rival Santander bought only large stakes of around 80 per cent, BBV limited itself to around 40 per cent interests, allowing it to buy into larger banks with the same amount of money,' he added. BBV aims at expanding its network and being present in all key countries in the region. Building on its experience in using IC to create business value, the bank intends to keep investment in IC a main goal, along with new partner relationships. 'We are investing to bring our new assets up to BBV risk management and information technology standards,' explained the CFO. Senior managers at BBV see that one key to creating business value in new international partners is investment in IC and consequent leveraging of this capability to attain strategic goals.

The Grower: Cemex[27]

Mexico's Cementos Mexicanos (Cemex) has employed a Grower strategy to transform its once country-based business into the third largest cement company in the world within a four-year time frame. To create new business opportunities and improve customer relationships, Cemex has attempted to build a global brand out of the traditional cement commodity business. It has done this by developing and leveraging two of its business capabilities—external relationships and IC.

Since 1990, Cemex has aggressively expanded its operations globally through the acquisition of cement and cement-related companies in Spain, the United States, Chile, Colombia, Venezuela, Panama, the Dominican Republic, Costa Rica, Haiti, Indonesia, the Philippines and Egypt. It has established a strong record for turning around underperforming and poorly managed companies, becoming adept at integrating new entities into its production and distribution operations. Close relationships with suppliers and distributors in these markets has also been a key business capability for the company. Providing financing, training, technical or operational support, Cemex has attempted to bring these entities closer to the company by helping to modernize their business processes.

A self-professed 'techie', the company's CEO, Lorenzo Zambrano, set out to develop his company's IC in the early 1990s, believing that information and technology would have a major impact on the way it competed in the industry. Heavy investment in state-of-the art communications technology and development of CemexNet which connects its 50 cement plants and 400 ready-mix operations throughout the world allows for centralized supervision of production and operational data, and quick identification of problems 24 hours a day. Detailed customer information is gathered and updated regularly to provide employees with accurate information.

Cemex also places a premium on employee education, devoting a minimum of eight per cent of total work time to training new employees. Included in this training is how to enter and use the information available to employees worldwide. Cemex's proprietary software programs enable its divisions to create virtual communities through which they can identify, share and improve upon the company's best practices. These programs assist the company in its efforts to further streamline business activities within its global operations network. Push technology automatically delivers information via the Internet to employees' computers giving executives real-time access to colleagues in similar departments around the world.

Development of IC has given Cemex an interesting way to improve customer delight—customers are guaranteed ready-mix cement deliveries within 20 minutes of schedule within designated geographic markets, regardless of weather conditions, and even in Mexico City's chaotic traffic. If there are delays, customers receive discounts of approximately five per cent. These guarantees have been made possible through a net-based logistics truck dispatch system and use of a Global Positioning System (GPS) to speed deliveries to customers. This system has also increased truck productivity by 35 per cent. Cemex's future plans include guaranteeing a delivery window of 10 minutes with free loads if late.

Recently Cemex developed business to business e-solutions for their largest distributors and major contractors in order to build solid partnerships along the supply chain. This year it also became the sole seed investor (US$20 million) in Miami-based PuntoCom Holdings (PCH), a Latin American e-business venture whose goal is to become Latin America's premier e-business development accelerator.

The Cutter: The Bank

Faced with financial losses, senior managers at The Bank have focused on a reactive strategy that places organizational priorities on reducing costs through branch consolidation, reduction in the number of employees, cost containment and process efficiency improvements. This strategy has led to an overriding focus on internal rather than external sources for business improvements over the last five years.

After merging with another major bank in 1993, The Bank's business approach focused on restructuring to integrate the new bank and streamline the two operations. The Bank decided to defer its growth plans to ensure optimal integration of the two banks.

In 1996, the integration projects were almost completed and The Bank started another initiative called VIVA. The initiative began with a major change in organizational structure. The Bank was separated into two banking units with separate P&Ls. 'Before VIVA, the bank operated as a single unit, and it was impossible to determine whether the retail unit was making or losing money,' commented one of the bank's executives. Financial analysis of the newly formed retail banking unit showed losses of 660 million euros.

The Bank's VIVA programme sought to address the retail banking unit's profitability. The first phase, which finished at the end of 1998, focused on cost-cutting and achieving efficiencies through the following four objectives:

- improving credit and risk management
- implementing a leaner and flatter organization
- redefining the roles of back-office system and IT infrastructure support
- transforming the distribution system.

Organizational restructuring and process improvements are the main capabilities identified for the VIVA programme, aimed at improving flagging business performance through a continued reactive cost reduction strategy. Although defining IT infrastructure support is identified as one objective of the programme, we know that The Bank has a long way to go to update its old IT infrastructure.

As we have seen in this case, an extremely cost-conscious company may not adequately invest in IT for new or future systems or applications. A Cutter strategy may also damage vital information capabilities. For example, structural changes such as downsizing tend to have a negative effect on behaviours by creating suspicion or mistrust among employees and managers. Political manoeuvering among managers in this climate may also affect the flow of information within a company. As information-based strategies increase in importance in all industries, and the need to have strong information capabilities becomes more vital, companies should seriously consider the potential erosion effect and opportunity cost of Cutter strategies. The side-effects of erosion may include a long period of rebuilding and recovery of information capabilities following a Cutter strategy.

The Cutter: US Food Manufacturer

One of the leading food manufacturing companies in the United States has followed a Cutter strategy since the mid-1990s, after a decade of new acquisitions and divestiture of non-strategic businesses. In the mid-1980s, it was the key player in one of the largest takeovers in the food industry, providing managers with the challenge of integrating the new company into the existing company structure and brand portfolios.

Throughout the 1990s, the company emphasized a reactive strategic bias through internal cost efficiencies to improve profitability by integrating, reorganizing and streamlining complementary businesses between the acquired company and the existing one. Senior managers' attention and priorities were on organizational restructuring and identifying the right people to keep. Due to the complexity of different IT systems and accounting structures and the possibility of more acquisitions and divestitures, the company delayed any decisions on developing IT guidelines, policies and standards or improving its information management practices. As a result, information management and IT use remain underdeveloped capabilities, which will continue to be neglected since the company has just begun process redesign changes. Senior management does not envisage any major improvements in information capabilities in the near future.

The Makeover: US Financial Institution

In 1994, under the direction of a new CEO, this institution began to redirect its strategy away from one primarily concerned with risk management and budget-based cost containment toward profitable growth through improved customer service and business accountability. Consolidation of the banking industry, as well as falling market share, prompted senior managers to take a serious look at how to redirect organizational efforts toward creating business value through a more proactive strategic bias.

To instigate the change, the senior managers first decided to tackle the enormous task of improving its customer information across all business units. They began by standardizing the company's financial reporting. Standardization would also help improve access to information. As one senior manager explained, 'When I first joined this company, if I asked for statistics on a client, I was told that I would have to wait while 15 other people approved the numbers before I could see them.' To streamline the quarterly customer reporting system, which took an average of 18 weeks to process, an IT system was installed to capture information in a unified way across the company. As part of this process, the company set reporting definitions and spent a great deal of time checking the quality of the information that would be used in the system. 'In the past, people in our organization did not trust the data that was reported to them,' commented one senior manager. 'There was the perception that data was "dirty", since there were many games being played with the numbers that were reported.'

Second, senior managers set out to improve the type of customer information that was collected by the sales force. This information would be used for two main purposes—to develop metrics on customer relationships to help the sales force identify the most profitable customers and services; and to create customized client services to differentiate the financial institution from others. The company developed a new IT system for remote distribution so that customer information could be accessed and reported more easily by the sales force. As one senior manager noted, 'We are now using our consulting capabilities to provide information to our customers to develop value-creating relationships with them.'

As we can see from this example, this Makeover company is in transition, moving away from its traditional, internally focused financial strategy to one that looks externally to create business value. Traditional customer relationships are being redefined to create new business opportunities and customer loyalty through improved customer service. Although the company is still dealing with a legacy of poor information behaviours, it is trying to move in the right direction. To achieve these goals, the company has invested in information capabilities to improve business performance.

The Makeover: European Retailer of Eyeglass Lenses and Frames

This company traditionally focused on delighting the customer through employee empowerment and person-to-person relationships. In 1997, senior managers faced two options for creating new business opportunities—international expansion through internal, organic growth or rapid expansion through acquisition of foreign, potential competitors.

Since time was short but competitors abundant, the company's senior managers favoured speed over caution and acquired a UK competitor. The acquisition doubled the number of employees and increased the number of stores from 200 to 700 overnight. This rapid international expansion forced senior managers to acknowledge that localization had gone too far because they had no supply chain management, central purchasing unit, IT infrastructure or IT platform. With the goal of improving operational information to compete on an international basis, the company is in transition—focusing on increasing IC investment, especially in the areas of IT practices and information management practices. Improving and building supply chain management, implementing regional purchasing and inventory management of eyeglass frames and planning a group-wide IT infrastructure on a cross-regional basis are currently underway.

ASSESSING YOUR COMPANY'S STRATEGY

As we have discussed in this chapter, senior managers' choices regarding company strategy—emphasizing either a proactive or reactive strategic priority bias, and executed through a mix of business capabilities—has business performance implications. Senior managers who are looking to improve their company's business performance, therefore, need to know where their own company falls within our three strategy groups in order to formulate an action plan to move toward greater business performance.

By completing the following two assessments, managers can quickly gauge their own company's strategy over the last five years.

Strategic Priority Assessment

On a scale of 1 to 10, with 10 representing the ideal, what were the strategic priorities your company achieved during the past five years?

Creating new business opportunities	1	2	3	4	5	6	7	8	9	10
Delighting the customer		1	2	3	4	5	6	7	8	9	10
Minimizing risk		1	2	3	4	5	6	7	8	9	10
Reducing cost		1	2	3	4	5	6	7	8	9	10

- Add together the scores for creating new business opportunities and delighting the customer.
- Add together the scores for minimizing risk and reducing cost.
- Subtract the first score from the second one. This is your strategic priority bias. If the score is positive, your company has a proactive strategic bias. If the score is negative, your company has a reactive strategic bias.

Creating new business opportunities + Delighting the customer = ... (1)
Minimizing risk + Reducing cost = ... (2)
Strategic bias = (1) – (2) = ...

Capability Mix Assessment

For a total of 100 per cent, assign a percentage to each of the following five business capabilities to represent their relative contributions to realizing strategic priorities in your company over the past five years. Refer to Figure 7.3 (p. 178) for definitions of each business capability.

	Contribution
Processes	
Organizational structure	
People	
External relationships	
Information capabilities	
TOTAL	**100%**

Rearrange the capabilities in order from the highest to the lowest percentage contribution in the following table:

	Contribution
1.	
2.	
3.	
4.	
5.	
TOTAL	**100%**

- What capabilities has your company emphasized to achieve strategic priorities over the last five years?
- Where has the most monetary investment and management attention been spent in your company?
- Does your company emphasize processes and organizational structure over IC in its capability mix, or does IC lead your company's capability mix? What has been the role of external relationships within this mix?

Is Your Company a Grower, Makeover, or Cutter?

- If your company has a positive strategic bias and a business capability mix that emphasizes IC and external relationships over other business capabilities, you are a Grower.
- If your company has a positive strategic bias, but your capability mix still emphasizes organizational structure and processes over IC, even though it has made improvements to IC, you are a Makeover.
- If your company has a negative strategic bias and your capability mix emphasizes organizational structure and processes over IC, you are a Cutter.

CONCLUSION

In this chapter we have shown the relationship between IC and a company's strategy. Although, ideally, a company intends to excel at all four strategic priorities, a competitive, constantly changing environment forces a company to adopt a strategic bias, which results in an emergent strategy that reflects what really happened.

We have explored how companies fall into one of three strategy groups—Growers, Makeovers or Cutters. Growers are companies that exploit their proactive bias by creating new business opportunities and delighting the customer, combined with the right business capability mix of emphasizing IC and external relationships. We have shown that IC plays a dominant role in the attainment of strategic priorities with our highest-performing group—Growers—and suggested that Makeovers, although in transition, have begun to invest more heavily in IC, while Cutters continue to lag behind.

Finally, as a first step to understanding the relationship of IC to your own company's strategy, we have provided a short diagnostic to enable you to evaluate your own company. This will provide the basis for discussing future challenges and prescriptions for change in the way managers shape future strategy in Chapter 8. Senior managers who are charged with shaping future organizational needs and outlining strategy need to know how to put together a capability mix that will provide them with competitive advantage. In the next chapter we explore how senior managers in each strategy group view their future capability mixes and how high-performing companies achieve future strategic priorities.

NOTES

1. Detailed discussion of the theoretical definitions and measurement of many of the constructs and relationships used as the basis of the research in these two chapters can be found in the Appendix of Marchand, D.A., Kettinger, W.J. and Rollins, J.D. (2001) *Information Orientation: The Link to Business Performance*, UK: Oxford University Press. Additionally, the new research summarily presented in these chapters is based on several University of South Carolina and International Institute for Management Development (IMD) working papers currently under review.

2. We realize that many authors make a distinction between 'resources' (i.e. physical, human capital or organizational resources (assets) available to a firm) and 'capabilities' (a firm's capacity to deploy these resources (assets) through competencies such as trustworthiness, flexibility, rapid response, etc.). See: Barney, J. (1991) 'Firm Resources and Sustained Competitive Advantage,' *Journal of Management* **17**(1): 99–120; Amit, R. and Schoemaker, P.J.H. (1993) 'Strategic Assets and Organizational Rent,' *Strategic Management Journal* 14: 33–46; and Schendel, D. (1994) 'Competitive Organizational Behavior: Toward an Organizationally Based Theory of Competitive Advantage,' *Strategic Management Journal* 154: 1–4. For managerial brevity, we assume that 'capability' refers both to the resources and the capacity to deploy these resources.

3. Resource-based theory maintains that competitive advantage arises from resources and attributes of a firm which cannot easily be imitated. See: Barney, J. (1991) 'Firm Resources and Sustained Competitive Advantage,' *Journal of Management* **17**(1): 99–120. These resources are strengths that firms can use to conceive of and implement their strategies. See: Learned, E.P., Christensen, C.R., Andrews, K.R. and Guth, W. (1969) *Business Policy*, Homewood, IL: Irwin; and Porter, M. (1981) 'The Contributions of Industrial Organization to Strategic Management,' *Academy of Management Review* 6: 609–620. A combination of resources and capabilities that are rare, valuable and difficult to imitate can create competitive advantage. See: Javenpaa, S.L. and Leidner, D.E. (1998) 'An Information Company in Mexico: Extending the Resource-Based View of the Firm to a

Developing Country Context,' *Information Systems Research* **9**(4): 342–361, December.

4. Like many researchers before us, we believe that a strategic model practical for managers should focus on strategic priorities that represent actions, rather than descriptions. For example, R. Miles and C. Snow's ((1978) *Organizational Strategy, Structure, and Process*, New York: McGraw-Hill) famous strategy typology classifies firms by their propensity for strategic action. Similarly, other scholars have used an action-based scheme to classify strategic priorities. See: Snow, C.C. and Hrebiniak, L. (1980) 'Strategy, Distinctive Competence and Organizational Performance,' *Administrative Science Quarterly* 25: 317–336; Miles, R.H. and Cameron, K.S. (1982) *Coffin Nails and Corporate Strategies*, Englewood Cliffs, NJ: Prentice Hall; Hambrick, D. (1983) 'Some Tests of the Effectiveness and Functional Attributes of Miles and Snow's Strategic Types,' *Academy of Management Journal* 26: 5–26; Cameron, K. (1986) 'A Study of Organizational Effectiveness and Its Predictors,' *Management Science* **32**(1): 87–111, January; and Segars, A.H., Grover, V. and Kettinger, W.J. (1994) 'Strategic Users of Information Technology: A Longitudinal Analysis of Organizational Strategy and Performance,' *Journal of Strategic Information Systems* **3**(4): 261–288.

5. Creating New Business Opportunities (CBO): This strategic priority is derived from Porter's differentiation strategy (see: Porter, M. (1980) *Competitive Strategy*, New York: Free Press) which endeavours to offer customers unique products or services, Miles and Snow's prospector strategy ((1978) *Organizational Strategy, Structure and Process*, New York: McGraw-Hill) characterized by a proactive external orientation, and Miller who identifies innovative differentiation as a discrete strategic priority ((1986) 'Configurations of Strategy and Structure: Towards a Synthesis,' *Strategic Management Journal* **7**(3): 233–249). Hence, creating new business opportunities consists of the continuous development of new products and services to gain and sustain competitive advantage.

6. Delighting the Customer (DC): Research on measuring the value of lifetime customers in both service and manufacturing industries shows the significant value of customer loyalty and retention (see: Heskett, J., Jones, T., Lovemann, G., Sasser, W. and Schlesinger, L. (1994) 'Putting the Service-Profit Chain to Work,' *Harvard Business Review*, March–April). Companies that take a customer-focused strategic priority attempt to show a strong direct linkage between customer satisfaction and business profit, such as with Miller's 'marketing innovators', Miller and Friesen's 'mature giants', and Kim and Lim's 'marketing differentiators'. See: Miller, D. (1986)

'Configurations of Strategy and Structure: Towards a Synthesis,' *Strategic Management Journal*, **7**(3): 233–249; Miller, D. and Friesen P. (1984) *Organizations: A Quantum View*, Englewood Cliffs, NJ: Prentice Hall; Kim, L. and Lim, Y. (1988) 'Environment, Generic Strategies and Performance in a Rapidly Developing Country: A Taxonomic Approach,' *Academy of Management Journal* 31: 802–827.

7. Reducing Cost (RC): Our definition of reducing cost is based on Porter's (1980) cost leadership, Miles and Snow's 'defenders' or Hambrick's 'efficient misers'. See: Porter, M. (1980) *Competitive Strategy*, New York: Free Press; Miles, R. and Snow, C. (1978) *Organizational Strategy, Structure and Process*, New York: McGraw-Hill; Hambrick, D. (1985) 'Strategies for Mature Industrial Product Businesses,' in J.H. Grant (ed.) *Strategic Management Frontiers*, Greenwich, CT: JAI Press.

   As quoted in Dess and Lumpkin, 'a cost leadership strategy suggests an internal orientation whereby a company concentrates on product efficiencies and cost control in order to be the lowest cost producer relative to competitors.' Ways to reduce cost depend heavily on industry dynamics and competitiveness and often no longer guarantee sustainable competitive advantage but, rather, are a necessity to stay in business. See: Dess, G. and Lumpkin, G. (1997) 'Entrepreneurial Strategy-making and Firm Performance: Tests of Contingency and Configurational Models,' *Strategic Management Journal*, **18**(9): 677–695.

8. Minimizing Risk (MR): Risk is a choice rather than a fate. The importance of forecasting, managing and, ultimately, minimizing risk is recognized as one strategy employed by managers. Companies minimize risk through the detection and subsequent management of potential business losses or harm and to secure competitive environments. While traditional theories on strategy (see: Porter, M. (1980) *Competitive Strategy*, New York: Free Press; and Miller, D. (1992) 'Generic Strategies: Classification, Combination and Context,' in P. Shrivastava, A. Huff and J. Dutton (eds) *Advances in Strategic Management*, Greenwich, CT: JAI Press) do not include the management of risk as a distinct strategic priority, Miles and Snow 'defender' typology includes risk minimization as a characteristic of companies wanting to establish stable and secure niches in their industries. See: Miles, R. and Snow, C. (1978) *Organizational Strategy, Structure and Process*, New York: McGraw-Hill.

9. Barney classifies firm resources into three broad groups: organizational capital resources, physical capital resources and human capital resources. See: Barney, J. (1991) 'Firm Resources and Sustained Competitive Advantage,' *Journal of Management* **17**(1): 99–120. Organ-

izational capital resources include formal reporting structures, planning, control and coordinating systems (see: Tomer, J.F. (1987) *Organizational Capital: The Path to Higher Productivity and Well-Being*, New York: Praeger); physical capital resources include technology or equipment (see: Williamson, O. (1975) *Markets and Hierarchies*, New York: Free Press); and human capital resources include training, experience, judgement and relationships of individual managers and workers (see: Becker, G.S. (1964) *Human Capital*, New York: Columbia). More managerially useful definitions of business capabilities were drawn from business change literature: Leavitt's 'Diamond Model', Galbraith's 'Star Model', and Kettinger and Grover's 'Process Change Model'. Leavitt describes the components of the organization as task, structure, technology and people. Galbraith more fully developed the people capability by emphasizing the role of culture and rewards as important aspects that must be addressed in order to implement a pursued strategy. Kettinger and Grover extended Leavitt's model by including business processes, IT and information resources as distinct business capabilities. See: Leavitt, J. (1965). 'Applying Organizational Change in Industry: Structural, Technological, and Humanistic Approaches,' in J. March (ed.), *Handbook of Organizations*, Chicago: Rand-McNalley; Galbraith, J. (1994) *Competing with Flexible Lateral Organizations*, New York: Addison-Wesley; Kettinger, W.J. and Grover, V. (1995) 'Towards a Theory of Business Process Change Management,' *Journal of Management Information Systems*, **12**(1): 9–30.

Finally, researchers such as Lorange and Roos have recognized external relationships as a business capability that has become more important in today's highly volatile and competitive business environment. See: Lorange, P. and Roos, J. (1993) *Strategic Alliances—Formation, Implementation and Evolution*, Cambridge MA: Blackwell Publishers.

10. We use the term 'external relationships' rather than strategic alliances (see: Lorange, P. and Roos, J. (1993) *Strategic Alliances—Formation, Implementation and Evolution*, Cambridge, MA: Blackwell Publishers) because we want to integrate those loose network relationships that are enabled through IT and can be best described as business networks. See: Venkatraman, N. (1994) 'IT-Enabled Business Transformation: From Automation to Business Scope Redefinition,' *Sloan Management Review*, **35**(2): 73–87. Lorange and Roos describe two ways of defining those alliances, either by degree of vertical integration (from a wholly-owned unit to informal network relationships) or by degree of interdependency between the parties involved (wholly-owned organization = high; informal network relationships = low). The authors distinguish between four generic motives for establishing external relationships, such as defending their core business,

catching up with new developments, remaining in a market where they only play a peripheral role, or restructuring.

11. The use of information and IT as a strategic resource has been recognized as an important business capability for many years. The advancement of communications and computing technologies has heightened the stature of IT from an operational resource unrelated to strategic goals to an integral ingredient in strategy formulation and implementation leading to competitive advantage. (See: King, W.R. (1978) 'Strategic Planning for Management Information Systems,' *MIS Quarterly* **2**(1): 7–37; Parsons, G.L. (1983) 'Information Technology: A New Competitive Weapon,' *Sloan Management Review*, Fall, 3–14; and McFarlan, W.R. (1984) 'Information Technology Changes the Way You Compete,' *Harvard Business Review* **62**(3): 98–103.)

Numerous studies have sought to raise managerial awareness of the competitive importance of IT in competitive strategies. (See: Ives, B. and Learmonth, G. (1984) 'The Information System as a Competitive Weapon,' *Communications of the ACM* **27**(12): 1193–1201; Porter, M.E. and Miller, V.E. (1985) 'How Information Gives You a Competitive Advantage,' *Harvard Business Review* **63**(4): 149–160; Wiseman, C. (1988) *Strategic Information Systems*, Homewood, IL: Irwin; and Parsons, G.L. (1983) 'Information Technology: A New Competitive Weapon,' *Sloan Management Review*, Fall, 3–14).

Others have provided extensive evidence of the critical role information resources can play in the realization of corporate strategy. See: Clemons, E.K. and McFarlan, W.F. (1984) 'Telecom: Hook Up or Lose Out,' *Harvard Business Review* **64**(4): 91–97; Ives, B. and Learmonth, G. (1984) 'The Information System as a Competitive Weapon,' *Communications of the ACM* **27**(12): 1193–1201; McFarlan, W.R. (1984) 'Information Technology Changes the Way You Compete,' *Harvard Business Review* **62**(3): 98–103; Cash, J.I. and Konsynski, B.R. (1985) 'IS Redraws Competitive Boundaries,' *Harvard Business Review* **63**(2): 134–142; and Clemons, E.K. and Row, M. (1991) 'Sustaining IT Advantage: The Role of Structural Differences,' *MIS Quarterly* **15**(3): 275–292.

More recently, Kettinger and Grover demonstrated that information resources leveraged with key business foundation factors can lead to sustainable competitive advantage. See Kettinger, W.J., Grover, V. and Segars, A. (1994) 'Strategic Information Systems Revisited: A Study of Sustainability and Performance,' *MIS Quarterly* **18**(1): 31–58. See: Kettinger, W.J., Grover, V. and Segars, A.H. (1995) 'Do Strategic Systems Really Pay Off? An Analysis of Classic Strategic IT Cases,' *Information Systems Management*, Winter.

In their 1998 research, Mendelsen and Pillai found that strategic use of an IT capability combined with the right 'information focus' (information management practices) strategies resulted in performance pay-offs. See: Mendelson, H. and Pillai, R.R. (1998) 'Clockspeed and Informational Response: Evidence from the Information Technology Industry,' *Information Systems Research* **9**(4): 415–433. December.

12. Although intended to measure a similar construct to IO, 'IC' in Chapters 7 and 8 was measured differently than information orientation as discussed in the rest of this book. Whereas the IO measure was derived using common factor analysis and reliability testing of multi-item measures, the IC referenced in Chapters 7 and 8 was captured as a single item measure. As with the four other business capabilities, we asked managers to aggregate IC as one idea and assign a percentage contribution of this capability to the realization of their strategic priorities. While we recognize that the single item strategy measures used in Chapters 7 and 8 do not hold the same level of construct validity or reliability as our overall IO and business performance measures, the face validity of these measures indicates that they provide important insights into the strategic thinking of a large sample of senior executives.

13. While the traditional resource-based view adopted the idea that resources and capabilities were static and directly matched to opportunities in the marketplace (see: Wernerfelt, B. (1984) 'A Resource-Based View of the Firm,' *Strategic Management Journal* 5: 171–180; Barney, J.B. (1986) 'Firm Resources and Sustained Competitive Advantage,' *Journal of Management* 17: 99–120; Grant, R.M. (1991) 'The Resource-Based Theory of Competitive Advantage: Implications for Strategy Formulation,' *California Management Review* **33**(3) 114–135), the modern view acknowledges that resources and capabilities are dynamic and can be developed to identify and respond quickly to changing business environments, as well as to shape new opportunities (see: Teece, D.J., Pisano, G. and Shuen, A. (1997) 'Dynamic Capabilities and Strategic Management,' *Strategic Management Journal* **18**(70): 509–533; Hamel, G. and Prahalad, C.K. (1994) *Competing for the Future*, Boston: Harvard Business School Press).

14. Resource-based theorists define firm resources and capabilities as being firm-specific and developed over time (see: Barney, J.B. and Hansen, M.H. (1994) 'Trustworthiness as a Source of Competitive Advantage,' *Strategic Management Journal* 15: 175–190; Collis, D.J. and Montgomery, C.A. (1995) 'Competing on Resources: Strategy in the 1990s,' *Harvard Business Review* July-August, 118–128) thus they cannot be disentangled from the firm's past experience and overall skills and knowledge of the management team (see: Amit, R. and Schoemaker, P.J.H. (1993) 'Strategic Assets and Organizational

Rent,' *Strategic Management Journal* 14: 33–46; Mahoney, J.T. and Pandian, J.R. (1992) 'The Resource-Based View Within the Conversation of Strategic Management,' *Strategic Management Journal* 13: 363–380).

Investments in capabilities tend to be irreversible and highly path-dependent, placing firms on the trajectory of capability development (see: Teece *et al.* (1997) 'Dynamic Capabilities and Strategic Management,' *Strategic Management Journal* **18**(70): 509–533).

15. Henry Mintzberg ((1973) *The Nature of Managerial Work,* New York: Harper & Row) indicates that senior managers recognize two aspects of strategy. Intended strategy is a rational planning response to competitive conditions in the environment and a course of action to respond. 'Emergent strategy' arises at various levels of the organization as people search for opportunities and engage in solving new or unexpected problems which may deviate from what was originally intended.

16. Miles and Snow ((1978) *Organizational Strategy, Structure and Process,* New York: McGraw-Hill) noted that the complexity of the strategy process can be somewhat simplified by searching for patterns in the behaviour of organizations. Observed patterns of emergent behaviour can be used to describe the underlying processes of organizational adaptation.

17. Van de Ven, A. (1983) 'Research on Organization Innovation,' School of Management, University of Minnesota and Hedburg, B.L.T., Nystrom, P.C. and Starbuck, W.H. (1976) 'Camping on Seesaws: Prescriptions for a Self-Designing Organization,' *Adminstrative Science Quarterly* 21: 45–65.

18. Porter ((1980) *Competitive Strategy,* New York: Free Press) characterizes two generic strategies that follow this pattern: differentiation strategy endeavours to offer customers unique products or services and is characterized by a proactive, external orientation; cost leadership strategy endeavours to create internal efficiency through risk minimization and cost efficiency and is characterized by a reactive, internal orientation.

19. Cameron ((1986) 'A Study of Organizational Effectiveness and Its Predictors,' *Management Science* **32**(1): 87–111, January) proved this point in his comparison of proactive and reactive managerial strategies. He found that proactive strategies and those with an external emphasis have a higher success rate than internal and reactive strategies.

20. Cameron ((1986) 'A Study of Organizational Effectiveness and Its Predictors,' *Management Science* **32**(1): 87–111, January) found that managers must implement a variety of strategies to ensure

effectiveness over time. Multifaceted managerial strategies were also more likely to lead to effectiveness than monolithic strategies.

21. From our study sample of 1,009 senior managers, we identified 169 senior management teams (SMT). Scores from managers within the same SMT were averaged to produce aggregate SMT scores. We next used a statistical cluster analysis technique to determine if there were meaningful groups of companies who achieved different strategic priorities at different levels. 'Cluster analysis' is a multivariate statistical procedure that starts with a data set containing information about a sample of entities and attempts to reorganize these entities into relatively homogeneous groups. Although several clustering algorithms exist, Ward's minimum variance criterion was chosen for this analysis based on its widespread use in social science research and its past use in strategic group analysis (see: Punj, G. and Stewart, D.W. (1983) 'Cluster Analysis in Marketing Research: Review and Suggestions for Application,' *Journal of Marketing Research*, **20**(3): 134–148; Harrigan, K.R. (1985) 'An Application of Clustering for Strategic Group Analysis,' *Strategic Management Journal*, **6**(3): 55–73). Although no formal criteria exist for determining the number of appropriate clusters, it is best to select the number of clusters based on *a priori* theory (see: Thomas, H. and Venkatraman, N. (1988) 'Research on Strategic Groups: Progress and Prognosis,' *Journal of Management Studies* **25**(6): 537–554). This is commonly referred to as descriptive validity of the cluster. Namely, can the resulting cluster structure be meaningfully labelled and do the resultant clusters have implications for existing or new theory? Our theory initially drove us to suspect that either two or three strategic priority grouping would exist. Based on past researchers such as Cameron ((1983) 'Strategic Responses to Conditions of Decline: Higher Education and the Private Sector,' *Journal of Higher Education* 54: 359–380) and Porter ((1980) *Competitive Strategy*, New York: Free Press) we might suspect that two discrete groups (proactive and reactive) would emerge. However, based on other prominent strategists such as Miles and Snow ((1978) *Organizational Strategy, Structure and Process*, New York: McGraw-Hill) we might anticipate that three groups (prospectors, analysers and defenders) would be found. The cluster analysis revealed that the three-cluster solution was most appropriate. ANOVA tests were run between the three cluster groups on IO and business performance. Tests showed significant statistical differences at the 0.05 level: Group 1 (the Growers—with the highest proactive bias) were significantly different from Group 2 (the Makeovers—with a moderate proactive bias) and Group 3 (the Cutters—with a reactive bias). Growers had statistically significant higher levels of IO and business performance compared to the other two groups. Although numerical

differences existed in the means of Cutters and Makeovers, these differences were not statistically significant.

22. Our finding of the existence of three cluster groups is consistent with Miles and Snow's ((1978) *Organizational Strategy, Structure and Process*, New York: McGraw-Hill) strategy types—prospectors, defenders and analysers—which differed with respect to risk disposition, innovativeness and operational efficiencies. Prospectors, like our Growers, have a proactive bias and exploit new business opportunities, facilitate innovation and focus on market and customer effectiveness rather than internal efficiencies. They are risk-takers, exhibit loose resource control and are less focused on cost efficiencies. Higher degrees of 'organizational slack' in these companies are permitted to facilitate innovation. Defenders, like our Cutters, have a reactive bias and resort to more stable environments with low risk, investing heavily in efficiency and tight resource control. They resort to price-cutting, employing more efficient logistical systems and making changes in production operations that lower costs. 'Organizational slack' is kept low with tight management control over operations. Analysers, like our Makeovers, are moderately proactive, and represent a hybrid of prospector and defender types. They typically make fewer and slower product/market changes than prospectors but are less committed to stability and efficiency than defenders. They typically minimize risk while maximizing the opportunities for profit. Hambrick's ((1983) 'Some Tests of the Effectiveness and Functional Attributes of Miles and Snow's Strategic Types,' *Academy of Management Journal* 26: 5–26) research found an entrepreneurial orientation of prospectors and an efficiency orientation of defenders, and Segars, Grover and Kettinger confirmed that firms exhibited characteristics of prospectors, defenders and analysers (see: Segars, A.H., Grover, V. and Kettinger, W.J. (1994) 'Strategic Users of Information Technology: A Longitudinal Analysis of Organizational Strategy and Performance,' *Journal of Strategic Information Systems* 3(4): 261–288).

23. While Cameron ((1983) 'Strategic Responses to Conditions of Decline: Higher Education and the Private Sector,' *Journal of Higher Education* 54: 359–380) found that proactive strategies generally produce higher business performance benefits, Hambrick ((1983) 'Some Tests of the Effectiveness and Functional Attributes of Miles and Snow's Strategic Types,' *Academy of Management Journal* 26: 5–26) found differences in performance tendencies among Miles and Snow's ((1978) *Organizational Strategy, Structure and Process*, New York: McGraw-Hill) three typologies. Based on our findings, it appears that Growers are similar to Miles and Snow's prospectors, having developed sufficient organizational slack which permits them to actively pursue strategies of

innovation, product growth and market focus while being less risk-adverse. When this Growers strategy is well executed it results in higher performance that in turn delivers additional slack resources. It appears that Makeovers have not yet achieved this level of business performance success and have, therefore, not developed slack resources.

24. Figure 7.8 provides us with the percentage allocation of each business capability of our three strategy groups. These percentages are the average numbers of all senior management teams that fall into one of the respective clusters. They represent the average 'profile' of a particular cluster.

25. Oliver argued that organizational decisions and activities are influenced by the social context, firm traditions and network ties (see: Oliver, C. (1997) 'Sustainable Competitive Advantage: Combining Institutional and Resource-Based Views,' *Strategic Management Journal* **18**(9): 697–713).

Resource and capability development requires not only an internally, but an externally, supportive environment. We would therefore expect to see an external relationship capability higher in Growers than in either Cutters or Makeovers given their strategic bias, which focuses more on external than internal strategic priorities.

26. It should be noted that the people capability was the highest in all three strategies. Past research would suggest several possible explanations: network analysis theory argues that firm strengths are embedded in human relationships and social structures (see: Hofstede, G. (1980) *Culture's Consequences: International Differences in Work-Related Values*, California: Sage Hills; Eisenhardt, K.M. and Schoohoven, C.B. (1996) 'Resource-based View of Strategic Alliances Formation: Strategic and Social Effects in Entrepreneurial Firms,' *Organization Science* **7**(2): 136–150; and Uzzi, B. (1997) 'Social Structure and Competition in Interfirm Networks: The Paradox of Embeddedness,' *Adminstrative Science Quarterly* **42**: 35–67). Social networks provide many information benefits in terms of access to information that might otherwise be unavailable, early exposure to information allowing pre-emptive action, better filtering of irrelevant information and legitimization of information (Burt, R.S. (1997) 'The Contingent Value of Social Capital,' *Administrative Science Quarterly* **42**: 339–365).

27. Marchand, D. (2000) 'The Rise of Cemex: Global Growth Through Superior Information Capabilities and Creative e-Business Strategies,' Lausanne, Switzerland: International Institute for Management Development (IMD). Case study.

8

FUTURE BUSINESS STRATEGY, THE IC MAXIMIZATION EFFECT AND COMPETING WITH INFORMATION

Information asymmetries exist whenever a company leverages information about customers, competitors and operations that is unusable or unavailable to its competitors. A valid illustration of this point was Dell Computers' ability in the 1990s to distinguish itself as the premier direct PC retailer to the corporate community worldwide.

Dell Computer Corporation[1]

Michael Dell's initial strategy was not to maintain a physical storefront, but to focus primarily on corporate purchasing through a combination of channels, including a direct sales force, call centre sales and services and the Internet. Dell recognized early that exploiting a direct model of doing business with customers meant the mass customization of products built on unique customer information and delivering superior customer service. These business capabilities would create significant customer loyalty and lock-in. Corporate customers (and consumers) would re-order when the next generation of PC chips from Intel or the next major software version from Microsoft were released, typically every 18 to 24 months. Over 10 years, this strategy permitted Dell to achieve enormous growth and profitability, to develop a superior company reputation, to increase market share against dominant players like Compaq, and to innovate with new products and services. Dell won an industry leadership position in a fiercely competitive industry.

However, industry leadership in competing with information is a temporary state and must be continuously re-won. Today's information advantage may become tomorrow's competitive necessity. For example, the information asymmetry that Dell established in its industry was at first scarcely recognized by the likes of Compaq, Hewlett-Packard and IBM. But eventually, recognition grew until in today's e-business-based direct sales marketplace, Dell's model is the primary business model for PC marketing and sales. IBM, HP, and Compaq have added direct sales capabilities via the Internet to supplement their sales force and wholesaler, distributor and retail channels. The competitive advantage that Dell once possessed is now threatened.

Dell has sought to renew its industry leadership by attempting to establish a second information asymmetry through selling peripheral products and services directly and with partners such as Amazon, which offers Internet services to business customers and consumers. The future will tell whether this second attempt to create information asymmetry will offer a sustainable competitive advantage.

As the Dell example above illustrates, we have entered an era in which changes in the use and importance of information, regardless of industry, require senior executives to think in entirely new ways about leveraging their competitive, customer and operational information. New mind-sets are necessary not only to add e-business capabilities to existing strategy, but also—even more importantly—to enable the company to leapfrog into new competitive positions of industry leadership.[2] Industry leaders look beyond performance today to assess the capabilities of the firm to handle challenges in information use that loom in the future.

Internet and electronic markets are beginning to drive industry shifts in financial services, retailing and other industries in which past information advantages enjoyed by companies with their customers, suppliers and partners are dwindling. As these changes have accelerated across services and manufacturing industries, every business has become an 'information business'. Future industry leadership depends on building and using information capabilities to create and sustain customer relationships, to detect competitive trends before other players do and to achieve operational efficiencies in time, cost and control.

Senior managers are now heeding the call and developing information-oriented strategies that direct their companies down a path that places information capabilities centre stage in their market and organizational behaviour. Pursuing this path will lead many managers in new directions and to new ways of thinking about relationships between business capabilities. Companies will seek to invent new ways to establish information asymmetries in the competitive marketplace. They will redesign organizational structures to control strategic decision-making centrally, but permit a mobile workforce to contribute remotely in multiple time zones and geographic locations. And they will establish capabilities to seamlessly exploit ever-accelerating IT opportunities in a smarter and faster way than competitors. A prerequisite of future industry leadership will be the plans that senior managers put in place today concerning how their company will compete in using information tomorrow.

What steps must companies take to work toward creating these information asymmetries? In this chapter we build on what we discussed in Chapter 7 to explore how senior managers in each of the three strategy groups envisage their future, and how they intend to leverage their investment in IC. We examine trade-offs within the business capability mix that senior managers may make in the future, and we introduce the IC maximization effect, which allows managers to save on or enhance other business capabilities. Last, we show that creating a tactical plan for the way a company can compete with information can help to drive the development of information capabilities and leverage the IC maximization effect for the future.

A STRATEGIC LOOK TO THE FUTURE

In Chapter 7, we found that companies fall into one of three strategy groups. Growers, the highest business performers, create business value through a proactive strategy of creating new business opportunities and delighting customers, combined with a business capability mix that focuses on higher investments in IC and external relationships. In contrast, Cutters rely on a reactive strategy that combines cost-cutting and risk management with a business capability mix that focuses on higher investments in maintaining a rigid organizational structure and business process efficiencies. Makeovers are in transition. Although they have begun to move toward a proactive strategic bias and improve their investment in IC, their business capability investment more closely mimics that of Cutters, rather than that of Growers—unable to leverage their capability mix, they have yet to achieve superior performance. Given the results of the emergent strategy comparison of the three groups in Chapter 7 (see Figure 7.7 on p. 185), we were interested to see how each group viewed changes to future capability mixes.

We asked senior managers to assign percentages (to make a total of 100 per cent) to relative contributions of each of the five business capabilities to the realization of its strategic priorities over the next five years. We found that, in the future, all three groups intend to follow very similar business capability mixes. As Figure 8.1 shows, each group has a similar capability mix, at consistent levels for each capability. It appears that senior executives from all three strategy groups realize the importance of information capabilities—all three groups have allocated most to IC (> 30 per cent) in the future. The lowest capability investment for all three groups is in organizational structure changes (< 10 per cent). Despite their past strategic paths, Growers, Makeovers and Cutters have come to the same conclusion regarding the strategy that they believe will result in the best business performance.[3] Information capabilities are at the heart of this strategy.

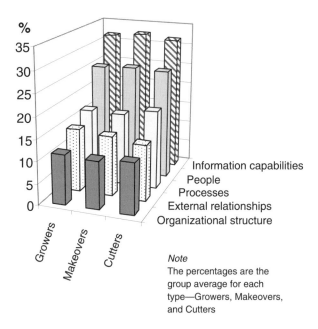

Figure 8.1: The capability mix in Growers, Makeovers and Cutters for future strategy

Increases in investment in information resources mean decreases in investment in other capabilities. How do companies plan to deal with the lack of resources for these other capabilities? We believe that there is a fundamental relationship between IC and other business capabilities that should be considered by managers when deciding which business capabilities to develop for the future. We call this the IC maximization effect.

DEFINING THE IC MAXIMIZATION EFFECT

Before the Information Revolution, companies had to find physical solutions to reaching customers, moving products or transferring paper-based information on customers or products. These companies had to simplify reporting structures, creating clear structural hierarchies to effectively coordinate communication, monitor contractual relationships and streamline the searching mechanism for people, information and knowledge. Decision rights resided primarily with a central authority and were passed down in vertical organizational structures.[4] Non-automated processes were defined around specific tasks associated with people and functions. Complex reporting and contractual structures such as those associated with business entities in a company's value chain were difficult to manage, and most often these structures were brought in-house, within the corporate boundaries, to minimize coordination costs.

The advent of information technologies and sophisticated information management practices, however, allowed managers to decrease their dependence on these traditional hierarchical organization structures, manual processes and relationships not only with people, but also with other business entities outside the organization. IT alleviated companies of the rigid organizational hierarchies needed to manage increasingly complex relationships. Flatter, networked structures that capitalized on local knowledge combined with shared corporate data began to emerge with the greater decentralization of decision-making and increased outsourcing of external relationships with customers, suppliers and partners.[5]

From the profiles of our strategy clusters introduced in Chapter 7, we can see these differences illustrated between Growers and Cutters. At the one extreme, Growers, who focus more heavily on the external environment to create business opportunities and satisfy customers, have more complex coordination and communication mechanisms to manage. They have relied on developing IC and stronger external relationships to overcome the problems associated with managing these more complex coordination structures and build in more participatory decision-making that capitalizes on local knowledge, information sharing and network-based controls. At the other extreme, Cutters seek to cut costs and minimize risk by streamlining organizational structures and processes to make them even more cost-efficient. A consequence of this streamlining is that Cutters are forced to maintain simpler coordination and communication mechanisms, through more centralized decision-making and the rationalization of production and financial costs.[6]

In essence, Growers have 'substituted' information technology, the associated information management practices, and workforce behaviours to support information use for the traditional hierarchical organizational structures that were needed in the past to ensure communication of accurate information and maintain control of operations.

The 'substitution' of capabilities is well-recognized in resource-based theory. According to scholars, substitution refers to the use of alternative resources or capabilities to achieve a goal or to produce outcomes which make that goal obsolete. This research recognizes that the substitutability of company capabilities and resources can result in a competitive advantage.[7] Quantitative research has shown not only that IT capital is a net substitute for both ordinary capital and labour, but that the ability of companies to take advantage of improvements in IC is determined in part by the substitutability of IC for these other factors of production.[8] Within this body of research, capability substitution can create sustained competitive advantage if competing companies cannot easily replicate a similar capability mix.[9]

When speaking to managers about current and future strategy during case study interviews, we observed that the greatest strategic changes in many companies seemed to be occurring to IC, indicating some level of capability substitution between IC and other business capabilities.

How do companies use information capabilities to substitute for other business capabilities?

To examine how companies use IC to substitute for other business capabilities, we looked at the differences between the past and future capability mixes of Growers, Makeovers and Cutters. We can represent this effect graphically by comparing percentage changes between past and future capability allocations in Figure 8.2. Bars appearing above the zero line indicate expectations of future percentage increases in that capability; bars below the zero line indicate expectations of future decreases in that capability in percentage points. We can see that all three groups intend to increase the contribution of IC to their capability mix by the greatest amount (> +5 per cent), while decreasing organizational structure by the greatest amount (> –3 per cent). All other allocations change by less than 2 per cent. This suggests that there is a degree of substitution of IC for organizational structure, as well as for other business capabilities to some extent. Although all three groups seem to substitute IC for organizational structure in the future, Cutters intend to substitute IC (> +8 per cent) for

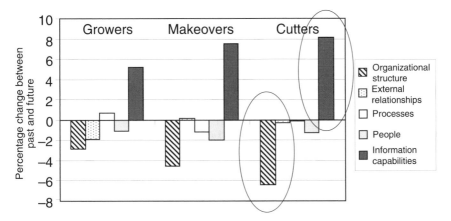

Figure 8.2: Information capabilities can save on or enhance other capabilities

organizational structure (< –6 per cent) to the greatest degree of the three groups. Growers substitute IC (> +5 per cent) for external relationships (–2 per cent) to the greatest degree of the three groups.

This is the IC maximization effect. Senior managers recognize that given limited resources they must make a rational choice to substitute IC for other business capabilities. Why is the IC maximization effect important for managers? Because a company's ability to substitute IC for its other capabilities allows it to either save on resources or to enhance existing capabilities.[10] Strategy researchers have found that the IC maximization effect confers several important benefits—savings (financial, resource or investment) and enhancements of both products and services.

The first benefit that investment in IC provides to a company is time savings by lowering costs of coordination. Within management research, IC has been found to lower coordination and transaction costs in three areas: communicating, searching and monitoring. For example, IC can improve communication by decreasing information overload thus allowing information to be collected centrally, processed by a single decision-maker and distributed throughout the company in the form of relatively simple commands.[11] Development of IC makes information processing less costly by creating common 'social conventions' and standard ways of collecting and communicating information that allow for more efficient management of projects and control of functional tasks. IC can lower the cost of knowledge transmission and reallocate it to decision-makers.[12] IC can reduce cost to companies by facilitating the searching costs associated with finding new information, filling job vacancies or finding appropriate solutions to problems. In addition, IC can decrease risk in contractual dealings by improving control over processes. Cost reductions in processes and performance measurement can be attained through more standard and real-time monitoring, thus improving decentralized decision-making.

IC maximization can also provide cost savings by substituting or 'making up' for underinvestment in other capabilities.[13] We can see this at work particularly with the advent of the Internet, where a lack of a global presence can be more readily overcome through web technologies that provide reach in international markets. In this case, IC makes up for a company's underinvestment in external relationships that could also provide a global reach of products and services.

The second idea associated with the benefit afforded by the IC maximization effect concerns how IC can enhance other capabilities.[14] In this case, performance improvements come not from cost saving associated with IC, but from the improvements associated with leveraging other capabilities. Management research shows that reallocating investment to IC can create substantial increases in productivity and performance of other capabilities. For example, IC can enhance communication networks among its people for better decision-making by facilitating communication to a greater number of people through a simple e-mail system, or a centralized project database can enhance employee knowledge to improve company awareness.

Figure 8.3 describes some scenarios in which IC can save on or enhance one or all of the other four business capabilities within an organization. For example, while IC can save on the number of people needed to complete difficult tasks, it can also enhance people's jobs by providing them with access to information and knowledge to improve their decision-making capability. Skills training can be improved by standardizing information and making it available through web technologies.

IC may be able to save on the need for highly structured, hierarchical reporting to facilitate effective communication and responsibility delineation. This freeing of structural boundaries—in virtual networks and virtual communities, for example—may in turn help to enhance the strategic priority of creating new business opportunities by encouraging the sharing and development of ideas between different management functions. In another company, supplementing traditional process tasks with information capabilities may enhance the company's ability to reduce costs, or information capabilities may be used to save on people.

Companies that can actually carry out readjustments in their capability mixes (resembling Growers) have much to gain. Today, with digital

IC	People (PL)	Processes (P)	Organizational structure (OS)	External relationships (ER)
Bottom line saves	• Knowledge is used more efficiently • Increased output • Less direct management • Fewer people needed	• Process simplification • Process standardization • Reduction in number of processes • Cycle time improvement • Just in time (JIT) delivery	• More local decision-making and more centralized control and coordination • Improved monitoring • Flatter OS • Less rigid OS	• Direct relationship with customer • Fewer suppliers • Less interface overhead • Lower coordination cost
Top line enhances	• Better business knowledge spread through the workforce • Makes work more interesting	• Make to order • Reconfigurable processes • Tight process links with other companies	• More virtual teams possible • OS quicker to change • More value in each layer/node	• Better relationships with suppliers/ delivery companies • Better servicing • Empower customer

Figure 8.3: The IC maximization effect

representation of information and access to this information from almost everywhere by means of IT-enabled systems, companies can substitute information for the movement of people, paper and products across geographical areas, time zones, markets and organizational boundaries. They can save on the need for rigid organizational structures with more flexible virtual networks of people, and replace physical processes with electronic ones.

What is the implication of this for senior managers' choices for investing in future business capabilities? Investment in information capabilities will not simply lead to more effective information use. It will also save on or enhance the other four business capabilities. The bottom line is that employee productivity, cost savings, partner relationships and process efficiency can all be improved through investment in information capabilities.[15] Let's look at how companies that have made the necessary changes to their business capability mixes are capitalizing on the IC maximization effect.

You Can Substitute Rigid Organizational Structure with IC

If you are a member of a large company, you have probably experienced a major restructuring programme within the last five years. Reductions in the number of middle management positions to attain a flatter organizational structure have often resulted in increased workloads for the remaining workforce. In many cases, this will have occurred without the parallel development of substitute ways to ease disruptions in communication hierarchies, networks and knowledge areas when many of these managers left the company.

The IC maximization effect has been shown to affect several aspects of organizational structure. First, IC allows for greater decentralization of decision authority by decreasing the cost of knowledge transmission and allowing the company to take better advantage of local information while maintaining overall corporate control. This not only affects a firm's information structure by reducing the burden of 'information overload' on centralized decision-makers, but encourages the use of teams over individual work.[16] Second, IC can decrease the need for vertical integration, affecting both the size and form of network structure available to the company.[17]

Our case research has shown that both start-up and established companies have been able to substitute IC for organizational structure, or hierarchy, by clarifying responsibilities and decision rights and moving some operations outside the organization.

SkandiaBanken

When designing a new direct banking venture to open for business in 1994, senior managers were more interested in making their own jobs more effective through information availability than in hiring many layers of managers and employees to execute responsibilities. Although business unit and area responsibilities were clearly defined and fell within the remit of senior managers, an overriding belief in transparency as a key behavioural value, along with open IT systems and well-defined information management processes, eliminated the need for further management layers. Secretarial positions were reduced to improve information flows and face-to-face communication among managers. Although all 250 employees were housed in one office building, the managing director insisted that the company maintain a formal information system to ensure easy and open access to company, employee and business unit information. This improved management control with wider spans of influence. Information in the formal information system was seen as accurate and up-to-date and was therefore trusted by SkandiaBanken employees.

SkandiaBanken also eliminated the possibility of being locked in to specific banking suppliers by interfacing its IT systems with financial industry systems and databases, instead of having to go through information middlemen, which would require further internal management of people and processes. In essence they are using IC to facilitate a market-based, as opposed to hierarchically-based, business model.

There is no doubt that start-up companies have the advantage of being able to avoid organizational hierarchies from the beginning. However, they too face similar issues as they mature. The Motley Fool, launched in 1996, is a fast-growing start-up in Virginia in the United States. It delivers simplified financial information—with a sense of humour—to about two million people via the Internet. Growing from 15 employees to more than 270 today, its challenge is to maintain its loose organizational structure through continued development of strong information capabilities.[18] Many established companies have been able to successfully substitute IC for organizational structure in their business. Oticon is a Danish company that has been making hearing aids for nearly a century. In 1988, faced with heavy losses, the company revolutionized the way it did business.[19]

First Oticon took down the walls—literally. All 150 employees were brought together to work in an open environment, without having assigned offices or desks. Then the company eliminated all titles, departments and divisions. People were assigned jobs on projects, and all work was done by temporary teams that were assembled when everyone gathered, with their files, in the same corner.

While Oticon was getting rid of its formal structure, it invested in a leading-edge computer system, with communication links to ensure frequent informal contacts between the Copenhagen headquarters and its operations in Europe and the United States. The company was an early adopter of e-mail and made heavy use of video-conferencing.

This organizational revolution, based on new patterns of information exchange, was a clear success. Product development took place more quickly, and Oticon became the first company to bring out digital hearing aids. The resulting financial success allowed the company to launch a number of takeovers, and by 1998 Oticon had become the world's third largest player in the hearing-care business.

You Can Enhance Processes with IC

Many companies have been able to use IC to break through boundaries or coordinate similar process tasks across functions and channels. The automation of common activities and the ability of a company to transform physical processes into virtual processes provide it with powerful ways to integrate once disparate and discrete functions. For example, electronic data interchange (EDI), efficient customer response (ECR) and continuous product replenishment (CPR) systems result in the substitution of IC for disjointed or manual business processes. IC substitutes for those processes that can be automated to simplify complex human-assisted tasks associated with channel or functional coordination and control.[20]

Banco Bilbao Vizcaya (BBV)

BBV wants to convince its customers to move to cheaper, electronic channels for their banking transactions, with a view to leveraging the branches as places to service and sell to individual customers. The bank has called this programme 'transactional migration'. It not only involves reducing transactional costs, but also eliminating back- and front-office functions at the branch level and training every branch employee as an account manager or customer representative to sell and service customers. Branches will become the centre of the value-adding activities—the other channels will support the branches. The account managers and customer reps will be trained to be proactive and follow up on customers' electronic operations. The graph in Figure 8.4 shows how the bank is considering transforming its branches.

Transactional migration and branch transformation do not mean losing contact with the customer—the programme is careful to emphasize the

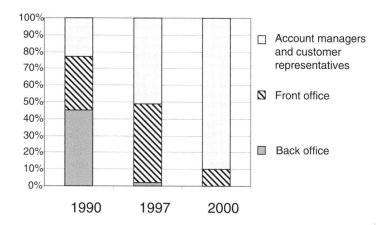

Figure 8.4:   BBV's branch transformation

importance of the branch in contacting the customer. As the head of retail banking pointed out:

> Retail banking is 'high-tech and high touch'. It's high-tech because the bank and the branch use every available technology in IT and telecommunications to enable the employees to manage their business; it's high touch because the customers need to have the sensation of being managed by people. The selling contact with the customer should be done by a person, not a machine.

Other companies, such as British Petroleum (BP), have capitalized on IC for internal process enhancements.[21] In 1994, its exploration and production company, BPX, felt that traditional information-sharing processes (documents, databases and meetings) were inadequate for effective problem-solving. The unit equipped each manager with a PC with video-conferencing equipment, multimedia e-mail, shared applications, a scanner and an electronic whiteboard. Sixty per cent of the project budget was dedicated to behavioural coaching to support this open approach to information exchange and management. This 'virtual teamworking' was such a success (with savings of up to $30 million in the first year) that the company made it available to all BP companies in 70 countries.

You Can Save on People with IC

The IC maximization effect also provides managers with the ability to save human capital and enhance people's effectiveness.[22] The effect might be an enhancement of current job roles by automating routine tasks, or cost savings through a reduction in redundant roles. IC can improve the ability of managers to monitor work, and improve incentives and performance measurements. Research has shown that companies that extensively use IC investments have a greater reliance on people skills and human capital.[23] As we saw in Chapter 6, SkandiaBanken's development of its information capabilities has allowed systematic and easy remote monitoring of employee performance. Yet greater decentralization of decision rights in a company encourages not only objective, but also more 'subjective', incentives based on unobservable tasks and decisions associated with teamwork. IC enables continuous incentive and training systems, as well as allowing the capture of employee knowledge in order to make it explicit for others to use throughout the company.

Egon Zehnder International

Established in 1964, Egon Zehnder International, based in Zurich, Switzerland, has become one of the best senior executive search firms in the world. It employs over 280 professional consultants in 55 locations, covering all major economies worldwide. Besides senior executive search consulting, it offers management appraisal studies and searches for board members and non-executive directors.

The company's chief financial officer (CFO) commented:

> Our whole business revolves around information. As an executive search firm, we work for clients all over the world—and they require global coverage and assistance in finding the right candidates for their global companies. All of our employees need to be able to access all the information available on a particular client—the company, industry, history, past searches and the like—as well as the possible candidates around the world.

To be able to access all information worldwide, Egon Zehnder uses a global system based on a distributed customized application database. A consultant noted:

> This system organizes information about past engagements in a very intuitive way. Before this system was in place, if I had to manage a new account, I had to call all our worldwide offices to see if our company had previously worked with the client. Now I can get this information on our centrally held consolidated database.

Egon Zehnder is able to save on people with IC in an efficient and effective way, using its distributed information management system. There are two major benefits:

- The company saves on consultant time, since it is much easier and quicker for a consultant to gather information worldwide.
- Customer information is retained inside the company. Before the system was in place, when a consultant left the company, all the information about his or her accounts and contacts would leave as well.

This story highlights a successful saving on people with information capabilities. However, Egon Zehnder had to go through various phases of implementation. 'Our first version, a pilot, was not developed with our consultants, and nobody in the company was using it. Then we changed the way we organized the information and we started rewarding people for entering information, and everything changed,' said the company's CFO. The company's senior managers became aware that information capabilities had to be well planned and had to follow the consultant's expectations about information use.

Skandia AFS[24]

Another company that has effectively substituted information capabilities for people is Skandia Assurance and Financial Services (Skandia AFS), a division of Sweden's Skandia Group. Skandia AFS manages over $85 billion in assets globally, mainly tax-advantaged long-term savings products. It has 200 offices in 24 countries.

During the early 1990s, Skandia AFS developed innovative ways of systematically assessing and managing the company's intellectual capital. As part of these efforts, managers devised new indicators for improving the visibility of knowledge assets. They also sought new ways of capturing and packaging these assets for transfer to others, as well as to cultivate them through training and information-sharing. They aimed at leveraging the knowledge of employees through rapid recycling of knowledge and increased commercialization.

In addition to a strong emphasis on leadership and values such as employee empowerment, Skandia AFS began to build knowledge-sharing tools that would support information collection and sharing among AFS companies. An application of the knowledge-sharing benefits of Skandia AFS's information technology investment was the prototype system used to speed the opening of offices in new country markets. The prototype consisted of a composite of standardized administrative modules—such as accounting procedures, predesigned products, information about funds management and underwriting, policy letters and pay-out information—which could be installed in new offices. It was estimated that prototypes reduced start-up time for new offices in new markets by as much as 50 per cent by decreasing the time needed to customize products for the local market. In essence, by sharing knowledge through greater use of IT systems, the office prototype reduced the number of people required to start up a new Skandia AFS office.

As this process accelerated, the learning and cost reduction benefits became even more apparent. As the chief information officer (CIO) noted:

> If you compare Switzerland, Germany and Austria—three similar offices—each one took less time to set up than the previous one. I would say that in terms of a balance between the contribution of people and the prototype in setting up a new office, it is now much less than 50:50. This is because we have successfully converted human capital into structural capital (the prototype system), which can be recycled.

You Can Enhance External Relationships with IC

If you can manage information about external relationships well, you don't always have to bring these resources in-house or acquire them. This is the result of using IC to enhance external relationships to better coordinate and communicate with suppliers, partners and customers.[25] IC can improve coordination and reduce the costs associated with mergers and acquisitions. IC allows for market-based solutions rather than hierarchical ones. Finally, IC allows for business diversification by improving coordination mechanisms.[26]

Wal-Mart, the giant US retailer, is one classic example of the use of IC to operate within a broader coalition of allies, venture partners and other affiliates. A pioneer in the use of electronic data interchange, Wal-Mart was able to change adversarial relationships with many suppliers into win–win collaborative relationships through better inventory management and replenishment systems.[27]

Skandia AFS[28]

Skandia Assurance and Financial Services (Skandia AFS) is a good example of a company that has used IC to enhance its external relationships. It does this through its 'federative' organizational structure.

While Skandia AFS concentrates on product marketing, packaging and administration, fund development and management are handled by specialized alliance partners operating outside the company (see Figure 8.5). Local brokers and banks, which subsequently assume the investment risks, handle Skandia AFS's fund distribution. These alliance partners also provide products to a variety of Skandia AFS's competitors. The strategy rests

Figure 8.5: Skandia AFS business concept: specialists in cooperation

on Skandia AFS's ability to manage alliances effectively with its partners, both upstream and downstream, and to be the 'best in class' in product marketing, packaging and administration.

Skandia AFS's organizational concept enables the company to keep core staffing quite low. Its global growth model is described as a federative structure, in which the specialists in the organization are tied together through a common value system but operate autonomously to develop client-based solutions. Skandia AFS refers to this arrangement as an imaginary organization, alluding to 'imagination and creativity', as well as to its imaginary (invisible) organizational structure of concentric rings (see Figure 8.6).

At the centre is an executive committee of 8, followed by a layer of 79 core competence leaders—mainly executive teams around the world—who meet once a year at a strategic advisory board conference. Surrounding the core are 3,000 Skandia AFS staff members, including employees handling information technology, logistics and administration. Surrounding the staff are 92,000 alliance partners, including agents, banks, brokers and independent financial advisors (IFAs). These partners handle fund management, customer contact, distribution and 'relationship development'. The largest circle includes the company's 1 million customers, who are mainly individual savers around the world, with over 1.6 million contracts.

This network of alliances means that the full Skandia AFS network leverages 29 people for every full-time employee, allowing the company to handle its burgeoning customer base without adding significantly to its fixed cost base. Skandia AFS believes this federative concept also allows the company to benefit from the new ideas that arise from this extended network.

Skandia AFS leverages IC to manage this alliance network. Investing two to four times more than the industry average in IT systems, Skandia AFS's objective is to use an 'international electronic knowledge networking and sharing system', which knits together employees and alliance partners and

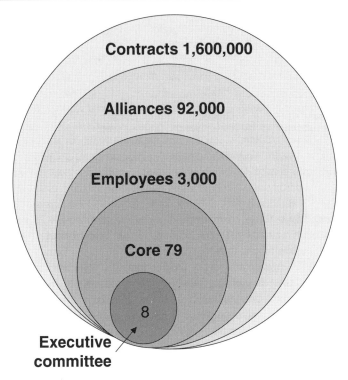

Figure 8.6:   Skandia AFS's federative structure

gives them access to knowledge inside and outside the company through a global network. The goal is to be able to enter the information system of any Skandia AFS partner from any other partner in order to transfer competencies. For example, Skandia's Assess system, which contains product and fund information, is used by over 15,000 brokers in the United States to show customers product attributes, as well as to print out applications on the spot for customers to sign in the broker's office.

Skandia AFS's management also focuses heavily on leadership and values to create an environment in which people's knowledge can be transformed into structural capital (information systems that capture and make explicit human expertise). Senior management wants to foster an organization with full 'work permits', in which people can collaborate freely in order to gain and share knowledge. The goal is to promote knowledge transparency, as opposed to mere knowledge transfer. In order to use their 'work permit', employees have to feel sufficiently empowered in their job. To monitor progress on how empowered employees feel, Skandia AFS includes several questions in its annual employee survey asking employees how much scope they believe they have to act—what they are allowed or not allowed to do. The result is an indicator—an empowerment index— that is subsequently included as an organization-wide indicator. Thus by leveraging information capabilities, Skandia AFS is able to enhance its external relationship capability across its alliance network, while increasing productivity and reducing the costs of coordination.

CLOSING THE INFORMATION CAPABILITIES GAP

As we have seen, Grower, Makeover and Cutter strategy groups have all recognized the importance of information capabilities and want to invest more heavily in IC than in other capabilities in the future. They all recognize and want to be able to attain the IC maximization effect. The ability of each strategy group to capitalize on the IC maximization effect, however, does not depend only on expressions of future intentions, but also on realistic assessments of how far a company has to go to attain the required information capabilities investment and consequent development.

All three strategy groups had different business capability contributions in the past. Figure 8.7 compares past contributions with future contributions for each business capability, displaying the gaps between past and future values. For example, Makeovers intend to increase the allocation to IC within their capability mix from 25 per cent to 33 per cent in the next five years, creating a gap of approximately 8 per cent.

What are the implications of the gaps? These gaps may represent required investment in money or time, or lack of organizational experience or human knowledge. All of these issues require change and attention in order for a company to be able to close the gaps. Larger gaps between past and intended future capability allocations will necessitate more radical changes in many aspects of the company. For example, as we can see in Figure 8.7, the largest changes to organizational structure will occur with Cutters, who have a larger gap than either Makeovers or Growers. This 'reduction' in organizational structure may mean some management reshuffling or cutbacks in some positions. Makeovers, for their part, who anticipate decreases in process allocation, may see less emphasis on business process re-engineering in the future.

The largest gaps for all three strategy groups occur between past and future information capabilities investment. Within these three groups, however, Cutters have the largest IC gap, intending to go from over 20 per cent to over 30 per cent within the next five years. Cutters, therefore, have the farthest to go in making the necessary changes to close the gap. The larger the gap, the greater the need for clear, tactical plans on how to make competitive use of new IC investments. This is because, as we have

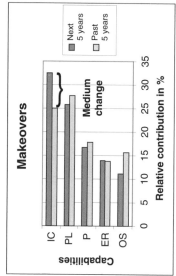

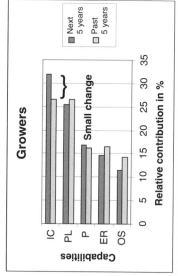

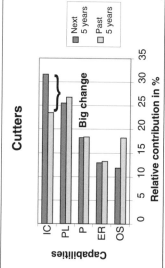

Figure 8.7: The business capabilities gaps

seen, intended strategies are often not achieved. Managerial values, attitudes and resources become more and more geared to the existing strategy such that changes are rare and painful.[29] Without a clear vision of how it intends to use IC to compete with information within its industry, a company is at greater risk of not investing in and attaining the development of future information capabilities to close the gap.

Growers have an easier journey ahead of them, since they have a smaller information capabilities gap than either Makeovers or Cutters. Companies in this group have already experienced some success in developing and leveraging information capabilities with competitive, customer and operational information, and will have an easier time instituting new changes in the future. These companies not only already possess the information capabilities on which to build, but they also understand how to create information asymmetry in the following ways:

- by gaining competitive foresight to exploit new markets
- by creating personalized products based on accurate customer information
- by improving the efficiency and efficacy of their business through the management of operational information.

As The Bank's strategy shows (see case study below), this company has a much harder—and longer—journey ahead to close the gaps between past and future information capabilities development compared with a Grower company, such as Dell Computers. This company, in contrast, already has well-developed information capabilities to continue to recreate information asymmetries.

Closing larger gaps in information capabilities is not impossible, but it does take time, and such companies must be prepared to follow the Dell example and develop clear plans through an IC strategy. Knowing where to go, and working out how to get there, are two different issues. In the next section we discuss how a company can develop plans to lead with information capabilities within its industry.

The Bank's Business Capability Mix

Despite the setbacks in The Bank's IC development (see Chapters 6 and 7), senior managers set their goals for the future. The second phase of restructuring, named profitable expansion, had four main objectives to:

- introduce new product strategies
- build multi-channel competence

- enhance sales effectiveness
- cross-sell financial service products.

As Figure 8.8 illustrates, attainment of these objectives would be based primarily on investments in IC, a large reduction in organizational structure and an increase in processes. The size of the gaps between past and future capability mixes indicates that The Bank has an enormous challenge ahead.

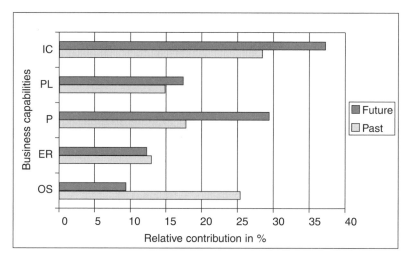

Figure 8.8:   Business capability mix for The Bank

Figure 8.9 shows at a glance how The Bank plans to decrease organizational structure by the greatest percentage. While it anticipates changes to IC, process changes in the future almost equal the IC change. With this heavy emphasis on future process development, it may not intend to leverage the IC maximization effect to the fullest extent.

Next steps

Changes to IC in the future will demand a clear, articulated plan to deal not only with an inadequte IT infrastucture, but also with the management of product and customer information. Most importantly, senior managers need to build a culture in which people within the company are transparent with their information, share it with others in The Bank, and proactively look for new ways of using information to create business value.

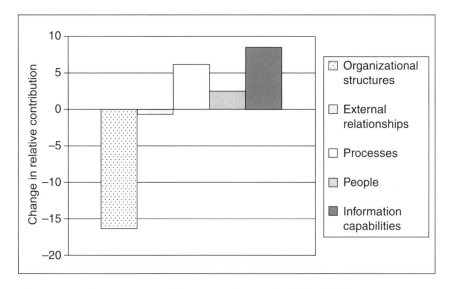

Figure 8.9: Business capability mix change for The Bank

LEVERAGING THE IC MAXIMIZATION EFFECT

How do senior managers initiate change within their organization to close the information capabilities gap and leverage the IC maximization effect? The following guidelines provide some suggestions for how to develop an IC strategic plan to address this issue within your organization.

Guideline 1:   Assess your company's future business capability mix

Before formulating an IC strategic plan, senior managers should assess the gaps between past and future capability mixes to define how their company views the future in terms of their capability mix and the extent of change required in the future.

Assessment of the Capability Mix Gap

Below is a worksheet to assist your company make such an assessment. To make a total of 100 per cent, assign a percentage to each of the following five business capabilities to represent its relative contribution to realizing strategic priorities in your company over the next five years. Place these values in the first column, 'future contribution', in the table below.

	Future	Past	Gap difference
Processes			
Organizational structure			
People			
External relationships			
Information capabilities			
TOTAL	**100%**	**100%**	

Copy your response from Chapter 7's Capability Mix Assessment into the second column, 'past contribution'.

Subtract the second column from the first column. This is your gap difference score. A positive score indicates an intended increase in that business capability in future. A negative score indicates a decrease in that business capability in future. For example: if a score is negative, effort must be focused on how to reduce a capability, substitute or switch it for something else, such as IC. If the score is positive, change efforts should be focused on using more of the capability or enhancing it.

Rearrange the gap difference scores in order from the highest to the lowest percentage change in the following table:

Gap difference

1.	
2.	
3.	
4.	
5.	

This should give you a snapshot of the areas where your company needs to focus effort.

Ask yourself the following questions:

- Does my company view investment in information capabilities as the leading business capability for the future?

- Will future changes to information capabilities require a concentrated effort within my company to ensure its development?
- What plans are currently in place to address the development of information capabilities? How do these need to be revised?

Guideline 2:   Examine the relationship between your company's strategic priorities and information capabilities as a key business capability, and ways to implement IC maximization.

How do senior managers initiate the shift in mind-set necessary for future change? A company must understand how it views strategy and its relationship to IC. As we have suggested in Chapter 7 and this chapter, there is a fundamental relationship between strategy and the ability of a company to build mature IO, create information asymmetry and improve business performance. Without an examination of all of these aspects, and an appreciation of how they interrelate with the existing mind-sets of senior managers, change is extremely difficult to address. Senior managers should ask themselves the following questions:

- Is your company a Grower, Makeover or Cutter?
- What is the right capability mix that your company should leverage to achieve strategic priorities in the future? What is the role of IC within this mix? Does your company assessment in Guideline 1 reflect this capability mix?
- Is your company currently thinking about how to implement the IC maximization effect? Are there opportunities now and in the future for your company to utilize IC to save on or enhance processes, organizational structure, people or external relationships?

As discussed in Chapter 2, the IO dashboard can be used as a guide for developing a future information capabilities strategy. As we will see in Chapter 9, a company-wide IO survey of all business units can also be used to identify IO pockets of excellence and IO black holes within the same company, to help guide senior managers in developing an information capabilities strategy.

Guideline 3:   Set the agenda for action, not just discussion

It is easier to talk about achieving strategies and capability mixes than it is to develop a path that leads to the implementation of these expectations. All too often, management discussions do not focus on realistic action plans.

Consider the European retailer of eyeglass lenses and frames discussed in Chapters 3 and 7. This company's major deficiency in its information capabilities over the past five years has been in IT practices and information management practices on a cross-regional basis. The problem is that so far senior managers have not done enough to implement a change programme to close the gap between past and future information capabilities development expectations. The IT director was ineffective in articulating a strategy and getting it accepted by group management, and was let go after only one year. No further investments in IT have been made to date, and no strategy for information capabilities has been articulated to improve the company's information management, even though aspirations remain high. These aspirations will remain wishful thinking until senior managers put together an action plan to address these issues.

Guideline 4:   Plan for industry leadership with competitive, customer and operational information

Although general improvements to information capabilities will improve your company's overall performance, fully leveraging the power of information to create information asymmetry within your industry can best be accomplished through tactical plans to compete with competitive, customer and operational information.

A close look at how your company plans to create industry leadership with these three types of information can help to drive the necessary IC investment and development to close the information capabilities gap and create a focused future information capabilities strategy.

Our research indicates that industry leadership in competing with information can be categorized in three ways:[30]

- Leadership in the use of competitive information—using information to compete more effectively in the marketplace. These leaders can acquire and use competitive information better than their rivals can to define a niche in the industry where others have tried and failed.
- Leadership in the use of customer information—using information about customers, as well as interacting with customers, to provide better products and services and retain their business. These leaders can gain and employ customer information to provide targeted knowledge about their products to meet the customers' emerging needs.
- Leadership in the use of operational information—using information that will boost operational effectiveness. These leaders can outpace competitors and satisfy customers with customized, faster and smarter ways of using operational information to respond to customer orders.

Competitive information

Companies become leaders with competitive information by becoming as close as possible to their customers, competitors, suppliers and partners.

ANX[31]

The Automotive Industry Action Group, made up of GM, Ford, Daimler-Chrysler, TRW, Bosch, Caterpillar, DANA and United Technology, established the Automobile Network Exchange (ANX) which was sold to Science Applications International Corp. in 1999. ANX is focused on moving most of the electronic interactions between thousands of automotive suppliers from private networks to a public data exchange infrastructure. This network allows parts suppliers, dealerships and financial service companies to share everything from CAD files and e-mail to order processing. The participants in ANX, who are competing in the same industry, recognized that, through collaboration, they could leverage the commonality of parts and designs and thus reduce costs. ANX is intended to enable 'coordination' in the motor industry as well as to increase the commitment and loyalty of motor industry players to each other. This also allows members to be more in tune with changes occurring within their competitive environments.

Customer information

Web technologies provide companies with innumerable opportunities to improve their customer information. Companies that traditionally have not had direct contact with the end consumer can now conduct direct one-on-one conversations with those consumers through the web. These technologies also provide ample opportunity to improve customer loyalty by providing customers with the information they require in a cost-effective, efficient manner.

Amazon, for example, has not only been able to capture customer behaviour, spending habits and preferences through its on-line bookstore, but has also been able to increase customer loyalty through partnerships with other major web sites. Like Amazon, many other web companies engage their customers in virtual communities around their products and services.

Operational information

Operational information focuses on how to improve the running of day to day business. Automation of routine tasks, such as American Express's automated telephone service for lost or stolen cards, not only improves operational efficiencies, but also improves employees' work performance by freeing them from these repetitive tasks. Collaborative software products, such as Lotus Notes, and the creation of intranets and extranets have also aided teamwork when members are separated by time and location. As we saw in Chapter 6, Norwich Union Direct's operational efficiency has been greatly improved by the sales reps' use of laptop computers, which are automatically updated with information received from the call centre's database, giving them an edge in service quality over competitors.

How should senior managers think about these three types of information? As a result of our research, we have produced Table 8.1, which presents some of the ways that companies with high IO have attained industry leadership in competing with competitive, customer and operational information. It can be used to kick-start your thinking about how you intend to compete with information within your own industry according to competitive realities. This table was developed through validated items on our survey instrument that show how senior managers view industry leadership in competing with information.

Table 8.1 Competing with information

What you can do	How you can do it
Competitive information	
Sense and anticipate competitive information to gain industry foresight and shape future industry strategy	Use scenarios whereby managers must continuously imagine future events or states that can evolve and to which they can respond
Collect and use information to ensure that partners are loyal by creating winning relationships wherever feasible	Use IC to engage in active cooperation with partners, either to strengthen partner links/loyalty or to co-opt potential competitors
Share information with suppliers by engaging in two-way information exchanges	Whenever possible, use extranets to work with suppliers, either by sharing information with them, by transacting business with them, or by collaborating with them on projects

What you can do	How you can do it
Exploit information from customers and partners to win new markets or operate more efficiently	Discover new business opportunities by continuously monitoring customer and partner information using new information technologies, such as data mining, intelligent agents, or web-based customer-tracking applications
Seek to eliminate unnecessary middlemen at all points in the value chain who do not add value to your company's information use	Examine all contacts with customers and suppliers and determine where you can establish direct digital links to reduce cost, increase choices, and create value

Customer information

Identify customer needs and personalize products	Attract customers to your company either physically or virtually and capture their personal needs directly or indirectly to offer customized products and services
Engage in two-way information exchanges with customers	Train your people to ask the right questions, either face to face or on-line
Enhance your products and services	Embed rich information in your products and services to increase their value
Push information to customers to encourage consumption	Use traditional media as well as web-casting and high bandwidth technology to push rich information to a broad customer base
Link customers in after-sales conversation	Develop a virtual community around your customers to increase loyalty and include rewards for continued interaction

(continued over)

Table 8.1 *(cont.)*

What you can do	How you can do it
Operational information	
Monitor information about business processes to make them more efficient	Implement a process information program to measure the efficiency of processes, to modify processes with changes in business practices, and to reward your people for improving your processes continuously
Push decisions in the organization down to the point at which the work takes place	Use IC either to fully automate routine and well-defined decisions or to employ automation to assist and monitor less skilled workers in making decisions that affect operational performance
Improve group work	Use IC to synchronize continuously, in real-time, the group or team activities in your company
Don't move things physically, move them virtually	Where feasible, cut high-cost travel, high-cost education and localized inventories by using teleconferencing, network-based learning, and network coordinated logistics

CONCLUSION

In the future, senior mangers will recognize that information capabilities will be even more important than in the past, as companies seek to leverage IC to save on or enhance other capabilities. The ability of a company to achieve the IC maximization effect will depend, to a large extent, on how far it has to go to develop these capabilities, i.e., the size of its IC gap. The determining factor will be a company's ability to implement a strategy that focuses on developing information capabilities in general, as well as its ability to focus company attention on how to compete with competitive, customer and operational information within its industry and competitive environment. In Chapter 9 we discuss the ways that companies can apply these ideas to multiple business units and/or in a global context.

NOTES

1. Marchand, D.A. and Boynton, A. (1999) 'Dell Direct in Europe: Delighting the Customer with Every Order,' Lausanne, Switzerland: International Institute for Management Development (IMD). Case study.

2. For example see: Hackbarth, G. and Kettinger, W.J. (2000) 'Building an eBusiness Strategy: Foundations of a Comprehensive Methodology,' *Information Systems Management*, Summer 2000; or Kettinger, W.J. and Hackbarth, G. (1999) 'Reaching the Next Level of E-Commerce: A Framework for Strategy Development,' London: *Financial Times*, invited article in Special Section on Mastering Information Management, 15 March.

3. While Miles and Snow (*Organizational Strategy, Structure and Process*, New York: McGraw-Hill, 1978) suggested that strategies tend to be enduring, Segars, Grover and Kettinger ('Strategic Users of Information Technology: A Longitudinal Analysis of Organizational Strategy and Performance,' *Journal of Strategic Information Systems* 3(4): 261–288, 1994) found that following the launch of a strategic information technology system, prospector and defenders changed their strategic orientation over time. These shifts were found to be rather dramatic, representing a fundamental change in strategic direction from earlier 'pre-system' operating philosophies. We witnessed a similar strategy mix shift in our findings in this study, with all three strategic priority groupings aspiring to assemble basically the same capability mix.

4. Dewan, Michael and Min found that firms which are more vertically integrated have lower IT investment given their simpler reporting and coordination structure. See: Dewan, S., Michael, S.C. and Min, C. (1998). 'Firm Characteristics and Investments in Information Technology: Scale and Scope Effects', *Information Systems Research* 9(3): 219–232, September. They go on to demonstrate that diversification within a company increases the need for coordination of assets across multiple lines of business and, therefore, increases the demand for more investments in IC.

5. Anand and Mendelson found that in firms in the information age, managers must consciously co-determine the right mix of IC and organizational structure. See: Anand, K.S. and Mendelson, H. (1997)

'Information and Organization for Horizontal Multimarket Coordination,' *Management Science* **43**(12). In their research, they found that managers of successful companies select coordination structures by jointly determining the company's decision authority structure ('who decides what') and its information structure ('who knows what'). Ideally managers will exploit IT to permit collocating of decision rights so that localized 'context' knowledge can be effectively exploited while also permitting the corporate-wide sharing of more general information that can be codified and applied across the company.

6. Miles and Snow and Segars, Grover and Kettinger recognized that prospectors have more complex communication mechanisms. See: Miles, R. and Snow, C. (1978) *Organizational Strategy, Structure and Process*, New York: McGraw-Hill; and Segars, A.H., Grover, V. and Kettinger, W.J. (1994) 'Strategic Users of Information Technology: A Longitudinal Analysis of Organizational Strategy and Performance,' *Journal of Strategic Information Systems* **3**(4): 261–288. To resolve this issue, they build more participatory organizational structures than defenders. In the information economy, these more complex communication structures have been mitigated by the coordination cost-reducing capabilities of IT and well-honed information management practices. At the other extreme, defenders tend to make substantial efforts to rationalize production and delivery with relatively simple coordination mechanisms through centralized decision-making and shaped by influences of production (process) and finance (cost).

7. Resource-based theory acknowledges the substitutability of firm resources to create, or erode, competitive advantage. See: Barney, J. (1991) 'Firm Resources and Sustained Competitive Advantage,' *Journal of Management* **17**(1): 99–120. Barney defines substitution as the use of alternative resources or capabilities to achieve a given criterion or to produce outcomes which make that criterion obsolete. For example, this may take the form of substituting a charismatic leader with a formal planning system to attain a similar strategic resource.

8. Dewan and Min found that IT capital is a net substitute for both ordinary capital and labour and suggest that the factor share of IT in production will grow to more significant levels over time: 'By substituting IT for labour or ordinary capital, organizations seek to capitalize on the vastly superior price and performance improvements in IT relative to these other inputs . . . The ability to take advantage of the economic opportunities created by improvements in IT is determined, in part, by the substitutability of IT for other inputs.' See: Dewan, S. and Min, C. (1997) 'The Substitution of Information Technology for Other Factors of Production: A Firm Level Analysis,' *Management Science* **43**(12): 1660–1675. December.

9. Scholars have argued that knowledge capabilities substitute for other firm capabilities and can create sustained competitive advantage if not replicated by competing firms (see: McEvily, S.K. (2000) 'Avoiding Competence Substitution Through Knowledge Sharing,' *Academy of Management Review* **25**(2): 294–311, April; Dierick, I. and Cool, K. (1989) 'Asset Stock Accumulation and Sustainabilty of Competitive Advantage,' *Management Science* **35**: 1504–1514; and Lippman, S. and Rumelt, R. (1982) 'Uncertain Imitability: An Analysis of Interfirm Differences in Efficiency Under Competition,' *Bell Journal of Economics* **13**: 418–438) and can result in higher financial returns. See: Coff, R.W. (1999) 'When Competitive Advantage Doesn't Lead to Performance: The Resource-Based View and Stakeholder Bargaining Power,' *Organization Science* **10**(2): 119–133.

10. While most management literature refers to the substitution of IC for other business capabilities, we use the term 'maximization effect' to represent the idea that managers not only recognize the 'saving' characteristics of IC for other company resources, but the characteristic of IC to enable or 'enhance' other business capabilities as well. For example, Ayers and Kettinger recognized that given the bounded resources possessed by an organization, it can substitute IT to reduce costs and maintain the same service or product quality, or it can use IT to enhance the product or maintain the same level of service. In addition, capital saved by the substitution of IT for other resources represents slack resources that may be dedicated to achieve a specific strategic priority. For example, IC substitution for people-intensive, hierarchical organizational structures may be dedicated to new product development, the opening of new markets or efforts to cement customer loyalty. See: Ayers, W.Q. and Kettinger, W.J. (1983) 'Information Technology and Models of Productivity,' *Public Administration Review* **43**(6): 561–566.

11. Communication costs can be decreased using IC, directly reducing the need for hierarchy and centralized decision control. Rather than provide all relevant information to all agents, IT allows information to be collected centrally, processed by a single decision-maker, and returned to agents in the form of relatively simple commands. See: Hitt, L.M. and Brynjolfsson, E. (1997) 'Information Technology and Internal Firm Organization: An Exploratory Analysis,' *Journal of Management Information Systems* **14**(2): 81–101, Fall. Desiraju and Moorthy found that IT's capacity for monitoring permits trading partners to better establish performance requirements to jointly set pricing and service levels and monitor joint investments. See: Desiraju, R. and Moorthy, S. (1997) 'Managing a Distribution Channel Under Asymmetric Information with Performance Requirements,' *Management Science* **43**(12): 1628–1644, December.

12. The idea that IC allows for companies to 'save' by lowering costs of coordination has been thoroughly dealt with in management literature. Considerable literature focuses on economic theory as a way to explain resource substitution, specifically of IC for other factors of production. These scholars developed coordination and transaction cost theories based on the notion that knowledge is distinguished as being general or specific (see: Hayek, F.A. (1945) 'The Use of Knowledge in Society,' *Economica* **35**(4)); specific knowledge is more costly to transfer, and general knowledge is correspondingly less costly to transfer (see: Jensen, M. and Meckling, W. (1992) 'Knowledge, Control and Organizational Structure', in L. Werin and H. Wijkander (eds) *Contract Economics*, Cambridge, MA: Basil Blackwell). IT can lower the coordination and transaction costs of some types of knowledge transmission by reallocating specific knowledge throughout the firm to reside with the people who need and use it internally and externally between firms. See: Aoki, M. (1990) 'The Participatory Generation of Information Rents and the Theory of the Firm,' In M. Aoki, B. Gustafsson and O. Williamson (eds), *The Firm as a Nexus of Treaties*, London: Sage; and Argyres, N.S. (1999) 'The Impact of Information Technology on Coordination: Evidence from the B-2 "Stealth" Bomber.' *Organization Science* **10**(2): 162–180, March-April.

13. For example, Nault found that IT can mitigate underinvestment in organization structure, so long as IT costs are not excessive. See: Nault, B.R. (1998) 'Information Technology and Organization Design: Locating Decisions and Information,' *Management Science* **44**(10): 1321–1335, October.

14. For example, Mendelson and Pillai found strong relationships between clockspeed (rate of change in an industry's external environment) and the use of information and information technologies that enhance real-time communication with team members, suppliers and customers. In dynamic environments, firms adopt IC to improve external relationships, processes and the information-processing capabilities of its people. See: Mendelson, H. and Pillai, R.R. (1998). 'Clockspeed and Informational Response: Evidence from the Information Technology Industry,' *Information Systems Research* **9**(4): 415–433, December.

15. It has been suggested that differences in unique complementary resources (resources leverageable with IT) among firms can be an important determinant in the competitive gains realized through development and deployment of strategic IT initiatives. See: Clemons, E.K. and Row, M. (1991) 'Sustaining IT Advantage: The Role of Structural Differences.' *MIS Quarterly* **15**(3): 275–292.

16. Hitt and Brnynjolfsson found that firms which are extensive users of IT exhibit decentralization of decision authority. See: Hitt, L.M. and Brynjolfsson, E. (1997) 'Information Technology and Internal Firm Organization: An Exploratory Analysis,' *Journal of Management Information Systems* **14**(2): 81–101. Fall. Other scholars have supported the idea that advanced IT leads to more decentralization of decision-making within firms. See: Zenger T. and Hesterly, W. (1997) 'The Disaggregation of Corporations: Selective Intervention, High-Powered Incentives and Modular Units,' *Organization Science* 8: 209–222; Johnston, R. and Lawrence, P.R. (1988) 'Beyond Vertical Integration—The Rise of the Value-Adding Partnership,' *Harvard Business Review*, July-August; Lawler, E.E. (1988) 'Substitutes for Hierarchy,' *Organization Dynamics* 17: 477–491.

17. Hitt (see: Hitt, L. (1999) 'Information Technology and Firm Boundaries: Evidence from Panel Data,' *Information Systems Research* **10**(2): 134–149, June) showed that increased use of IT is associated with substantial decreases in vertical integration, supporting the idea that IT affects firm boundaries by decreasing coordination costs. See: Malone, T., Yates, J. and Benjamin, R. (1987) 'Electronic Markets and Electronic Hierarchies,' *Communication of the ACM* 30: 484–497; Gurbaxani, V. and Whang, S. (1991) 'The Impact of Information Systems on Organizations and Markets,' *Communication of the ACM* 34: 59–73; Clemons, E.S.P. and Reddi, M.C.R. (1993) 'The Impact of Information Technology on the Organization of Economic Activity: The "Move to the Middle" Hypothesis,' *Journal of Management Information Systems* 10: 9–35. Brynjolfsson *et al.* found that increases in IT investment by US firms have been associated with a decline in firm size. See: Brynjolfsson, E., Malone, V., Gurbaxani V. and Kambil A. (1994) 'Does Information Technology Lead to Smaller Firms?' *Management Science* 40: 1628–1645.

18. Accenture (2000) *Outlook Special Edition: The Information Edge*, July.

19. Accenture (2000) *Outlook Special Edition: The Information Edge*, July.

20. Desiraju and Moorthy suggest that IC can substitute for process by showing that performance requirements may improve a distribution channel if the manufacturer sets the performance requirements and both manufacturer and retailer jointly invest in information systems to monitor the retailer's compliance with requirements. See: Desiraju, R. and Moorthy, S. (1997) 'Managing a Distribution Channel Under Asymmetric Information with Performance Requirements,' *Management Science* **43**(12): 1628–1644, December.

21. Accenture (2000) *Outlook Special Edition: The Information Edge*, July.

22. IT has been linked to the ability to leverage and exploit pre-existing business and human resources via co-presence and complementarity responsibilities and decision-making. See: Clemons, E.K. (1986) 'Information Systems for Sustainable Competitive Advantage,' *Information Management* **11**(3): 131–136; Clemons, E.K. and Row, M. (1991) 'Sustaining IT Advantage: The Role of Structural Differences,' *MIS Quarterly* **15**(3): 275–292; Ross, J.W. *et. al.* (1996) 'Develop Long-Term Competitiveness Through IT Assets,' *Sloan Management Review*, Fall: 31–42; Powell, T.C. and Dent-Micallef, A. (1997) 'Information Technology as Competitive Advantage: The Role of Human, Business and Technology Resources,' *Strategic Management Journal* **18**(4): 375–405.

23. Hitt and Brynjolfsson found that firms which are extensive users of IT have a greater reliance on skills and human capital and emphasize subjective incentives. See: Hitt, L.M. and Brynjolfsson, E. (1997) 'Information Technology and Internal Firm Organization: An Exploratory Analysis,' *Journal of Management Information Systems* **14**(2): 81–101, Fall.

24. Marchand, D.A. and Roos, J. (1996) 'Skandia Assurance and Financial Services: Measuring and Visualizing Intellectual Capital,' Lausanne, Switzerland: International Institute for Management Development (IMD). Case study.

25. IC has been shown to enhance external relationships by improving communication with suppliers and partners and solidifying strategic partnerships. See: Keen, P.G.W. (1991) *Shaping the Future: Business Design Through Information Technology*, Cambridge, MA: Harvard Business School Press. Malone prepared one of the most forceful arguments that a greater use of information and communication technologies leads to a greater reliance on markets to organize economic activity between buyers and suppliers. See: Malone, T., Yates, J. and Benjamin, R. (1987) 'Electronic Markets and Electronic Hierarchies,' *Communications of the ACM* 30: 484–497.

26. Nault found that so long as IT costs were not excessive, the joint profitability of three types of organizational design (central authority, decentralized nodes and a mixed mode of both central and decentralized nodes) is increased by IT. See: Nault, B.R. (1998) 'Information Technology and Organization Design: Locating Decisions and Information,' *Management Science* **44**(10): 1321–1335, October. Dewan, Michael and Min found that firms which are less vertically integrated (that is, use alternative organizational structures) have a higher level of IT investment. See: Dewan, S., Michael, S.C. and Min, C. (1998) 'Firm Characteristics and Investments in Information Technology: Scale and Scope Effects,' *Information Systems Research* 9(3): 219–232.

27. Bradley, S.P., Ghemawat, P. and Foley, S. (1996) 'Wal-Mart Stores, Inc.' Boston: Harvard Business School Publishing. Case Study # 794024.

28. Marchand, D.A. and Roos, J. (1996) 'Skandia Assurance and Financial Services: Measuring and Visualizing Intellectual Capital,' Lausanne, Switzerland: International Institute for Management Development (IMD). Case study.

29. Miles, R. and Snow, C. (1978) *Organizational Strategy, Structure, and Process*. New York: McGraw-Hill.

30. The three categories of leadership in the use of competitive, customer and operational information belong to a comprehensive construct which we termed 'industry leadership in competing with information'. The following discussion is based on the confirmatory factor analysis findings as discussed in Chapter 9 of Marchand, D.A., Kettinger, W.J. and Rollins, J.D. (2001) *Information Orientation: The Link to Business Performance*, UK: Oxford University Press.

31. Bushaus, D. (2000) 'Trade the ANX Way,' *Information Week*, 6 March.

9

IMPLEMENTING INFORMATION CAPABILITIES GLOBALLY: A PORTFOLIO APPROACH

In this chapter we shift our discussion from managing and competing with information capabilities in a single company or business unit to the context of companies with multiple business units acting on a local, regional and/or global basis. What should be the focus of information capabilities improvement efforts in companies with multiple business units? What roles do corporate or home office managers play in improving the IO and business performance of different business units in the same or in different industries and locations around the world?

For companies with multiple business units, the senior management team at the headquarters or home office must consider the relative performance of not one, but many, business units and how their individual performance affects the overall performance of the group or company worldwide. These business units may all be at different stages of IO maturity and business performance and may envisage different ways of competing with information in the future. How can corporate headquarters raise the overall IO level of the group or global company? How can it develop a global or company-wide IO strategy to move all business units to a higher level of IO and, consequently, better business performance and industry leadership in competing with information?

The responsibility for addressing these questions clearly rests with the group or company-wide management team, since it exercises the role of the parent in overseeing the creation and execution of corporate strategy to create business value on a global basis. We examine the steps that can be taken by senior managers at the group or global level to improve the overall levels of IO in their business units and for the company as a whole. In doing so, we also discuss the different types of organizational approaches with multiple business units—multinational, international, transnational, regional and global companies. How should corporate managers and business unit managers behave toward each other in defining business strategies and developing information capabilities to increase business unit and corporate performance?

Our research indicates that our way of measuring IO applies to all companies with multiple business units. In addition, we believe that every business unit needs to improve its IO if the overall group or company-wide IO is to result in improved business performance. Our discussion is just as important for those companies that have developed organically on a business unit basis as for those that have grown through mergers, acquisitions and diversification strategies.

In this chapter we extend the concept of portfolio management to include more than just decisions about the range of businesses in which the company should invest its money. Portfolio decisions are also about where and how a company should focus overall its management time, resources and attention. Our new approach to portfolio decisions will address the following key questions:

- How does a company with multiple business units invest globally in information capabilities?
- How should corporate and business unit managers deal with information capabilities relative to their senior management team competencies?
- How can corporate and business unit managers select the right mix of strategic priorities and business capabilities to improve performance in individual business units and company-wide?
- How can corporate and business unit managers find the right balance between the need for business unit flexibility to manage strategic priorities and business capabilities with the need for standardization across the group?

We start with the case of a worldwide financial services company (GFS Group) to illustrate the importance and implications of an IO assessment within a global company with multiple business units. We then discuss how to achieve the right mix of strategic priorities and business capabilities to result in improved performance among many business units, using a large European electronics corporation as an example. Lastly, we present steps to foster effective information use in a global company through a global information capabilities strategy.

INFORMATION ORIENTATION (IO), BUSINESS PERFORMANCE AND INDUSTRY LEADERSHIP OF A GLOBAL COMPANY

In this section we introduce the GFS Group, one of the world's leading financial services companies. The GFS Group played a major role in our international study, with senior management teams (SMTs) of 48 business units—including corporate headquarters—from 32 countries participating in our research survey. Its participation enabled us to revalidate our overall study results within a global company. We found that the IO model holds for the GFS Group and can be used in global companies as a business measure of their information capabilities among business units and the home office. Using our statistical analysis techniques, we confirmed that managers in a global company hold the same ideas about information behaviours and values, information management practices and IT practices as those in our overall study sample. In addition, they also perceive the interactive links between the three information capabilities and IO as explained in Chapter 1.

Global Financial Services Group (GFS Group)

GFS Group has a worldwide presence with business units in more than 60 countries reaching over 30 million customers. The Group operates in four core businesses—non-life insurance, life insurance, reinsurance and asset management. The group covers almost all types of non-life insurance around the world, for individuals as well as for commercial businesses. The range of life insurance services includes solutions for individuals and businesses, which increasingly involve the group's asset management operations. In the highly competitive reinsurance market, GFS Group has specialized in two areas, offering a full spectrum of reinsurance in the areas of finite risk and traditional reinsurance, as well as alternative, structured solutions to meet the investment needs of corporate customers. At the end of 1998, the group had some US$ 375 billion in assets under management.

Although GFS Group's performance has been strong, it needs to transform itself from a profitable insurance company to an integrated financial services group to remain among the leaders in the financial services industry worldwide. In spring 1998, the group chief executive officer (CEO) launched several strategic initiatives, including a group-wide business and IT strategy review called 'Power IT'. He was eager to identify how IT could be used as a strategic weapon to create competitive advantage for the new integrated financial services business model.

Beginning in August 1998, the Power IT initiative focused on building sustainable business/IT partnerships through:

- group-wide sharing of information and intelligence
- efficiencies in IT processes and new development activities within and among the business units and the group's head office
- effective and creative use of new technology
- world-class execution of IT.

GFS Group's Information Capabilities

A project team was set up to oversee the Power IT review over the next 12 months. While this team was conducting an external business and technology assessment as well as an internal Strengths-Weaknesses-Opportunities-Threats (SWOT) analysis of the group's current IT capabilities, we invited GFS Group's CEO to participate in our study.

Forty-eight GFS regional, divisional and corporate senior management teams participated in the study. As we suspected, the results determined that GFS business units varied widely in their levels of IO and their business performance. Figure 9.1 depicts the same IO benchmarking tool as introduced in Chapter 2. However, instead of benchmarking GFS against the study sample we benchmarked GFS business units against each other. We can see that business units fall into all four benchmark categories. While some business units are self-aware winners, with high IO and corresponding high business performance, others are blind and confused, with low IO and low business performance. Yet other business units fall into the info-oriented laggard and winner at risk categories.

Taking a Portfolio Approach to Improving IO in GFS Group

The existence of different levels of IO among multiple business units within a global company demands differentiated ways to improve IO company-wide. Thus corporate managers must use an appropriate portfolio approach if they want to raise the overall threshold of IO globally across the business units of the company. By continually improving the overall IO and performance levels within each business unit, a company will be able to move all its business units into the 'winning' quadrant.

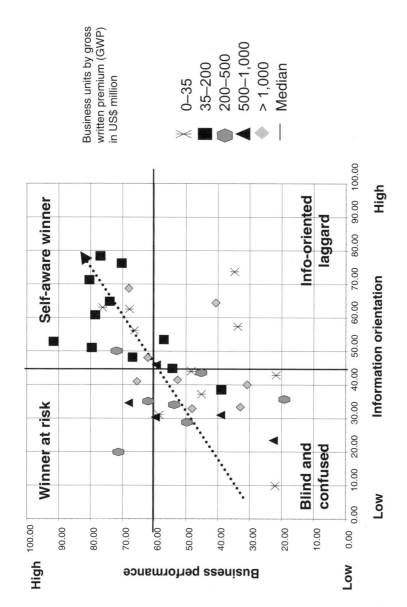

Figure 9.1: SMTs of the GFS Group: information orientation to business performance

Transforming Power IT into IO Power

Since our research results indicated that many of the GFS business units had low IO and were less mature in the behavioural aspects of information use, it became obvious that GFS had to rethink its mainly technology-centric Power IT initiative. The project manager acknowledged a need to broaden the project's scope:

> Our study results about IO and its link to business performance really redefine the task in hand. We definitely need a more integrated approach to deal with our IT practices and the other information capabilities such as information behaviours and values. Otherwise, the chances are low that we will get business value out of this.

If a company with multiple business units undertakes a similar analysis, the overall profile will have the same implications as those we found for GFS Group. A company with multiple business units must adopt a portfolio approach to developing the information capabilities of individual business units in order to achieve higher IO and business performance. In the next section we discuss the mix of strategic priorities and business capabilities that lead to superior performance in companies with multiple business units.

CREATING THE RIGHT MIX OF STRATEGIC PRIORITIES AND BUSINESS CAPABILITIES TO ACHIEVE SUPERIOR PERFORMANCE IN A GLOBAL COMPANY

As we noted in Chapter 7, there is a strong relationship between the emergent strategic priorities achieved by a business unit or company and the capability mix it draws upon. Corporate executives, in general, are charged with moving their business units to superior performance by delivering high shareholder value. Business unit managers—usually working within the context of company-wide vision and direction—customize a unique strategy and mix of business capabilities to address specific market requirements.

In an ideal business environment, corporate strategy and business unit strategy would be synchronized to leverage a proactive bias through the right capability mix. However, competitive pressures may lead corporate executives to follow strategies that may not be consistent with the business conditions and strategies of their business units (and vice versa). Thus there is often a divergence between the strategic priorities and the capability mix suggested by corporate managers and those actually implemented at the business unit level.

As we discussed in Chapter 7, the emergent strategy of Growers focused externally on creating new business opportunities and delighting the customer. This strategy emphasized information capabilities and external relationships as important business capabilities for implementing their proactive bias. This mix of capabilities is the most effective in achieving superior business performance. Cutters, in contrast, have a reactive bias and focus internally on reducing costs and minimizing risk, relying more on business processes and organizational structure to implement their emergent strategic priorities. Although reducing costs is often required, these companies do not emphasize building information capabilities and do not achieve higher business performance over the long term.

Possible Gaps between Corporate and Business Unit Strategy

In companies with multiple business units, which operate on a local, regional or global basis, different strategies and mixes of business capabilities will be pursued by individual business units and perhaps by corporate managers as well. How should a corporate executive team evaluate the consistency or divergence between its views and those of a business unit?

Figure 9.2 suggests four possible scenarios given proactive (Grower) and reactive (Cutter) strategies at the corporate and business unit levels. Makeovers, the third of our strategy groups, are not treated as a separate group in this discussion because they already appear to be in transition towards a Grower strategy, and most probably have a Grower strategic vision and mind-set. This figure shows the synergies, problems and possible solutions that might occur when corporate executives and business unit managers advocate the same or different strategies. In two of these scenarios, both teams have a similar strategic vision resulting in either a 'dynamic duo' (a positive synergistic relationship) or a 'downward spiral' (a short-term fix or a long-term negative impact). In the other two scenarios, there exists a disconnect between corporate and business unit strategies, resulting in the business unit 'not getting the message' or adhering to a different set of strategic assumptions and hoping to positively influence corporate strategy through 'skunk works', following a strategy that runs counter to the corporate mentality.

Corporate Grower: Business unit Grower

This is the dynamic duo partnership. In this block, corporate executives and business unit managers share an enthusiasm for growth strategies to

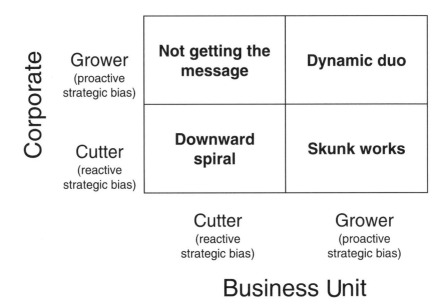

Figure 9.2:   Gaps between corporate and business unit strategy

sustain their marketplace leadership. Both are concerned about developing information capabilities to increase their IO levels. This synergy represents the best relationship scenario, since building commitment to IC initiatives is not needed to the same degree as in our other three groups. Companies who are able to foster a similar mind-set regarding the strategic uses of information capabilities in all business units can more readily capitalize on the IC maximization effect, thus creating cost savings and enhancements to other business capabilities. Companies exhibiting these relationships also find innovative uses of information capabilities to improve their businesses.

Corporate Grower: Business Unit Cutter

In this case, there is a divergence between corporate executives, who want to grow the company, and business unit managers, who continue to engage in systematic cost reduction in their units—they are not getting the message. While corporate managers see the importance of IO in relation to current business performance, business unit managers are preoccupied with concerns related to organizational structure and process redesign. Corporate teams wanting to improve this situation first need to examine the cause for the disconnect in strategic vision. For example, is the business unit isolated from corporate influence, either by geography or lack of clear, substantive communication? Is there a lack of confidence in the business unit in the ability of a Grower strategy to create performance improvements or in the corporate team itself? Often management buy-in to new strategic initiatives needs to be demonstrated with specific examples. Since reducing costs is important to these managers, specific examples of how information capabilities can reduce costs within their business unit can help build buy-in. Incentive systems often play a role in supporting the wrong business strategy. Are business unit managers' rewards tied primarily to internal, operational metrics, or to those focusing on external measures, such as customer satisfaction or success at bringing new products to market? In the worst case, leadership in these units may need to be replaced to create meaningful strategic change.

Corporate Cutter: Business Unit Grower

While corporate executives advocate cutting costs, some business unit managers engage in a contrary growth strategy within their business unit. They may be trying to make up for lost revenues at the corporate level by growing their way out of the problem, as opposed to cutting costs like their other business unit colleagues. In this situation, business unit managers work on information capabilities and external relationships, while corporate managers concentrate on changes in organizational structures and internal processes to increase efficiency. These business units managers can go so far as to implement a successful 'skunk works' operation following a growth philosophy that runs counter to the corporate cutter mentality. In addition to showing business unit performance benefits, skunk works managers hope to influence the corporate strategy and approach. Depending on the degree of freedom given to them by corporate executives, business unit managers may find themselves frustrated by the tensions arising over this issue. When skunk works operation arise, corporate teams need to recognize the learning potential that can be leveraged from these business units. These 'rogue' units may have learned how to make the difficult transition from Cutter to Grower strategies and this successful change model needs to be transferred to other business units throughout the corporation.

Corporate Cutter: Business Unit Cutter

The downward spiral relationship displays agreement on cutting costs, which leads the company and/or business unit either to short-term benefit with improved profitability or—if sustained—to a downward spiral. This downward spiral influences investment and development of information capabilities. Unless savings are immediately reinvested in new capability development, cost-cutting strategies more often than not reduce IC budgets. Decreases in IO levels as a result negatively impact business performance which leads to further cost-cutting strategies in an attempt to respond to marketplace challenges. Companies experiencing this downward spiral have no one to blame but themselves—business units are often following the strategic orders of a blind and confused corporate office. A total lack of Grower tendencies within the portfolio of business units may indicate a corporate culture that does not tolerate dissent or encourage innovation. Industry realities may also encourage this extremely reactive strategic bias. Companies in this situation have an opportunity to unleash radical change initiatives since the 'burning platform' will force company employees to jump off or pull together to put out the fire.

Corporate and Business Unit Divergence in a Large European Electronics Corporation

In this corporation, we observed a divergence between emergent corporate and business unit strategic priorities and business capabilities.

Feeling price pressure from the Japanese and Americans, corporate executives wanted to reduce costs to push consumer prices to competitive levels. They sought to achieve this strategy primarily by means of process improvements without having to lay off large numbers of employees. They did not see information capabilities as a major lever of change, nor did they build to achieve the IC maximization effect to save resources and enhance their strategy, and, consequently, experienced low business performance. The corporate office neither saw opportunities for growth nor the need to change its capability mix in the future.

Corporate Cutter: Business Unit Cutter—the downward spiral

Mirroring its corporate leaders, a US business unit in a seemingly fast-growing telecommunications market segment pursued a cost-cutting strategy, with a similar emphasis on process improvement and low emphasis on IC. Following this course resulted in low business performance. The business unit managers recognized that they needed to create business opportunities in the future and tried to move away from their cost-cutting strategies of the past. However, corporate executives questioned whether they were 'doing the right thing' and whether they were 'aware' of the cost-cutting steps necessary to make a transition to a more growth-oriented approach. The problem was exacerbated by the fact that, at the time, the corporate office did not see any clear way for the company as a whole to achieve growth.

Corporate Cutter: Business Unit Grower

A northern European business unit specializing in analytical instrumentation and software for industrial process control actively pursued a growth strategy in a climate of company-wide cost cutting. Working closely with R&D departments of some of the world's largest companies, it was compelled to think about creating new business opportunities in instrumentation and customized software to meet specialized customer demands. In contrast to corporate head office and most other business units, it focused on external relationships and information capabilities to effect its strategies. This mix resulted in high business performance. Thus a skunk works operation can prosper amid cost-cutters. In the future, this business unit intends to continue on this path by further substituting information capabilities for organizational structure. It hopes that further investments in its employees, who will be enabled with better information capabilities, will help it stay ahead of the pack by constantly creating new business opportunities.

As we have seen from these three examples, corporate executives can use our corporate/business unit strategy matrix to assess where they stand in relation to each of their business units. This can be an eye-opening evaluation. Depending on the links, tensions will be revealed. These tensions will be healthy if a corporate Cutter is willing to learn from business units that pursue a growth strategy. They will also be healthy if a corporate Grower is able to identify Cutters among its business units and can make sure that through managerial intensive care these business units are pulled toward participating in corporate growth efforts and improving their IO levels.

Makeovers, being on the right track already, need specific attention in terms of aligning their capability mix to better fit the proactive bias they want to pursue. These business units, however, may be more susceptible to influence than their proactive Grower counterparts, since changes to their strategy have not yet resulted in improved business performance. Makeover business units must make sure that competing priorities, either from the corporate level or within their own business unit, do not divert attention or resources away from their growth path.

Tensions, however, may also become quite unhealthy. In cases where corporate executives and business units both choose strategic priorities and capability mixes that go hand in hand with lower IO and lower business performance—that is, follow a Cutter strategy—group-wide results will tend to be pulled down further and further. In addition, corporate executives may deem their view of strategic priorities and business capabilities to be the 'right' view. Some business unit managers, whether they disagree or not, will follow the corporate view. We have seen clearly in this section that an emphasis on growth supported by information capabilities offers long-term possibilities for business success.

MANAGING INFORMATION CAPABILITIES IN A GLOBAL COMPANY

As we observed in the case of GFS Group, global companies need an information capabilities strategy that is not solely IT-based. GFS Group had to rethink the scope of its Power IT initiative to include a focus on information management practices and information behaviours and values to improve information use throughout the group. Other large global companies have also reached the conclusion that building IT capabilities alone is not sufficient—a company needs to address the way it uses information among its business units.

In this section, we present six practical guidelines that a company with multiple business units can follow to create an information capabilities strategy on a group-wide basis. These guidelines should be initiated by corporate managers, but should involve the managers of business units as well. For business unit managers, the aim is to gain better understanding of the business strategy and information capabilities of their unit compared to other business units in the company and to the expectations of the corporate head office. For corporate managers, the intention is to understand their business unit portfolio as well as the relationship of their corporate strategic priorities and capability mix to the business conditions and approaches of their business units.

Guideline 1:   Determine the strategic bias and capability mix of your group/company at the corporate and business unit levels, share the results, and work toward becoming the dynamic duo

A company with multiple business units should determine the strategic bias and capability mix of the corporate executive team as well as those of the business unit management teams. This can be done using the strategic priority and capability mix assessments in Chapter 7. Next it is important to analyse why a specific management team decided on an existing mix of strategic priorities. What are the mind-sets of senior managers that drive the strategic orientation? Is it fear about not being able to offer products and services at a competitive price? Is it a vision of gaining market share through excellent customer service?

This should then make it easier for managers to understand the mindsets that drive the relationship between corporate headquarters and individual business units. Are corporate and business unit relationships top-down, so that corporate management dictates the direction business units are expected to follow? Or does corporate management decide on a strategic direction, but take the individual context of each business unit into account?

The same evaluation process can be applied to the mix of business capabilities and their relationship to strategic priorities. Which capabilities—and in what proportions—do the corporate executive team and the business units use to try to implement their strategic priorities? Do business units with the same strategic bias use a similar capability mix to execute their strategic priorities? What is the relationship between the development of information capabilities and other business capabilities?

In one of our case studies, a business unit's inability to implement effective information capabilities was directly linked not only to its past Cutter strategy, which focused on streamlining acquisitions and mergers made throughout the 1990s, but also to the corporate level's inability to establish an information capabilities improvement strategy. The business unit's chief information officer (CIO) explained:

> Decision-making is extremely slow in this company because it is based on a model of consensus. As a result, there have been no major policy decisions made about IT. We are far behind in IT infrastructure investment and have many different—and sometimes incompatible—systems throughout the organization. There is no recognition of the problems we face in this area at a corporate level.

Discussions of strategic priorities and business capabilities between the corporate level and business units, if held in a climate of trust, will form an important basis for all subsequent change activities, whether they are concerned with defining business strategy as a whole or with improving specific capabilities.

Ultimately, a series of dynamic duo partnerships (see Figure 9.2) is optimal—with both corporate and business unit managers pursuing a growth strategy, using information capabilities and external relationships to implement them. This approach—as our research has shown—will lead to better business performance across the whole company.

Following this first guideline defines the framework within which improvements to a company's information capabilities on a group-wide basis will be most effective and thus have positive impacts on business performance.

Guideline 2: Evaluate information capabilities on a group-wide basis, openly discuss results, and do so periodically

The next step to raising a global company's information capabilities is knowing where the corporate headquarters and the individual business units score on information orientation (IO). A survey of all business units, using the IO dashboard outlined in Chapter 2, will provide an overview of the entire company.

By discussing the IO dashboard of each business unit with the respective business unit management team, corporate executives are in a position to collect a complete picture of their group's information capabilities. They can compare business units according to different information capabilities—information behaviours and values, information management practices and IT practices—to analyse where business unit and group capabilities are strongest or weakest. It is useful to conduct these discussions openly, since it is corporate executives, together with business unit managers, who will have to find the right initiatives to improve each business unit's information capabilities and thus the IO of the overall group.

Since business units within a global company face different competitive realities, it is important to customize plans for each business unit to determine how best to compete with information within its industry and environment. This can best be achieved by engaging business unit managers in constant communication with headquarters during the development of an information capabilities strategy. These strategies must then be implemented in the respective business contexts of the different business units. It is the task of the corporate level to synchronize the business unit efforts and try to foster synergies wherever possible.

As discussed in Chapter 2, the global company must regularly assess the group's information capabilities, since corporate and business unit managers must decide on the sequence of IO improvements over time to achieve better performance in the business units, which will lead to better group performance. By carrying out a periodic assessment, along the lines of Figure 2.5, the corporate level will gain feedback on which IO initiatives have worked best, and/or where regrouping on business strategy and information capabilities is necessary.

Guideline 3: Carefully analyse your company's pockets of excellence: learn from the winners

By plotting the relationship between IO and business performance for the corporate team and each business unit on a chart, as we did for the GFS Group in Figure 9.1, one can obtain an immediate picture of how all the business units are distributed. There are four different categories, as outlined in Chapter 2: self-aware winners, winners at risk, info-oriented laggards and blind and confused.

There may be times when it is necessary for corporate managers to take top-down decisions. A multi-business/multi-unit company doing an evaluation of the mind-sets and performance of its business units may decide to reallocate managers from high-performing teams to low-performing teams in order to energize and educate low-performing managers, to share best practices on building information capabilities and to improve the overall performance of the group.

This was the case with the large electronics corporation. The corporate office moved the managing director of a self-aware winner business unit, which relied heavily on implementing strategy through information capabilities, to a blind and confused business unit. At the same time, it wanted to start regular information capabilities meetings among the management teams, at which the managers of selected high-performing business units would discuss IC improvements with the managers of low-performing units. The corporate office scheduled three meetings, each focusing on a specific information capability—information behaviours and values, information management practices and IT practices. During these meetings, change strategies were developed for low-performing units. The aim was to have an IC-experienced 'buddy' team that could support the change process of the low IO unit.

In addition, the corporate office expected the high-performing business units to share experiences and best practices with each other to sustain and further develop their high information capabilities. Results from these discussions were then recorded in an IC best practices database, which was organized according to our IO model and was available to all corporate and business unit managers.

Guideline 4:   Determine how your business units can compete with competitive, customer and operational information within your industry

Corporate headquarters, together with all business units, must formulate a tactical plan for competing with information that will also help to guide appropriate information capabilities investment. If it is necessary to raise the overall IO levels of all the business units and, subsequently, the company as a whole, general improvements to all three information capabilities are required. This will, however, not be enough to create effective industry leadership in competing with information in the future.

Whilst becoming a high IO company improves business performance, only concrete steps toward competing with competitive, customer and operational information as outlined in Chapter 8 will set the targets to provide the right basis and context for improving business performance. For example, a business unit decides that it wants to create competitive advantage by moving into e-business. It plans to expand its current customer base for existing products by targeting a different customer segment from its traditional one. To accomplish this, it not only has to improve its operational information to create the infrastructure to support this new venture, but it must also be able to monitor competitors' moves in the area and create a way to tap into this new customer segment through improved customer information. Investment in and development of information capabilities should directly support this business unit's strategy for competing with information.

Guideline 5:   Capitalize on the IC maximization effect

Corporate offices and business units can identify areas where information capabilities can result in savings or enhance service or product levels by substituting for other business capabilities. If your company has been a Cutter in the past, it should determine where information capabilities substitute for existing resources in business units. Careful analysis of current use of business capabilities (processes, organizational structure, people and external relationships) can help to identify suitable areas for information capabilities deployment and change among business units.

For example, many Cutter companies find that operational process changes—such as centralization of administrative processes, development of standard financial measures or streamlining of order fulfilment and supply chain processes—put in place to pursue a cost reduction strategy create opportunities to kick-start information capabilities development and implementation in their business units. With careful foresight and planning, these process and IT system changes within business units—and across the company—can provide opportunities to implement shifts in information capabilities such as improved sharing and transparency of information use across processes, while lowering the non-value added activities of people. In this case, improved processes and information behaviours also save employee resources and time.

Alternatively, with a bit of creative thinking and planning, shifting IT spending from operational and business process support to IT for innovation support may create, in some business units and business functions, substantial improvements in information use. This is especially true for marketing departments, product development groups and sales organizations in which using IT for innovation support—coupled with a recognized need for excellent information and an external focus on markets and customers—may enhance the development of information capabilities. IC maximization, in this case, does not necessarily lead to savings, but for no—or very little—additional cost enhances other business capabilities.

Coupling improvements in information capabilities with improvements in external relationships can have a substantial impact on the business performance of business units and the company or group overall. Although coordinating external relationships is not always easy and it may require significant behavioural changes to manage processes, relationships and information flows across partnerships, joint ventures and alliances, there is the potential for long-term savings and benefits. New business capabilities, including information capabilities, can be introduced from outside the company to ignite or accelerate Grower strategies in business units that were previously Cutters. This is especially important in cases in which the corporate team is a Grower and interested in higher IO to improve performance, but the business units have formerly been Cutters. Waiting for these business units to transform themselves from within may not be feasible, so external relationships can be used to enhance information capabilities improvements and create higher IO.

Guideline 6: Continuously balancing business flexibility and standardization through IT practices is essential to improve information capabilities group-wide

Global companies with high IO are constantly trying to create the right mix of business flexibility and business standardization. Business flexibility provides business unit or product managers in global companies with the freedom to decide how to tailor their products and services as well as their demand/supply chain processes to the specific needs of local markets. As long as these managers can operate profitably by creating customer value in their business unit or country, they are the people who typically decide their information capabilities approach and define the mix of business capabilities to achieve their strategic priorities.

Business standardization, in contrast, reflects the concurrent need to find ways of reducing the operating costs of the global business and all its units by seeking to share best business practices or adopt common business processes and IT infrastructure wherever feasible. In addition, business standardization may be necessary for a company to leverage its human knowledge across the company and business units or to share information and collaborate on projects for the benefit of the global company.

Business standardization is usually facilitated through a company's IT practices, which—as we discussed in Chapter 6—contribute to information capabilities in terms of value creation for the company as a whole. Depending on the degree to which a company operates on a local, regional or global basis, a mix of IT practices can be implemented at different geographical levels. Figure 9.3 summarizes five different approaches according to these criteria. We have used the same categories for IT practices already introduced in Figure 6.3—IT practices that are necessary to compete, essential to operate and distinctive—based on the extent to which they add value by making a company's information use more effective.

Approach A: Multinational

This approach clearly emphasizes flexibility over standardization— investments in IT practices are made locally, regardless of their return on effective information use; that is, the value that they add to the business on a business unit by business unit or country by country basis. The advantages of this approach are local flexibility and autonomy for management decision-making, processes and operations, as well as the opportunity for corporate management to focus on company-wide financial performance and brand management. The disadvantages are obvious— investments in systems are duplicated in each business unit, but the systems may not be the same, making them incompatible across units and/or between countries. Thus the multinational company suffers from poor information-sharing and lack of transparency, both of which are important information behaviours and building blocks for mature information capabilities.

Approach B: International

In this approach, the corporate office, usually in the form of the chief information officer (CIO), tries to develop shared services and systems among business units and to promote standards for data and voice networking to enable regional and global communications and information-sharing. Typically in such a company, the CIO reports to the chief financial officer (CFO) and his or her authority is based on persuasion, not top-down mandate. The advantages of this approach are synergies for IT practices to build necessary information capabilities and greater awareness of best practices in the company. But adoption of company-wide IT policies and standards by business units is voluntary. The problems with this approach are twofold—IT practices investments are viewed as costs by business unit and company managers, and corporate decision-making is slow, since policies and standards are based on reaching consensus among diverse business unit managers and IT directors.

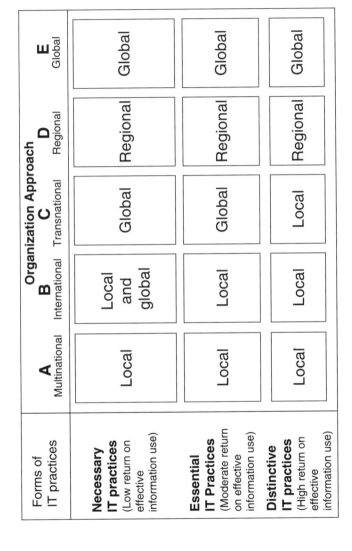

Figure 9.3: Balancing business flexibility and standardization through IT practices

Approach C: Transnational

The third approach aims to meet the needs of bottom-up business culture, where flexibility in adopting processes and systems is required for growth and innovation. It also satisfies the need for company-wide synergies to reduce the costs of necessary and essential IT practices by providing global IT systems and infrastructure that permit anyone in the company to communicate anywhere, any time. Decisions for distinctive IT are at the business unit level, but the company relies on a culture of 'beg, borrow or steal' for sharing best practices across business units. While this approach maximizes high levels of business flexibility with standardization, problems might arise if the globally implemented IT practices become unresponsive to business users over time and/or fall behind in adapting to technological changes.

Approach D: Regional

'Regional' here, for example, means treating Europe as one country or Latin America as a single entity. This approach clearly represents a top-down focus. Advantages lie in cost savings, since even investments in IT practices with a high return on effective information use are made over a large area or region. Common processes and systems are implemented—and people, processes and structures are aligned—regionally, not locally. Systems might even be implemented on a global basis if applicable. Disadvantages are the length of time it takes for implementation and the difficulty of changing operations once a regional approach to business has been established.

Approach E: Global

In this approach value creation is not so much based on business flexibility as on global brands and operations. Companies in this category possess very strong top-down cultures. They operate truly global markets, selling the same products in geographically and culturally diverse parts of the world. To coordinate rapid worldwide product roll-outs requires consistent and accurate information to support global decision-making. Common processes and systems to support managerial decision-making globally reduce costs and save time, since they only have to be implemented once worldwide. Disadvantages lie in the highly top-down culture and in the strong consistency, which make it difficult to adapt to non-incremental business changes.

Choosing the Best Approach

How does a corporate executive team determine the best approach for achieving business flexibility and standardization for all of its business units and corporate head office? Three key questions need to be addressed:

- Which approach permits your company to create business value and lower overall costs at the same time?
- Do your IT practices permit your company to be more rather than less flexible in responding rapidly to business change?
- Do your company's IT practices enable your employees and managers to share information and communicate rapidly anywhere, any time and with any person or partner?

The best approach is the one that helps you to manage your company in a global economy with maximum customer focus and business flexibility, while reducing operating costs and standardizing the administrative functions and IT practices that do not create direct business value. Let's look at two contrasting company examples.

In the case of a large company specializing in motor car windscreen and window replacement, corporate executives realized that their business unit by business unit approach to investments in IT did not create the flexibility for value creation they had expected. Through participating in our study they learned that IT practices were only one of three important information capabilities. They used the investment framework for evaluating IT practices maturity, outlined in Chapter 6, to classify their IT applications and immediately formed different work groups to look for ways to find synergies through standardization across the group of 10 business units. A CIO was appointed whose responsibility it was to implement standardization projects, which are now well underway. He said:

> The best thing about it is, this way, I can squeeze in discussions about improvements to the other information capabilities as well without having to explain the whole complexity of IO and its positive effect on business performance. By going through this process of balancing flexibility and standardization, we can now make business unit managers aware and improve information behaviours and information management practices as well.

Conversely, the corporate management of a US food manufacturing company, which in the past had grown through repeated acquisitions, has for years delayed taking decisions about investment in IT practices for standardization purposes. Because of the acquisition strategy, senior managers are faced with incompatible IT systems supporting different parts of the company, but they have been reluctant to make huge IT investments for standardization only to have to change them with future acquisitions. Driven by a cost-cutting strategy that measures business performance solely on profitability measures, senior managers continue to postpone IT investments and continue to permit the duplication of IT systems throughout the company's many businesses, leading to low IT practices and low IO overall.

CONCLUSION

In this chapter we have discussed the challenges of information capabilities management facing corporate executives of companies with multiple business units. The example of the GFS Group has shown that there cannot be a single information capabilities strategy for the whole group. Rather, a company has to take a portfolio approach to raising the overall IO level. In addition, the relationship between the strategic biases of corporate headquarters and individual business units influences the development of differentiated IC improvement efforts. Finally, we presented six guidelines to consider when building and pursuing a company-wide information capabilities strategy.

V

PUTTING INFORMATION CAPABILITIES INTO PRACTICE STARTS WITH YOU

10

THE PERSONAL CHALLENGE TO LEAD WITH INFORMATION CAPABILITIES

Building IO maturity begins with you as a manager—your mind-set, your behaviours and the practices that are connected to effective information use in your business. How managers focus and channel human energy with information and IT impacts directly on business performance. Managers do not fail because they lack intelligence or motivation. They fail because they cannot face reality about events, products or people. They cannot hear bad news, or they cannot seek new ideas and information.

If 'managing' means 'controlling' people, information, resources and processes, most managers, because they are controllers, think that they are succeeding. But managers who cannot be candid and truthful and who cannot face their mistakes and learn from them will fail. To lead, managers need to know how to use information. Leading means sensing new knowledge and focusing on the right information to run the business today and to change it tomorrow. Most of all, it means inspiring people in the business to use information and knowledge effectively.

In this chapter we present seven key principles that managers can follow to improve the information capabilities and IO maturity of their business unit or company through their personal conduct and behaviours. What is your personal IO maturity in leading your people? What can you do to improve your information capabilities to inspire your people to practice what you do, not just what you say?

Based on our case research and many years of advising senior management, we have learned about the fundamental differences between senior managers in companies where information capabilities lead to superior business performance and in those where their information capabilities do not effectively contribute to business performance.

In companies with high IO, the senior managers lead by knowing which information creates value for them, their people and their business—and how. They are aware, even obsessed, with sensing and using the right information. They continually challenge their own information management practices, information behaviours and values and IT practices. They have a keen sense of urgency about 'what we don't know'. They worry about how to use information more effectively to:

- sense the reality of the outside world, and
- change their business practices to exploit that emerging reality.

Managers in these companies focus on facing reality by being open to new ideas, treating bad news as good news, and instilling and celebrating the right information behaviours, information management and IT practices in themselves, their staff and their companies. These managers gain credibility among their staff by practising the behaviours and values of effective information use that they fully expect others to practis as well. Table 10.1 summarizes the lessons learned from the management style of high-performing companies.

In companies with poor information capabilities and low IO, however, the senior managers talk about good behaviours and values as well as information management and IT practices, but focus on managing by controlling people, events, processes and resources. Their behaviours and values seem disconnected from their words about personal integrity, information sharing and being open to bad news or frankness—even when the truth hurts. In these companies, managers speak about the positive business benefits of using information or IT effectively, but do not practise what they preach at work. They often treat information as a political weapon to compete with other managers, rather than as an asset the company can use to improve its business results. They speak about IT's key role in making the business more competitive, but do not use the technology themselves. Or they believe that the Internet and e-business are for others, not for them. They urge their subordinates to be open and candid with them, but selectively employ information to control other people's decisions and actions. In conversations with managers in these companies, there is an air of unreality, since they speak about information, people and IT as important for competitive survival, but act each day in ways that contradict or undermine the achievement of good information capabilities. Are you an IO leader? See Table 10.1 to find out.

Table 10.1   Are you an IO leader?

Information orientation begins at the top. It takes more than authorizing an IT investment and training staff to use information. It calls for different behaviours, values and practices. Whenever an organization asks people to think and act differently, the leader has to model and be a symbol of the new behaviours.

Your employees will look at what you do, not what you say. Are you prepared to 'walk the talk' on information orientation?

- **Do you set the standard for the behaviours and practices you want your people to adopt?** Do you share sensitive information? Do you actively seek out information and new ideas? Do you accept, even welcome, bad news? Do you learn from your mistakes, and share that learning with others?

- **Do you understand the possibilities and limitations of information technology in your business?** Do you use technology (computers, the Internet, e-business) in your daily life? Do you see the IT function and the CIO as part of your business? Do you understand that the Internet and e-business are already a competitive necessity rather than a source of potential competitive advantage?

- **Do you know how to use information effectively?** Do you ask yourself the questions that management guru Peter Drucker[1] poses for information leaders: 'What information do I need myself? From whom? In what form? In what time frame?' and 'What information do I owe to the people with whom I work and on whom I depend? In what form? In what time frame?'

- **Do you create the right expectations for your people?** Do you try to understand the mind-sets—the distinctive viewpoints, needs, agendas and expectations—that influence your employees, customers, suppliers, partners and competitors? Do you use this insight to promote an inclusive understanding of your core business strategies for growth and the mix of business capabilities required? Do you give your employees and managers clear criteria and measures to guide them when they make decisions?

- **Do you understand the conditions under which your company must improve its information capabilities?** Are you working from a reliable assessment of the scope of your company's challenge and the precise source of its weaknesses? Have you set challenging targets for your staff to reach?

The way in which managers face their business reality each day and the way they talk about and behave with information to achieve better business performance either builds or diminishes information capabilities in their company. The seven principles that follow should help managers to lead their company and business unit to IO maturity and superior business performance. They will also serve as a platform for analysing why the personal mind-sets and behaviours of managers influence the information capabilities of their people and directly affect the performance of their business unit and company.

SEVEN KEY PRINCIPLES TO IMPROVE INFORMATION CAPABILITIES

Principle 1: Managers must personally set the standards for information behaviours and values in their company and business unit

Integrity, transparency, sharing information and a positive view of control all depend on the mind-set and personal example of managers. If they do not practice these behaviours and values, their employees will not have sufficient trust and confidence that managers will use information and behave consistently. Acting on these behaviours and values also enhances the manager's personal credibility in making changes that can lead to improved information behaviours and values in their staff.

General Electric Company (GE)[2]

Jack Welch, the CEO of General Electric Company, captures the essence of why high integrity, a constructive view of control, transparency and sharing are vital to people's behaviours and values in his company.

For Welch, the key to being a good business leader is to 'engender enthusiasm' in people to enable them to have more freedom and more responsibility: 'What we are looking for . . . is leaders who can energize, excite and control rather than enervate, depress and control.' Welch believes that managers must be team members and coaches, who must facilitate idea generation and information-sharing rather than 'controlling'. This implies that managers must develop personal integrity in themselves and their people. They must also manage their people to inspire them to contribute their knowledge and share ideas. 'To be blunt, the two quickest ways to part company with GE are, one, to commit an integrity violation, or, two, to be a controlling, turf-defending, oppressive manager who can't change and who saps and squeezes people rather than excites them and draws out their energy and creativity.'

Thus, for Welch, not compromising on integrity is critical to building an atmosphere of trust and confidence. It encourages the sharing of ideas and information and promotes responsibility, rather than control: 'I dislike the traits that have come to be associated with "managing"— controlling, stifling people, keeping them in the dark, wasting their time on trivia and reports, breathing down their necks. You can't manage self-confidence into people.'

In addition, Welch believes that integrity enhances the ability to face reality and act quickly and decisively on it. Moreover, facing reality means learning from mistakes, since most managerial mistakes come from not facing and dealing with reality. Thus Welch sees a direct connection between integrity and transparency as well as a link between integrity, control and sharing by building trust and confidence in people.

Welch also places enormous emphasis on 'keeping business simple' by not complicating decisions unnecessarily and by being clear about which performance criteria and measures count for employees and managers:

'Numbers aren't the vision—the numbers are the product. We always say that if you had three measurements to live by, they'd be employee satisfaction, customer satisfaction, and cash flow. If you've got cash in the till at the end, the rest is all going to work, because if you've got high customer satisfaction, you're going to get a share. If you've got high employee satisfaction, you're going to get productivity. And if you've got cash, you know it's all working.'

With straightforward and understandable measures, managers and employees can focus on what is important in a business and how to generate ideas and information to create business value. For Welch, the secret to innovation is always to assume that there are better ideas outside of the company that employees must sense and share proactively, wherever in the company they can make a difference:

'The operative assumption today is that someone, somewhere, has a better idea; the operative compulsion is to find out who has that better idea, learn it and put it into action—fast . . . The quality of an idea does not depend on its altitude in the organization . . . An idea can come from any source. So we will search the globe for ideas. We will share what we know with others to get what they know. We have a constant quest to raise the bar, and we get there by constantly talking to others.'

In sum, managers should not expect their staff to be proactive with information-seeking and new ideas unless they are too. This is true for GE, as well as for the European Business Electronics Unit we saw in Chapter 5. Senior managers feel that they are not at the centre of high-tech business intelligence in their own country, so they make continual visits to Silicon Valley and other high-tech centres to proactively seek out information. This permits them to be more innovative and to engage in new product development back home.

If managers themselves did not go on these visits, it is unlikely that their staff would feel compelled to act on the business intelligence that they return with. By personal example, these managers create a hunger for new ideas and information for their business and inspire their people to respond to the new information to improve their business results.

Principle 2:   Managers must not only know how to use information technology, but must also understand the role of IT in their business and communicate this to their staff

Without a basic understanding of what information technology can do, managers may either overestimate its value, by relying on the knowledge of others, or underestimate its value, by not applying their own managerial judgement appropriately. Percy Barnevik, the former CEO of the ABB Group, characterized his managers in the early 1990s as 'BCs' or 'ACs', depending on whether they were born before or after the (personal) computer. He suggested that this demarcation signalled a dramatic shift in managerial attitudes toward using information technology. Those born before the personal computer, BCs, were unlikely to experience and think naturally about the transformational impact of IT on their business and their life as a manager.

Those born after the personal computer, ACs, were more likely to view IT as a natural tool in their professional life and also appreciate its transformational role in the business. While this distinction may be viewed today as old hat, it nevertheless captured the view that using IT was vital to understanding it in the business. No future managers can afford not to view IT as an essential tool for doing the business and changing the business at the same time.

This is particularly important in the era of e-business, when managers must be able to imagine the many ways to use IT and the Internet to transform their business. If managers neither care about nor understand the Internet and thus miss the potential for e-business in their industry, they probably cannot see—and therefore will not support—the actions their company must take if it is to win in the 'new economy'.

As we noted in Chapter 6, there are distinct differences between low IO and high IO companies in the managerial mind-set toward IT and the use of IT. In companies with low IO, senior managers perceive IT in two very different ways. Inside the company, IT is treated as a cost and a support function for basic operations and business process support. Managers tend to view the IT function and the chief information officer (CIO) as somehow disconnected from the real business. There is a constant need for the IT function to justify its existence, separate from the business units and the more established functions of the company such as human resources and finance.

These same managers, however, naively view the Internet and e-business as potential sources of competitive advantage for their company, even though the company is unlikely to have the information capabilities to support alternative models of e-business. Since the managers are new to the Internet and e-business both personally and professionally, they do not realize that a large part of Internet and e-business is, generally speaking, already a competitive necessity in their industry, as opposed to a competitive advantage. In many of these companies an IO credibility gap exists, since their current information capabilities are unlikely to sustain their future expectations about competing in their industry.

In contrast, in companies with high IO, senior managers understand that IT practices are vital to achieving superior performance, but remain realistic about treating IT as a necessary, but not the only, source of competitive advantage in their company. They know that, without the right information behaviours and values and information management practices, IT alone will not make the difference between achieving competitive necessity and competitive advantage.

These managers also have realistic expectations about e-business and the Internet in their industries. They understand that the companies that will win in the e-business economy will be those that exploit e-business opportunities today in their existing business and prepare for the disruptive effects of e-business in their markets in the future. For example, in 1998, Jack Welch was one of the first CEOs of a major global company to establish an e-business unit within every major business division of GE. The mandate for these e-business units was 'To Dell' or 'Be Delled' in their respective industries, that is, to explore ways to disrupt their industries with e-business strategies before competitors and new entrants could do so.

As we noted in Chapter 6, companies with high IO expect to use IT, including the Internet, now to compete. However, to get ready for tomorrow's disruptive e-business competition, they are also targeting business investments in information technology. Senior managers in these companies do not view IT as separate from the business, but as part of leading a successful company in the e-business era. Since they have good personal and company experiences with IT, they are in a position to systematically improve their companies' information capabilities, and they are ready for industry leadership challenges. They seek to exploit the business potential of IT and e-business for top business performance. Their mind-sets, experiences and attitudes toward IT and e-business are in line with their expectations for IT in building information capabilities that will enable their companies to stay ahead in their industries.

Principle 3: Managers must know how to effectively use information, not just know how the company uses information to create business value

During the last twenty years, companies have used IT widely for operations and business processes. The IT industry has also pushed the personal use of IT with PCs, cell phones, pagers and other digital appliances.

Historically, however, information management in business has largely focused on accounting and finance, marketing and sales, manufacturing and logistics. There has been little effort to improve personal information management—how managers and knowledge workers sense, collect, organize, process and maintain information. Companies have given managers and knowledge workers more power to make important business decisions and take on added responsibility, but few understand how well these people use and manage information in their everyday working lives.

We call this development the information paradox. On the one hand, personal information management in a company is an important part of organizational and individual success. Management guru Peter Drucker has concluded:

> For the knowledge worker in general, and especially for executives, information is the key resource. Information increasingly creates the link to their fellow workers and to the organization, and their 'network'. It is information, in other words, that enables knowledge workers to do their job.[3]

On the other hand, managers spend little time or attention improving how they and all their staff—not just knowledge workers—use information to network more effectively with each other. Managers have either relied on administrative staff and IT specialists to understand which information they needed about the business or they have abdicated their information responsibilities in favour of decisions based on gut feeling and intuition. Lack of information about problems and situations, they claim, can be a virtue.

To break out of this information paradox, managers must take responsibility for the information that they use and share to create business value. Managers cannot expect their company to be good at using information if they do not take personal information responsibility themselves. In companies with high IO, managers create value by taking responsibility for their use of information. They do not expect—nor do they want—administrative staff or IT specialists to make decisions about what information they need to understand. Since a good deal of information needed by managers is located outside the company and is relatively informal and ill defined, they have to take personal responsibility for sensing, processing and sharing it with other managers and employees.

Further, to evaluate the personal information practices and effectiveness of other managers and knowledge workers, managers must develop their own good personal information practices. Since knowledge work is carried out by individuals in teams and projects, managers cannot talk about good information practices without demonstrating them. Since a good deal of a manager's work is public and shared, behaviours and values of individual managers are under constant scrutiny. So fellow managers and workers can see first-hand how well a manager senses outside intelligence and shares it with others while he or she performs, not simply see it in the decisions the manager says are based on his or her information activities.

Peter Drucker has suggested that managers must ask two questions of themselves regarding their personal information responsibilities:

- 'What information do I owe to the people with whom I work and on whom I depend? In what form? In what time frame?'
- 'What information do I need myself? From whom? In what form? In what time frame?'[4]

By periodically answering these two sets of questions, managers can become more aware of their information responsibilities to others and of others' to them. They can be in a better position to understand which types of information they require to manage their business and to create business value. This focus on knowing what you want and knowing how to share and use it is also important to enable people in the company to understand how they share and use information and which information is most significant for executing their responsibilities. This principle of reciprocity, carried out each day at an individual level, creates a climate for understanding which information and which information practices are critical to running and changing the business.

For example, the principle of reciprocal information responsibility means that managers and employees must take the lead in the design and implementation of new information practices and IT systems for the business. As we noted earlier, managers cannot abdicate this responsibility to administrative staff and IT specialists, only to complain later that 'they' did not deliver. Managers must recognize that they are in the best position to know what they want; ultimately, it is they who must take personal and organizational responsibility to see that they get it.

To escape the information paradox—and ensure that personal information awareness and use can translate into information effectiveness

company-wide—managers have to assume their information responsibilities if they expect their employees to do the same.

Principle 4:   Managers must create the right expectations for their people in changing business strategies and the mix of business capabilities

Managing involves influencing the mind-sets of people in a company and
people with whom the company does business—customers, suppliers,
partners and competitors. Mind-sets are the distinctive viewpoints,
needs, agendas and expectations that directly influence how individuals
perceive their work and engage in it. In shaping their people's viewpoints
and expectations about the business, managers can act in two ways. On
the one hand, they can work toward understanding the mind-sets of
others and candidly exchange views and expectations about what a business should do and how. On the other hand, they can act before they
understand other people's viewpoints and expectations. In this case,
management becomes (negative) control and, to achieve their priorities
and implement change, managers are forced to engage in explicit acts of
persuasion and power plays.

While you may believe that managing in the real world involves both
types of behaviours, it is clear that companies with high IO emphasize the
first one. As a manager, you cannot foster the right information behaviours, follow the right strategies and get the right mix of business
capabilities without first understanding the viewpoints of others before
and as you act. For these reasons, companies such as BBV and Hilti focus
on understanding and shaping the mutual viewpoints, expectations and
information capabilities of their people, which is consistent with their
strategy of being Growers.

For example, the first and second 1,000-day Programmes at BBV, as
discussed in the Introduction, were aimed at developing a clear understanding among all managers and employees of the link between having
the right mix of business capabilities—including information
capabilities—and successfully focusing on customers for cross-selling financial products and services. All BBV employees are aware of the links
between building the right business capabilities and achieving superior
business performance. A basic responsibility of senior managers is to
manage the mind-sets of their employees in terms of how the bank operates to achieve growth and customer value. This includes what the employees are expected to do in their work, how the bank uses product and
customer information in selling to and serving customers, and how it
rewards individual, team and company performance.

This persistence of managers in promoting inclusive understanding of the core business strategies for growth and the mix of business capabilities required to achieve these strategies over a period of years is a distinctive element of a company with high IO.

In contrast, companies with low IO exhibit one or both of the following tendencies. Like The Bank, discussed in earlier chapters, they may emphasize a narrow and manipulative view of control. In this setting, managers speak about the 'traditional' mind-sets of their staff and the need to overcome reactive behaviours and ways of doing business. Managers often recognize the mind-set issues in their company, but press for more control over their staff as a way of managing change. For Cutters, the focus on control is critical to make sure people behave in appropriate ways in the midst of downsizing and restructuring. Managers are not candid with their staff and take decisions behind the scenes, since the climate for mutual understanding and frank dialogue is low or non-existent.

For Makeovers, the focus on control is not as narrow, but can be confusing. In this case, managers are trying to achieve a new proactive strategic viewpoint but still have a capability mix which resembles that of the past. It is difficult to know or understand exactly what managers expect or which approach to building business capabilities is needed. Thus employees and managers might live in a climate of mixed messages, with confusion over priorities and uncertainty about which business capabilities to improve.

The second tendency of companies with low IO is to create a credibility gap between their business strategies and the business capabilities to execute these strategies over time. These are companies that promise customers a lot in services and products, but for a variety of reasons are not in a position to deliver fully, since they have diluted or failed to build the right mix of business capabilities. For example, if a Cutter, like The Bank, pursues this strategy over several years, we know that the company will seriously dilute or erode its information capabilities, especially the information behaviours and values of its staff. Senior managers in the company may suddenly announce that customer delight and creating business opportunities are the critical strategic priorities. However, following several years of redundancies and de-layering, the information capabilities to deliver their new, intended strategy will be seriously lacking. If senior managers persist in these objectives without recognizing the urgent need to build appropriate information capabilities, their employees may view their strategy statements as either unrealistic (we can't deliver on the promises) or, at worst, highly cynical (how can we deliver on our promises to customers without the right business capabilities?).

Another manifestation of the credibility gap, as the case study below shows, occurs when a company effectively sells its information capabilities to customers over time, but for whatever reason cannot effectively implement them.

Global Freight Forwarding Company

A leading global freight forwarding company has, over the last ten years, been unable to implement an integrated freight forwarding IT system on a worldwide basis. In the late 1980s, the company outsourced the project to a consultancy, that, over seven years, was unable to achieve any results. In the mid-1990s, the company organized an internal team to implement the same IT system. After four years, the company was ready to implement two pilot sites for the global system—still a long way from a global approach.

In the meantime, the senior managers had succeeded in repositioning their company in the minds of their best and global customers. To delight customers and work effectively with other companies on multinational accounts, the company sold its integrated global freight forwarding system and Internet capabilities to customers around the world. The customer response was favourable. Multinational customers had long clamoured for the real-time global monitoring of their shipments and direct interfaces with the company's Internet site for other services.

The company's managers succeeded in selling information capabilities that they did not have in place to large customers and are now compelled to deliver on these capabilities in any way they can. The company's new CEO has drawn one moral from this story: 'If you promise high IO, you had better have the information capabilities to deliver it!'

Principle 5: Managers must not simply be advocates of good information capabilities for their business, but they must also understand the conditions for implementing IC in their business

If you want to improve information capabilities in your business, there is no room for wishful thinking. Senior managers can advocate stretch targets for enhancing information capabilities, but they must work out if conditions in their business give their people a realistic chance of gaining substantial improvements. In our company research, we identified four types of cases where senior managers advocate improvements in information capabilities, but may or may not fully appreciate the conditions in their company to make such improvements happen.

Type A: Ambitious and Highly Focused on Building Information Capabilities

Companies with high IO did not always possess high information capabilities. They grew them. In established companies such as BBV and Hilti, the seeds of information capabilities were already planted in each company's way of doing business before the 1990s. In the case of BBV, both the focus on the branch at the centre of retail banking and the early development of IT systems to support customer and product information management were established in the early 1980s. At Hilti, the direct sales force model and the intense focus on customers were in place before the 1990s. However, in both companies, the arrival of new CEOs in the mid-1990s, coupled with their urgent and intense focus on building information capabilities to meet ambitious growth targets, led to a five-year journey of consistent improvements in each information capability.

At the beginning of their journeys, the two companies identified stretch targets for both business performance improvement and changes in information capabilities. At the time, an external observer might have concluded that their goals were not in line with their business capabilities—a correct conclusion. However, senior managers set their goals very high knowing that even if they fell short of the stretch target, they would exceed the accepted rates of improvement in their industries. In both cases, 'stretch' meant that as these business leaders raised their business targets each year, they aggressively pursued improvements in information capabilities. Although on the face of it the goals of these companies might have seemed ambitious, they were in fact realistic, given senior managers' understanding of the business conditions of their companies. Thus, over five years, both companies made remarkable improvements in their information capabilities and business performance.

Type B: Ambitious, but Missing Key Information Capabilities

In some cases, senior managers take a strong stand on one or other information capability, such as information behaviours and values, but do not understand their company's deficiencies in others, such as IT practices. As we saw in Chapters 3 and 7, this was the case with the European retailer of eyeglass lenses and frames, which started in the 1980s as a small French company with a very customer-centred service approach. Information practices and behaviours were highly localized in the store, yet transparent and proactive; the focus of the business was on store management and operations.

In 1997, when the company acquired a large UK competitor, the number of employees doubled to about 8,000 and the number of stores more than trebled to 700, across 17 countries. The CEO, who had previously believed that, 'IT was not in the genes of his company', had to face the prospect of significantly improving IT practices for operations and business process support. This meant expanding information management practices from store operations to regional supply chain processes and shifting localized information values and behaviours to those of a broad-based, 700-store retail operation.

In this case, the CEO became aware through our IO dashboard that, given the high IO scores on information behaviours and values in the company, business performance could be significantly improved by aggressively attacking deficiencies in IT and information management practices across the company. In the light of its service focus, winning brands, people culture and entrepreneurial growth, this company could close the gap between advocating ambitious business improvements and creating the business conditions for high IO.

Type C: Urgent Information Capabilities Turnaround Required, but Conditions Are Poor

Managers are very keen to improve their information capabilities, but either do not understand the actions to take with their people, or focus from the start on the wrong information capabilities. In Chapter 4, we noted that changing information behaviours and values can take years to improve significantly in established companies. Many companies have a long history of poor information behaviours and values. These may be caused by senior managers' approach to command and control, vertical and highly fragmented approaches to IT and information management practices, or people cultures that breed suspicion, lack of information-sharing and use of information as a political weapon.

For example, in Chapter 4 we mentioned the case of the major US financial services company that before the mid-1990s had experienced poor information behaviours and values on the part of many CEOs over several years. One CEO, in particular, had behaved autocratically toward managers and had been dismissed for falsifying performance information given to the board of directors. Because of the low levels of information integrity, transparency, sharing and formality displayed by several CEOs over more than a decade, efforts by the company's current CEO to improve information behaviours and values had met with mixed success. While he and members of his senior management team would like to rapidly improve information capabilities in the company, and have personally taken steps to change their behaviours and values, lower level managers and employees regard their efforts towards change with doubt and suspicion. In this case, good intentions alone will not lead to major improvements in information capabilities.

Type D: Changing Business Expectations, but Low Information Capabilities—the Danger of Wishful Thinking

Companies with low IO clearly face the greatest challenges in linking managerial expectations about business performance or information capabilities improvements with the reality of conditions in their business. A company that has performed poorly over the last five years and has low IO, coupled with either a Cutter (such as The Bank) or Makeover approach to business strategy, faces a major credibility gap with its employees and its customers.

If the senior managers advocate a Grower strategy and begin talking about customer delight and new business opportunities, they must at the same time be sure to outline the specific steps—as suggested in Chapters 3 to 6—to substantially improve the three information capabilities concurrently. Without decisive and well-executed steps to improve their own and their people's information behaviours and values, coupled with clear changes in IT and information management practices, these managers run the greatest danger; that of wishful thinking. They announce changes in business strategy, but underestimate the weakness of the company's information capabilities and the steps they must take in order to correct them aggressively to improve the bottom line.

Principle 6: Managers need to have the courage and foresight to disrupt a successful business model in order to capitalize on future potential—they cannot wait to see what the future holds.

The decision to grow a company by exploiting new business opportunities and delighting customers requires senior managers to anticipate the future and build business capabilities that fit the future view of the business, not necessarily the current one. Inventing a new business approach while running an existing business challenges the mind-sets of managers in two ways:

- First, they must decide to disrupt their existing business model for an uncertain future one—their attachment to the existing business model damages their chances of successfully adopting the new model over time. 'Creative destruction' sounds good until your management team tries it.

- Second, they and their people are reaping the benefits of the existing model while taking actions to undermine them for unclear and risky new ones. This situation places the people who run the existing business in a difficult position. After all, why put today's benefits at risk when the threat of future competition is unclear? In this case, senior managers in established companies face a dilemma. If they wait until the future threats become known, they lose time and the opportunity to make the first move for early advantage. If they act when the potential threats are not yet clearly perceived, they risk taking the wrong steps and building inappropriate business capabilities.

As we noted in Chapters 7 and 8, the Grower strategy makes companies leverage information capabilities for their current and future business success. Today, in the era of e-business, the decision to augment or transform information capabilities involves rethinking current business approaches or inventing entirely new ones. Managers must take advantage of the IC maximization effect—using information capabilities to enhance or save on other business capabilities such as processes, people, organizational structure and/or external relationships. To do so, senior managers are faced with three major options for designing new business approaches and coping with existing ways of doing business.

Approach A: Exploit Information Capabilities Fully in a Start-up

A senior management team that starts to exploit information capabilities in a start-up operation separate from its traditional business is unencumbered by a legacy of organizational structures, processes, people and low IO.

SkandiaBanken

When senior managers of the Skandia Group decided to launch a new direct bank in the 1990s in the Swedish banking market, they were able to invent a pure model: direct banking, cross-selling products and attracting customers with higher interest rates on savings and responsive, flexible services. SkandiaBanken, through its affiliation with the Skandia Group, was able to gain immediate brand recognition. Yet the new direct business model leveraged information capabilities wherever possible to substitute for unnecessary management layers, overly complex business processes, vertical reporting structures and an extensive system of physical branches.

In addition, the direct model exploited weaknesses in the more established banks in the Swedish market by positioning itself as a low-cost, but highly customer-focused, bank in which customers were treated as individuals, not accounts. Moreover, early on SkandiaBanken advertised its customer and service integrity and its competitive savings rates as a direct response to the image of low customer and product integrity of established banks. A series of bank 'bail-outs' in the early and mid-1990s, and lower returns on customer accounts, provided Skan-diaBanken with a market window in which to exploit its direct business model and its unique information capabilities in the Swedish marketplace.

For an established company, designing a start-up operation offers the advantages of a pure model for fully exploiting information capabilities. However, while the new enterprise may succeed, the existing business units of the established company may not benefit from synergies between the pure business model and the current ways of doing business.

Approach B: Add New Information Capabilities to the Existing Business

Many senior managers in established companies today believe that they can have their cake and eat it. They think that they can leverage new e-business models and information capabilities without changing their existing business approach. These managers think that they can have the best of both worlds, but they risk getting the worst. In such cases, it is difficult for managers and their employees, having grown up with and benefited from the traditional way of doing business, to fully support a new e-business model that may threaten or disrupt the way they currently do business.

For example, we saw in Chapter 8 how Dell Computers, during the 1990s, successfully exploited a direct business model for selling desktop and portable PCs and servers against companies such as Compaq, IBM and Hewlett-Packard, who have traditionally sold PCs through whole-saler, distributor and retailer networks. The established companies have aimed at preserving their traditional external relationships with whole-salers, distributors and retailers, but at the same time, they have adopted direct ways of selling—similar to Dell's—through call centres and the Internet, bypassing their own business partners to sell direct to consumers and businesses.

These attempts to straddle intermediary and direct channels have met with mixed success. Compaq has consistently lost market share to Dell over the last five years. IBM has had major difficulties in making its PC division profitable. Hewlett-Packard has been slow to adopt direct ways of doing business and selling its PC products over the Internet. With one foot firmly planted on the side of tradition, doing business through retail channels, and the other foot placed tentatively on the side of the direct e-business model, which was successfully leveraged by Dell in the PC industry, these companies have found it difficult both to sustain the benefits of their existing business model and capture the benefits of the new direct e-business. Their managers have been reluctant to disrupt the accepted ways of doing business with powerful retail partners for an uncertain direct, e-business future. When company managers straddle the dock and the departing boat, any wrong move can leave them stranded in deep water.

Approach C: Transform Your Business Model with New Information Capabilities

The most challenging position for managers is to transform a traditional business into a company competing with new information capabilities. These companies require multi-year journeys and major changes in people, structures, processes and external relationships, as we have seen in the Hilti and BBV case studies. In the mid-1990s, the senior managers of both these companies began bold and consistent efforts that were to continue for the next five years to transform their company's business approach with new information capabilities. We believe there are three reasons for their success.

- First, their senior managers understood that their Grower strategy required a determined effort to implement new information capabilities to achieve business success. There was to be no compromise on the journey to systematic improvement.
- Second, these managers did not believe that their traditional way of doing business could be combined with new IC-based methods. Instead, they sought to redefine their existing approaches to information capabilities and integrate the new Internet and e-business models. For Hilti, this required a new approach to delivering value to customers through their direct sales force supplemented with call centre and Internet capabilities. For BBV, this meant fully integrating their branches with direct ways of doing business, including Internet and call centre banking.

- Third, these managers and their employees believed that superior execution of their information capabilities each day was the source of their company's competitive advantage. While many company managers may aspire to Grower strategies, companies such as these believe that competitive advantage is a product of both good strategy and superior execution in day-to-day business. Their pursuit of operational excellence with information capabilities, and the right strategies, linked to determined efforts by their managers and people always to 'make good better', permitted these companies to fight today's competitive battles effectively and prepare for future success. Unlike management teams in many established companies, these managers never know enough, never anticipate enough, and never execute well enough. They are always seeking information and ideas in the outside world to achieve superior performance.

Our conclusion is that managers who transform their companies with information capabilities need courage, determination and consistent striving. Their personal example is paramount in changing mind-sets and behaviours and in winning the support and understanding of their people.

Principle 7:   Managers who lead their company toward high IO are in the best position to implement the e-company in the new e-business economy

There were many predictions of the virtual organization during the 1990s. At the beginning of the twenty-first century, however, we do not know the many forms the virtual organization will take. How will the Internet and e-business evolve? Will they require new forms of organization based on knowledge and information, not things? Will the 'e-company' be an organization at all? Or will it simply be temporary aggregations of knowledge workers delivering business value by continually realigning themselves in projects, deals and relationships through global networks?

What we do know is that whatever shape the e-company takes in the new economy, a company's ability to achieve superior business performance will be based on the right mix of business strategies and capabilities leading to high IO. The reasons for this are threefold:

1. E-companies Will Be Growers

   E-companies will have to survive by being Growers, not Cutters or Makeovers. The companies will focus on two key strategies. First, they will need to continually reinvent their products and services to create business value. E-companies will be aggressive learning organizations because they have to be. Their managers and staff will need to be proactive in generating and using new ideas and information faster and better than competitors. Second, e-companies will need to delight each and every customer they have—real-time and on-line. Customizing individual products, sensing customer needs and responding one-to-one will require these companies to design their business processes with the utmost flexibility. Customer relationships and services will be customized and unique because they have to be.

2. E-companies Will Fully Leverage the IC Maximization Effect

E-companies will employ the IC maximization effect as a competitive weapon—they will enhance or save on the traditional resource capabilities such as people, organizational structure, processes and external relationships. These companies will substitute information and digital processes for physical processes wherever feasible. They will minimize organizational structures that block appropriate information and knowledge-sharing across functions, processes and organizational boundaries. They will save on people by cutting activities, tasks and responsibilities that add no value and by leveraging people's willingness to make their knowledge explicit and usable, to benefit the company and themselves. Finally, to exploit the full business value of new forms of network-based competition, cooperation and co-opetition, they will seek to 'Internetwork' people in companies with partners, customers and even competitors.

In short, e-companies will succeed by inventing new ways of fully leveraging the IC maximization effect in their business models.

3. E-companies Will Require High IO to Stay Ahead of the Pack

There is no guarantee that going virtual or direct in the future will help a company to achieve competitive advantage. Despite what many academics, consultants and managers have claimed over the last ten years, new entrants and established companies in diverse industries will adopt many or all of the elements of this organizational model. So being an e-company in the future will be more of a competitive necessity than a competitive advantage. The leading companies in an industry will be compelled to react and respond to the business capabilities adopted by their competitors or new entrants. Like leading marathon runners, these companies will be forced to run faster and harder to maintain their lead. They will have to execute the business capabilities of the e-company just to stay in the lead pack.

The few companies that attain competitive advantage in and across industries will be those that exploit their Grower strategies and the IC maximization effect to achieve high IO and superior business performance. Only these managers and companies will be able to stay ahead of the lead pack in their industry. Which characteristics of the e-company they adapt or invent will depend directly on their journey to continuously improve their IO maturity. As we noted in Chapter 8, these will be the companies whose managers have built information capabilities in the past and who expect to sustain their industry leadership in competing with information in the future.

CONCLUSION

When we began this book, our aim was to make visible a previously invisible dimension of business management. We wanted to give you as a manager the lens, the metric and the ways of managing information, people and IT in your company to attain superior business performance. The lens is the IO model. The metric is the information orientation of your company or business unit. The management path to leveraging information capabilities, the IO maturity framework, is what we have learned in our two and a half year international study about how senior managers in a global sample of companies lead their staff to use information and IT to improve business results.

Leading a company on a journey to achieve high IO and attain superior business performance takes hard work, persistence and personal commitment. Knowing this, our intention was not to start a new management fad or offer a quick fix solution. To undertake the journey you will have to develop the right mind-set about effective information use in your business. You will have to begin to measure your information effectiveness. And, you must lead and inspire people along the way—your company will be the better for it.

NOTES

1. Drucker, P. (1999) *Management Challenges for the 21st Century*, New York: Harperbusiness.
2. Slater, R. (1998) *Jack Welch and the GE Way: Management Insights and Leadership Secrets of the Legendary CEO*, New York: McGraw-Hill.
3. Drucker, P. (1999) *Management Challenges for the 21st Century*, New York: Harperbusiness.
4. Drucker, P. (1999) *Management Challenges for the 21st Century*, New York: Harperbusiness.

INDEX

EXECUTIVE DEVELOPMENT FROM IMD
Institute of Management Development

IMD is one of the world's leading business schools. Located in Lausanne, Switzerland, IMD has been developing managers for over 50 years. Based on IMD concepts, each book in this inspirational series provides a complete practical toolkit for success.

Competing with Information

A Manager's Guide to Creating Business Value with Information Content

Edited by Donald Marchand, IMD

The first in the series, this book shows why companies that cope well with information management are in a strong market position. It focuses on how successful information can create real business value in four ways: minimising risk, reducing costs, delighting customers and creating a new reality. It details the 'what, why and how' of information management and looks at the four key net strategies: Internet, Intranet, Extranet and the industry net.

0471 89969 0   2000   352pp   Hardback

EXECUTIVE DEVELOPMENT FROM IMD
Institute of Management Development

IMD is one of the world's leading business schools. Located in Lausanne, Switzerland, IMD has been developing managers for over 50 years. Based on IMD concepts, each book in this inspirational series provides a complete practical toolkit for success.

Focused Energy
Mastering Bottom-Up Organization
Edited by Paul Strebel, IMD

Deriving its ethos, structure and core values from an IMD Executive Development course and featuring case studies including Citibank, AT&T and Shell this, the second book in the IMD series lucidly explains what a bottom-up organization is and why these flatter, energy-rich structures are the key to value creation in the future. Paul Strebel charts the different paths to achieving a bottom-up structure, then explains how managers can combat its pitfalls by sharing information, co-ordinating laterally and developing strategy from within.

0471 89971 2   2000   320pp   Hardback